DATE DUE		

AMERICAN WOMEN FICTION WRITERS 1900–1960

VOLUME ONE

AMERICAN WOMEN FICTION WRITERS

1900–1960

VOLUME ONE

Edited and with an Introduction by

Harold Bloom

CHELSEA HOUSE PUBLISHERS

Philadelphia

ON THE COVER: Beatrice Whitney Van Ness (American, 1888–1981), *Summer Sunlight*, ca. 1936. Oil on canvas, 39" x 49". The National Museum of Women in the Arts, gift of Wallace and Wilhelmina Holladay.

CHELSEA HOUSE PUBLISHERS

EDITORIAL DIRECTOR   Richard Rennert
PRODUCTION MANAGER   Pamela Loos
PICTURE EDITOR   Judy Hasday
ART DIRECTOR   Sara Davis
SENIOR PRODUCTION EDITOR   Lisa Chippendale

WOMEN WRITERS OF ENGLISH AND THEIR WORKS:
   American Women Fiction Writers, 1900–1960: Volume One

SERIES EDITOR   Jane Shumate
CONTRIBUTING EDITOR   Tenley Williams
ASSOCIATE EDITOR   Therese De Angelis
INTERIOR AND COVER DESIGNER   Alison Burnside
EDITORIAL ASSISTANT   Anne Merlino

The Chelsea House world wide web site address is
http://www.chelseahouse.com

5 7 9 8 6 4 3

Library of Congress Cataloging-in-Publication Data

American women fiction writers / edited and with an introduction by
   Harold Bloom.
       p.   cm. — (Women writers of English and their works)
   Includes bibliographical references and index.
   ISBN 0-7910-4480-7 (v. 1). — ISBN 0-7910-4496-3 (pbk. : v. 1)
     1. American fiction—Women authors—History and criticism.
   2. American fiction—Women authors—Bio–bibliography. 3. Women and
   literature—United States.   I. Bloom, Harold. II. Series.
   PS374.W6A455 1997
   813.009' 9287—dc21
     [B]   97-6310
                                                                              CIP

CONTENTS

AMERICAN WOMEN FICTION WRITERS 1900-1960

VOLUME ONE

THE ANALYSIS OF WOMEN WRITERS

HAROLD BLOOM

I APPROACH THIS SERIES with a certain wariness, since so much of classical feminist literary criticism has founded itself upon arguments with that phase of my own work that began with *The Anxiety of Influence* (first published in January 1973). Someone who has been raised to that bad eminence—*The Patriarchal Critic*—is well advised that he trespasses upon sacred ground when he ventures to inquire whether indeed there are indisputable differences, imaginative and cognitive, between the literary works of women and those of men. If these differences are so substantial as pragmatically to make an authentic difference, does that in turn make necessary different aesthetic standards for judging the achievements of men and of women writers? Is Emily Dickinson to be read as though she has more in common with Elizabeth Barrett Browning than with Ralph Waldo Emerson?

Is Elizabeth Bishop a great poet because she triumphantly meets the same aesthetic criteria satisfied by Wallace Stevens, or should we evaluate her by criteria she shares with Marianne Moore, but not with Stevens? Are there crucial gender-based differences in the representations of Esther Summerson by Charles Dickens in *Bleak House*, and of Dorothea Brooke by George Eliot in *Middlemarch*? Does Samuel Richardson's Clarissa Harlowe convince us that her author was a male when we contrast her with Jane Austen's Elizabeth Bennet? Do women poets have a less agonistic relationship to female precursors than male poets have to their forerunners? Two eminent pioneers of feminist criticism, Sandra Gilbert and Susan Gubar, have suggested that women writers suffer more from an anxiety of authorship than they do from influence anxieties, while another important feminist critic, Elaine Showalter, has suggested that women writers, early and late, work together in a kind of quiltmaking, each doing her share while avoiding any contamination of creative envy in regard to other writers, provided that they be women. Can it be true that, in the aesthetic sphere, women do not beware women and do not suffer from the competitiveness and jealousy that alas do exist in the professional and sexual domains? Is there something in the area of literature, when practiced by women, that changes and purifies mere human nature?

I cannot answer any of these questions, yet I do think it is vital and clarifying to raise them. There is a current fashion, in many of our institutions of higher education, to insist that English Romantic poetry cannot be studied in the old way, with an exclusive emphasis upon the works of William Blake, William Wordsworth, Samuel Taylor Coleridge, Lord Byron, Percy Bysshe Shelley, John Keats, and John Clare. Instead, the Romantic poets are taken to include Felicia Hemans, Laetitia Landon, Charlotte Smith, and Mary Tighe, among others. It would be heartening if we could believe that these are unjustly neglected poets, but their current revival will be brief. Similarly, anthologies of 17th-century English literature now tend to include the Duchess of Newcastle as well as Aphra Behn, Lady Mary Chudleigh, Anne Killigrew, Anne Finch, Countess of Winchilsea, and others. Some of these— Anne Finch in particular—wrote well, but a situation in which they are more read and studied than John Milton is not one that is likely to endure forever. The consequences of making gender a criterion for aesthetic choice must finally destroy all serious study of imaginative literature as such.

In their *Norton Anthology of Literature by Women*, Sandra Gilbert and Susan Gubar conclude their introduction to Elizabeth Barrett Browning by saying that "she constantly tested herself against the highest standards of male-defined poetic genres," a true if ambiguous observation. They then print her famous "The Cry of the Children," an admirably passionate ode that protests the cruel employment of little children in British Victorian mines and factories. Unfortunately, this well-meant prophetic affirmation ends with this, doubtless its finest stanza:

XIII

They look up with their pale and sunken faces,
    And their look is dread to see,
For they mind you of their angels in high places,
    With eyes turned on Deity.
"How long," they say, "how long, O cruel nation,
    Will you stand, to move the world, on a child's heart,—
Stifle down with a mailèd heel its palpitation,
    And tread onward to your throne amid the mart?
Our blood splashes upward, O goldheaper,
    And your purple shows your path!
But the child's sob in the silence curses deeper
    Than the strong man in his wrath."

If you read this aloud, then you may find yourself uncomfortable, on a strictly aesthetic basis, which would not vary if you were told that this had been composed by a male Victorian poet. In their selections from Elizabeth Bishop, Gilbert and Gubar courageously reprint Bishop's superb statement explaining her refusal to permit her poems to be included in anthologies of women's writing:

> Undoubtedly gender does play an important part in the making of any art, but art is art and to separate writings, paintings, musical compositions, etc., into sexes is to emphasize values in them that are *not* art.

That credo of Elizabeth Bishop's is to me the Alpha and Omega of critical wisdom in regard to all feminist literary criticism. Gender studies are precisely that: they study gender, and not aesthetic value. If your priorities are historical, social, political, and ideological, then gender studies clearly are more than justified. Perhaps they are a way to justice, or at least to more justice than women have received throughout thousands of years of male domination and aggression. Yet that is a very different matter from the now vexed issue of aesthetic value. Biographical criticism, like the different modes of historicist and psychological criticism, always has relied upon a kind of implicit gender studies and doubtless will benefit, as other modes will, by a making explicit of such considerations, particularly in regard to women writers.

Each volume in this series contains copious refutations of, and replies to, the traditionally aesthetic stance that I have advocated here. These introductory remarks aspire only to a questioning, and not a challenging, of feminist literary criticism. There are no longer any Patriarchal Critics; they are all dinosaurs, fabulous beasts fit for revival only in horror films. Sometimes I sadly think of myself as Bloom Brontosaurus, amiably left behind by the fire and the flood. But more often I go on reading the great women writers, searching for the aesthetic difference that yet may prove to be there, but which has not yet been found.

INTRODUCTION

WILLA CATHER, A HALF CENTURY after her death, remains the greatest of American women novelists. Her nearest rival, Edith Wharton, stemmed from Henry James, as Cather did, but always wrote in James's mode, as Cather did not. Though she continues to be widely read, Cather seems to me somewhat underestimated, particularly in recent criticism, which is perhaps too much centered upon her sexual orientation. Only a few modern American novelists of her own era—Dreiser, Faulkner, Fitzgerald, Hemingway—are of her eminence, though among these she has affinities only with Fitzgerald. Her best books—*My Ántonia* (1918), *A Lost Lady* (1923), *The Professor's House* (1925)—should have a permanent status in American fiction. Their high and deliberate artistry as subtle studies of loss allows them to sustain many rereadings. Her most ambitious novel, *Death Comes for the Archbishop* (1927), remains an impressive work, but its curiously classical hero, Archbishop Latour of Santa Fe, lacks the passion necessary for someone who is projected as an American epic protagonist, as a new version of the frontier mythos.

In her Jamesian essay, "On the Art of Fiction," Cather formulated a memorable aesthetic credo: "Any first-rate novel or story must have in it the strength of a dozen fairly good stories that have been sacrificed to it." That is a useful formula for testing *My Ántonia* and *A Lost Lady*, nostalgic reveries haunted by the shades of stories that might have been told, of embraces that could have been attempted, of lives that should have been experienced. Jim Burden, the narrator of *My Ántonia*, has a reverence for the past, for his own childhood, that is a kind of secular religion, of which the girl Ántonia is the goddess. Cather's surrogate, Burden is properly named, both because he is heavily laden by his memories and also because the novel is *his* prose poem, with a burden or refrain that is Vergilian: "The best days are the first to flee." For Burden, the present itself is past, and the future merely an occasion for looking backwards. Whether or not there is an ironic distance between Cather and Burden is rather ambiguous and is still subject to critical dispute. If the irony is there, then it reflects an ambivalence within Cather towards societally imposed reticences that her art strives to accept. I can recall no passages in Cather in which a woman's longing for a man is persuasively represented. Yet this scarcely matters; the burden of *My Ántonia* is one in which yearning for the past and desiring a lost woman are perfectly fused together.

Cather's art, praised by Wallace Stevens for its "pains to conceal her sophistication," achieved an apotheosis for the short novel *A Lost Lady*, where another ambiguously male protagonist, Niel Herbert, recalls his lost lady (never more than an image) as the vision that has governed his life:

Her eyes when they laughed for a moment into one's own, seemed to provide a wild delight that he had not found in life. "I know where it is," they seemed to say, "I could show you!" He would like to call up the shade of the young Mrs. Forrester, as the witch of Endor called up Samuel's, and challenge it, demand the secret of that ardour; ask her whether she had really found some ever-blooming, ever-burning, ever-piercing joy, or whether it was all fine play-acting. Probably she had found no more than another; but she had always the power of suggesting things much lovelier than herself, as the perfume of a single flower may call up the whole sweetness of spring.

Flaubert and James alike might have admired that paragraph, with its intimation that fiction also, at its best, suggests things much lovelier than itself. Cather as a person had her opacities; as a writer she had the rare power to evoke, through perceptions and sensations, the image of a possible ecstasy of existence, even though that image had to be placed firmly in the personal (and national) past.

DJUNA BARNES

1892-1982

DJUNA BARNES was born June 12, 1892, in Cornwall-on-Hudson, New York. She was the second child of an English violinist and aspiring poet, Elizabeth Chappell, and an American father, Wald (Buddington) Barnes, who was variously a musician, painter, and writer. When Djuna was five years old, her father's mistress, Fanny Faulkner, moved into their home, and throughout her childhood, Djuna would spend much time caring for an increasing number of siblings and half-siblings. The family moved many times before settling on a farm in Huntington, Long Island.

The Barnes family led a bohemian life. The children were kept out of the school system in the belief that public education would keep them from greatness. Djuna read novels and immersed herself in poetry and painting; later she attended Pratt Institute and the Art Students League. Her grandmother, Zadel Barnes, who lived with the family and later helped Djuna begin a career as a journalist, was an advocate of free love and a feminist who had been active in the suffrage movement. There is speculation that Djuna had a sexual relationship with her grandmother; Djuna also claims to have been violently raped at age 16. Whatever the truth—and surely some terrible event or events did occur—an intense bitterness toward human experience and toward her family would suffuse all her work.

In 1912, because of the increasing poverty that accompanied the expanding family, Djuna's parents divorced. She moved with her mother and younger brothers to New York City. There she wrote for the *Brooklyn Eagle* to support her family and, by the 1920s, was a popular contributor to *Vanity Fair, The New Republic*, and *Smart Set*. Many of the articles were unsigned, however, and remain uncollected.

In 1915, Djuna left her mother's home to live in Greenwich Village, and she published her first book, *The Book of Repulsive Women*. She wrote one-act plays, presented by the Provincetown Players. With a sense of sexual freedom since girlhood, Djuna Barnes had lovers of both sexes.

Barnes went to Paris as a magazine correspondent in 1921. Part of the wave of expatriate writers from America, she came to know Gertrude Stein, James Joyce, Robert McAlmon, and Ezra Pound. *A Book*, a collection of poems, stories, and drawings, was published in 1923. She depicted Mina Loy and Natalie Barney in *Ladies Almanack*

1

(1928), a parody of Elizabethan language and Parisian lesbians. *Ryder* was published the same year. *Nightwood* (1936), considered her greatest work, brought the attention of T. S. Eliot. A later admirer of Barnes's work was Dag Hammarskjöld, who cotranslated *The Antiphon* into Swedish and had it performed at Stockholm's Royal Dramatic Theatre.

Intensely private and reclusive, Djuna Barnes lived, from 1940 until her death, on Patchin Place in Greenwich Village. Although Barnes was a friend of James Joyce, was sponsored by T. S. Eliot, and was the subject of lectures by Dylan Thomas, it was her bitterness toward her family that informed *The Antiphon* (1958), her greatest work after *Nightwood*. A picture of cruel family dynamics, the play centers upon the Djuna figure, who has sacrificed all for art and is murdered when her mother crushes her skull with a curfew bell. One of Barnes's brothers claimed that *The Antiphon* was written as revenge against her family; Djuna responded only that "justice" was her motive.

In 1959, Barnes was elected to the National Institute of Arts and Letters. She continued to write, publishing poetry and *Creatures in an Alphabet*, a bestiary printed posthumously in 1982. Djuna Barnes died in New York City on June 19, 1982.

CRITICAL EXTRACTS

JOHN HAWKES

Recently *Time* magazine, pernicious as ever, dismissed the *Selected Writings* of Djuna Barnes by saying that the best of her work, *Nightwood*, offered little more than "the mysterioso effect that hides no mystery," and even Leslie Fiedler has described Djuna Barnes' vision of evil as effete. Yet all her myth and fear are mightily to be envied. Surely there is unpardonable distinction in this kind of writing, a certain incorrigible assumption of a prophetic role in reverse, when the most baffling of unsympathetic attitudes is turned upon the grudges, guilts, and renunciations harbored in the tangled seepage of our earliest recollections and originations. It is like quarreling at the moment of temptation. Or it is like working a few tangerines on a speedily driven lathe. Djuna Barnes is one of the "old poets," and there is no denying the certain balance of this "infected carrier" upon the high wire of the present. She has moved; she has gone out on a limb of light and indefinite sexuality and there remains unshakeable. She has free-wheeled the push bicycle into the cool air.

Djuna Barnes, Flannery O'Connor, Nathanael West—at least these three disparate American writers may be said to come together in that rare climate of pure and immoral *creation*—are very nearly alone in their uses of wit, their comic treatments of violence and their extreme detachment. If the true purpose of the novel is to assume a significant shape and to objectify the terrifying similarity between the unconscious desires of the solitary man and the disruptive needs of the visible world, then the satiric writer, running maliciously at the head of the mob and creating the shape of his meaningful psychic paradox as he goes, will serve best the novel's purpose. Love, for Djuna Barnes, is a heart twitching on a plate like the "lopped leg of a frog"; for Flannery O'Connor it is a thirty-year-old idiot girl riding in an old car and tearing the artificial cherries from her hat and throwing them out the window; for Nathanael West, love is a quail's feather dragged to earth by a heart-shaped drop of blood on its tip, or the sight of a young girl's buttocks looking like an inverted valentine. Each of these writers finds both wit and blackness in the pit, each claims a new and downward sweeping sight and pierces the pretension of the sweet spring of E. E. Cummings. Detachment, then, is at the center of the novelist's experiment, and detachment allows us our "answer to what our grandmothers were told love was, what it never came to be"; or detachment allows us, quoting again from *Nightwood*, to see that "When a long lie comes up, sometimes it is a beauty; when it drops into dissolution, into drugs and drink, it has a singular and terrible attraction." But mere malice is nothing in itself, of course, and the product of extreme fictive detachment is extreme fictive sympathy. The writer who maintains most successfully a consistent cold detachment toward physical violence . . . is likely to generate the deepest novelistic sympathy of all, a sympathy which is a humbling before the terrible and a quickening in the presence of degradation.

—John Hawkes, "Fiction Today," *Massachusetts Review* (Summer 1962), excerpted in *Twentieth-Century American Literature*, ed. Harold Bloom (New York: Chelsea House Publishers, 1986), 306–7

ALAN WILLIAMSON

Djuna Barnes' work is permeated by the dualism of day and night, which is expounded at length, if somewhat cryptically, in the great monologues of *Nightwood*. In the day, which is the world of everyday life, men behave as if they were immortal, as if a human being were a determinate, knowable and rational entity, and as if human communication, through language and, more profoundly, through love, were valid and satisfying. In the world of night, which underlies the day and which man enters through suffering, all these assumptions prove false. Man is "but a skin about a wind, with muscles clenched against mortality" (*Nightwood*). Under man's rational consciousness lies the subconscious, an unfathomable jungle of dark forces which determine his life and which he cannot know or control. In his unconscious nature, any man is capable of every crime: "There is not one of us who, given an eternal incognito, a thumbprint nowhere set against our souls, would not commit rape, murder and all abominations." Man is made aware of his unconscious self in dreams, in which his irrational impulses project themselves without fear of restraint or consequences. "We wake from our doings in a deep sweat for that they happened in a house without an address, in a street in no town, citizened with people with no names with which to deny them. Their very lack of identity makes them ourselves."

Human communication is also a deceptive surface. Language, as a process of definition and abstraction, falsifies reality by denying the elements of change and mystery: it gives "a word (for a thing) . . . and not its alchemy." Communication in love is equally unsatisfactory. Love is ⟨. . .⟩ the direst need of the unconscious, and yet it is thwarted by the very nature of the unconscious as a sealed and impervious inner life unknown to the conscious selves which try to communicate.

> We swoon with the thickness of our own tongue when we say, 'I love you,' as in the eye of a child lost a long while will be found in contraction of that distance—a child going small in the claws of a beast, coming furiously up the furlongs of the iris.

To paraphrase this typically intricate and economical simile, in trying to articulate love in language, as in the spectacle of a civilized child lost in the jungle who has reverted to an animal, we feel the magnitude of the distance between the rational consciousness and the animalistic forces of the unconscious.

Djuna Barnes' vision of love is thus in a sense Proustian: the torment of love lies in the knowledge that the beloved has a secret inner life in which the lover can never participate. The lover is jealous not of the known, but of the suspected rival. The emblem of love is the lover watching over the sleeping beloved, realizing that he can never know what is going on inside her at this moment, that she may be betraying or killing him in a dream, and at the same time knowing that he is equally capable of betraying or killing her in his dreams. The tragic paradox of love lies in the fact that the unconscious, which is the source of the desire for love, is incapable of possessing or of being possessed: it betrays the beloved in dreams, as it may force the conscious self to betray her in life. Love, in its stark futility, becomes, for the lover, a kind of death: "The night into which his beloved goes . . . destroys his heart."

Thus man struggles in a world whose surface placidity is radically contingent on irrational hidden forces; he is isolated and constantly vulnerable to the destructive power of death, love and the darkness within himself. Djuna Barnes focuses the enigma of man's predicament and renders it significant in terms of a myth which bears a close kinship to the Christian myth of the Fall, but which offers little possibility of Christian redemption. The ecclesiastical tone which T. S. Eliot took in defending Djuna Barnes suggests strongly that he perceived a Christian habit of thought, if not doctrinal Christianity, in a writer who contended that "No man needs curing of his individual sickness; his universal malady is what he should look to."

—Alan Williamson, "The Divided Image: The Quest for Identity in the Works of Djuna Barnes," *Critique* (Spring 1964), excerpted in *Twentieth-Century American Literature*, ed. Harold Bloom (New York: Chelsea House Publishers, 1986), 309

JAMES BAIRD

Kenneth Burke recently made a fresh start with *Nightwood*, contending that the book "aims at . . . a kind of 'transcendence downward.' . . ." He finds an intention to make the plot absolute, in a series of "[Biblical] Lamentations, much as though this were the primal story of all mankind." One is not persuaded that Burke admires the book. But his rigor with the content is a good augury. He is concerned with the Scriptural mode of the work. Had he comprehended the preceding novel *Ryder*, he would have noticed the Scriptural mode in its beginnings. It would be mad to say that Djuna Barnes intended to write a substitute Testament for humankind. What she did intend was a dismissal of Scriptural authoritarianism by deliberately crafted Scriptural frames, each playing with Biblical language, each designed to present sardonically the Law as an insufficient revelation of the nature of man, and, first for her, that of woman. Burke surveys too little. But his study proposes that Djuna Barnes was intent upon novelistic structure. We should remember that she wrote in an American era of the novel when *consciousness* was all. (O'Neill, of course, tried to use some ill-digested Freud to "expand" the American drama, without notable success.) Djuna Barnes wished to bring to the American novel the full burden of the dark of the mind, the night, the subconscious. She intended to be an American surrealist. Clearly she thought of herself as unique. She was unique; and today she belongs in the unique company of some of our new writers.

The doctrines of the surrealists have spread very slowly into Protestant America. T. S. Eliot noted in his introduction to *Nightwood* the perseverance of the Puritan morality, its dismissal of the images of sleep as nonfigurative in the life of the "successful" man. The American future may come to evaluate the psychedelic age as prophecy. Vonnegut, Pynchon, and Hawkes, as examples from this American present, suggest the coming on of a new morality, and a new mode in an art of fiction as full exposition: the totality of the dark and the light, subconscious and conscious, the mind at the full. In the renascence of Djuna Barnes she will be read with our new novelists. The reading will not advance affinities to Poe, and, at the other end of the spectrum, to Joyce. Poe wrote his tales as symbols of the "furnishings" of one mind, his own. Djuna Barnes intended to expose the human condition, as she saw it, by fictive analogies. As for Joyce, one should simply note with André Breton, the chief French spokesman of surrealism, that Joyce is not a true surrealist. "Joyce labors to keep himself within the framework of *art*. He falls into novelistic illusion." The distinction rests in the insistence of surrealism upon an exposition of universals. Thus, despite the distance between Poe and Joyce, each is intent upon art as illusion, a privacy of vision ending with the limits of each sovereign imagination. The point is that the vision does not refer, as though it were a self-contained picture from Synthetic Cubism, beyond itself. In the intent of Gertrude Stein, the deep privacy of the fiction, the poetry, the plays, there is a comparable evidence of the self-contained. All of this is to say that the work of Djuna Barnes is designed to refer beyond itself. Related to the tenets of surrealism, her work urges the need for a new morality and the need for a new scripture describing the phenomena of the human mind. . . .

Breton wrote in his *Second Manifesto of Surrealism* (1930): ". . . we are not afraid to take up arms against logic, if we refuse to swear that something in dreams is less meaningful than something we do in a state of waking. . . ." So Djuna Barnes, speaking through Matthew O'Connor in *Nightwood*: ". . . they [the French] think of the two [wakefulness and sleep, day and night] as one continually . . . Bowing down from the waist, the world over they go, that they may revolve about the Great Enigma. . . ." When Matthew later contends against "that priceless galaxy of misinformation called the mind, harnessed to that stupendous and threadbare glomerate called the soul. . . ." he extends the "French" wisdom of his author, looking, at her behest, into the depths of an older culture with a profounder knowledge of *mind* and *soul*. Was it that Americans were kept in relative ignorance by the stern rubrics of Puritan "logic" and by the wider and pervasive Protestant denial of the mystery, the Great Enigma, which all faithful readings of Scriptural Law must reject? Did these biases prohibit in America a knowledge of the truth of human existence, as though we were iron-bound to Scriptural Law which was itself born of the sleep and the dream of men? Is it foreign to Americans to contend, with Matthew O'Connor in *Nightwood*, "To our friends . . . we die every day, but to ourselves we die only at the end"? Gide said very much the same; so has Sartre. Professional surrealism is not the absolute source for either of these Frenchmen. But the angle of vision of recent French metaphysics and French art is there. Djuna Barnes, without any doubt, reflected most strenuously in her unique explorations the French modes which she knew. We suppose a continued dedication on her part to French thought as she published *The Antiphon*, her verse play, in 1958. This is a dedication to art as antiphon, the answer from the life of the subconscious; and one finds here, in this substantial example of her surrealist style, a recapitulation which stretches back to Baudelaire.

—James Baird, "Djuna Barnes and Surrealism: 'Backward Grief,'" *Individual and Community* (1975), excerpted in *Twentieth-Century American Literature*, ed. Harold Bloom (New York: Chelsea House Publishers, 1986), 307

DONALD J. GREINER

⟨T⟩he following is suggested as a working definition of black humor: it makes no attempt to minimize the terror of the post-World War I universe; it uses comedy to encourage sympathy as well as to expose evil; it suggests futurity; it celebrates comic distortions as an indication that anything is possible; and it is related to the poetic use of language. Three primary characteristics remain especially significant: extreme detachment on the part of the author; the comic treatment of horror and violence; and disruption or parody of conventional notions of plot, character, theme, and setting. The result is highly conscious, unrealistic, militantly experimental comic fiction.

Nightwood is one of the first American novels to reflect the working definition, yet apparently only Sharon Spencer has mentioned its comic spirit. Briefly commenting on the chapter "Watchman, What of the Night?" she describes the dialogue between Dr. Matthew O'Connor and Nora Flood as "intense, extremely funny, and extremely ludicrous. . . . The setting is the doctor's rented room in a cheap Paris hotel, a room that is in itself so terrifying and ridiculous that it might inspire pages of analysis of its 'black comedy.' " The black humor of *Nightwood* is, indeed, particularly illustrated in the grotesque, violent characters, the detached attitude toward the descriptions of outrageous clothes and houses, and the parody of the novelist's role.

These comic elements are part of Barnes' larger thematic concern with modern man's separation from a more primitive animal nature—at first glance, hardly the theme for a humorous novel. Only Robin Vote is united with her bestial side, yet she wanders through Europe from city to city and from lover to lover in a futile effort to attain full humanity. In *Nightwood*, humanity, day, and present contrast with beast, night, and past. Thus Robin is introduced as an "infected carrier of the past" and as having "the eyes of wild beasts." Her various love affairs with Felix, Nora, and Jenny illustrate a search for someone to tell her that she is innocent, for, as Barnes suggests, awareness of innocence leads to consciousness of moral values and, in turn, to humanity. Robin's three principal lovers, however, are unable to help her achieve the human state. Caught up in their own senses of alienation, and goaded by selfish love of

Robin, they become animal-like themselves in their desperation to appropriate the bestial woman.

The numerous love affairs are destructive, painfully pursued, and selfishly concluded, for each character searches for a lover who might alleviate his sense of incompleteness. The longed-for reunion between animal and human states never takes place, and the characters are left with an impossible choice: to be primarily human, which means the painful awareness of alienation, or to be primarily animal, which means the longing for moral consciousness. Barnes suggests that the scale has tipped too far on the side of humanity, and she would probably agree with Dr. O'Connor's advice to Nora: "Be humble like the dust, as God intended, and crawl."

The discussion of theme might suggest to the unprepared reader that *Nightwood* is anything but comic. Happily, however, Barnes has not written a novel of unrelenting gloom. Her sense of humor is evident from the beginning, and her use of funny elements with a depressing theme reflects the perplexing mixture so vital to black humor. . . . Recognition of the comedy, however, depends upon the individual reader, for Barnes maintains total authorial detachment. Hedvig and Guido are not singled out as comic dupes, as characters who deserve only our laughter. Seen in the context of the novel, they are no more grotesque and ridiculous than the major characters who are damned by alienation and cursed by thwarted love. . . .

None of these people can be called characters in the conventional sense. They do not "live," nor are they "round," and the reader is never encouraged to identify with them. Like the characters in many contemporary black humor fictions, Barnes' people are static and subordinated to theme. *Nightwood* provides insight into the disordered human condition by conveying generalizations about love, bestiality, and religion, and it avoids the reader's expectations of verisimilitude and character development. In most instances Felix, Nora, Robin, and Jenny act as vehicles for the poetic prose, for the "saving beauties of language"; they are not essential to Barnes' ideas nor to her means of expressing them. Specific details and descriptions are purposely omitted so that upon finishing *Nightwood* one cannot define what the characters wear or how they look. Poetic generalizations about homosexual or heterosexual love in the midst of discussions about bestiality, the night, and religion do not need living characters or realistic events. O'Connor's reaction to Jenny perhaps best expresses the reader's complex feelings about the characters in experimental black humor fiction: "That poor shuddering creature had pelvic bones I could see flying through her dress. I want to lean forward and laugh with terror."

—Donald J. Greiner, "Djuna Barnes' *Nightwood* and the American Origins of Black Humor," *Critique* (August 1975), excerpted in *Twentieth-Century American Literature*, ed. Harold Bloom (New York: Chelsea House Publishers, 1986), 308

JAMES B. SCOTT

To approach *Nightwood* from a structural viewpoint or to regard it as a "poetic" novel, is at once helpful and limiting; for, in either case, we are viewing the work externally as a form, or as a succession of "devices." Robin is the *raison d'être* of *Nightwood;* she dictates its form and inspires its poetry. She is the central reality about which the artifices of character, place, and situation function as the canvas flats, the "props," and the supporting characters of a play. But it would be idle for us to define Robin. Just as she herself is a mass of contradictions, what she represents extends itself into the often contradictory physical and spiritual characteristics of mankind. She is both the "Soul" of *Nightwood* and the "Soul," naturalistically presented, of man.

Robin is the essence of Self, or the selfness of the Self, made incarnate. Man, naturalistically seen, is an animal; he has an (evolved) animal body but no "Soul" in the Platonic sense wherein it is traditionally conceived that individuals contain within them an essence of self that transcends mortality. That Platonic "Soul" is thought to live forever, and it forms the basis for the promise of eternal life upon which so many religions build their theological structures. But, if man is regarded naturalistically, that quality of "essence," or "soul," must die with the body. Hence Robin is also the promise of death; for that elusive but palpable *real* sense of self, will, after all, cease at the moment of death, together with all longing for it. Robin is "eaten death," according to the doctor; and his remark is reinforced by the aura of decay that emanates from Robin's skin when she is in her trancelike sleep. Her slow life burns coldly like that of fungi, an "earth flesh" suggestive of our mortality; for we are all dying from the moment of our birth.

But Robin is also myth-engendering. She is first introduced to *Nightwood's* pages amid the jungle she has created in her hotel room, under whose profuse plants and birds she lies in a deep sleep. Felix, "out of delicacy," steps behind the palms while the doctor attends to Robin. Felix is thus placed where Acteon concealed himself to observe Diana, where the Elders observed Susanna, and where countless swains have observed and fallen in love with endless nymphs. For Felix must surely fall in love with Robin as he observes her. If man's true history is lengendary, as the doctor insists, Robin embodies that legend; for she is a "carrier" of the primal origins that man has all but forgotten during the long civilizing process.

—James B. Scott, *Djuna Barnes* (New York: G.K. Hall & Co., 1976), 115–16

LOUIS F. KANNENSTINE

Nightwood, appearing in 1936, suddenly towers over all of Djuna Barnes's previous work, excelling it in organizational perfection, intensity of conception, and power of phrasing—the same broad qualities that would later distinguish *The Antiphon* and, less imposingly, *Spillway*. But it should not be assumed that it is discontinuous from the earlier work, a result of a sort of literary immaculate conception. It is in fact the convergence and refinement of Miss Barnes's hitherto somewhat contrasting styles and scattered themes. *Nightwood* is a distinct advance in treatment of narrative and character, achieving a new unity and reaching a plateau upon which Miss Barnes has since insisted upon remaining. It goes beyond the early versions of the short stories in its extreme concentration and richness of ambiguity, and it is also much more successful in transcending literary period and fictional genre than was *Ryder*.

The greater unity of *Nightwood*, to give but one preliminary example, is apparent in Miss Barnes's management of parody and the new prominence given to Matthew O'Connor. *Ryder* meant to disrupt and parody its own narrative by insertion of dialogue in play form, poems, and illustrations. It aimed for scattered effects rather than one dominant effect. *Nightwood*, however, manages to achieve an intense single-mindedness comparable to that of the *Spillway* stories in their final version, and the urge to parody is strictly contained in the doctor's inexhaustible flights of rhetoric. This is not to say that, with the doctor offstage, Miss Barnes is incapable of regarding Felix Volkbein's passion for nobility and the Catholic church, or Jenny Petherbridge's "squatter" tactics, without irony. The fact is that these attitudes culminate in O'Connor's own vision, and the parodic tone belongs to his choral monologues. So if, say, Burton's *Anatomy of Melancholy* is echoed somewhere in the novel, it is in the doctor's own words that it, along with the spirit it represents, is parodied. It is this associative resonance that *Ryder* and *Ladies Almanack* never fully achieved.

But this is only one element that contributes to the greater cohesiveness of *Nightwood*. A particular new factor in Miss Barnes's work that appears here is a preoccupation with the nocturnal, with sleep and dreaming, which, insofar as the characters in the novel become immersed in it, provides a new perspective upon the familiar themes of the earlier work: the nature of time and history, the condition of women and particularly women in love, the Bleeding Heart as a religious and secular symbol for universal suffering, and the "middle condition" as the measure of being. It is possibly the last of these that furnishes the broadest understanding of the novel's exceedingly close and complex texture.

In *Spillway*, the state of being at halt, neither here nor there, is one of intolerable anguish. Yet for Madame von Bartmann, it is the source of illumination, of the tragic vision of life. In the intermediate position, dualities are abolished. The distinctions that the rational intelligence habitually makes, as it analyzes and categorizes experience, become erased. The characters in

Nightwood hover between night and day, dream and reality. It is a middle region that they inhabit, and implicit in their situation are the novel's intertwined themes. This condition also determines the form of the novel, giving rise to its unique structure, imagery, and language.

   —Louis F. Kannenstine, *The Art of Djuna Barnes: Duality and Damnation* (New York: New York University Press, 1977), 86–87

CAROLYN ALLEN

In *Nightwood*, what readers hail as stylistic innovation begins not so much with Barnes's desire to experiment as with her recognition that current modes of discourse were inappropriate for her subject. In *Nightwood*, she eschews the language of rationality, often nominal in emphasis, dichotomous in argument, and factual in description, because it cannot adequately portray her subjects, the power of the night, of irrationality and the unconscious; and the nature of love, particularly love between women. To evoke them, Barnes uses instead an indirect, associative style that depends on reader intuition rather than on logic. The style of *Nightwood* tries to avoid naming directly, and so concentrates on not-naming, on using syntactic and semantic structures that signal indirection. Direct description would, for example, place in too distinct a relief a woman like Robin Vote, the novel's central force, who is best conceived as a presence rather than as a character. In passages describing her there is a syntactic preference for the passive voice suitable to her title, "la sonambule," and frequently for negation in keeping with her "presence-in-absence." In addition, love between women, in which self-knowledge comes from loving one who is different from yet resembles the self, requires a language tending toward synonymy rather than antonymy. Appropriately then, the principal mark of Barnes's style is the analogy, the terms of which are basically alike though superficially different. The talk of the two main speakers, Matthew and Nora, is heavily metaphoric as if single words or direct description were inadequate to convey the nature of their subjects, the discoveries and despairs of love. The syntax is complicated, heavily embedded and often appositional, another suggestion that single phrases alone cannot name what is occurring. Throughout individual passages and among widely separated sections, words and phrases are repeated, sometimes with a shift in meaning, and the reader must associate these words with earlier occurrences of them in order to see how Barnes depends on lexical sets rather than on narrative or characterization to convey her ideas.

Ironically and purposefully, the novel's highly metaphoric and oblique style makes a crucial point: words do not work. For Matthew and Nora, talk, even elaborately constructed talk, does not convince or sustain or serve in experiences of extremity. Although conversations about the night world are the substantive center of the novel, speakers have either collapsed into chaos or fallen silent before its conclusion.

Traditional plot development is of scant interest to Barnes, and in *Nightwood* it operates as pretext rather than context. ⟨. . .⟩

⟨. . . One⟩ of the most singular features of *Nightwood* is the way Barnes makes interior feeling a topic of exterior conversation. The metaphoric language in which Matthew and Nora discuss abstract mental constructions calls on techniques often associated with interior monologue. One critic mentions Barnes's "frequent employment of the interior monologue" even though the novel's monologues are actually exterior and conscious. Some passages seem interior because states of mind are the principal subject of conversation and because the talk about them is removed from what we ordinarily associate with everyday conversation; people do not usually talk like Matthew, though interior monologues in novels may employ his degree of metaphor. Furthermore, the style of *Nightwood* as a whole is so idiosyncratic that it often seems as if Barnes were writing an essay instead of a novel. All the characters talk in the indirect style used in the narrative descriptions. Though in one sense Barnes keeps her reader at an impersonal distance by her indirection, in another she creates a personal voice which the characters all share. It is difficult to avoid thinking of a single metaphor-maker behind Matthew's and Nora's voices and narrative passages. As a result, the largely undifferentiated and highly self-conscious language may be thought of as Barnes's own "interior monologue" though formally there is nothing interior about it. Like Joyce and Faulkner, she is interested in what goes on in the mind, but instead of mimetic "streams" of consciousness or unconsciousness she relies on indirection in narrative observation, characterization, and figurative language.

> —Carolyn Allen, " 'Dressing the Unknowable in the Garments of the Known': The Style of Djuna Barnes's *Nightwood*," *Women's Language and Style: Studies in Contemporary Language*, no. 1, 1978. E.L. Epstein. L&S Books, reprinted in *The Critical Cosmos Series: American Fiction 1914 to 1945*, ed. Harold Bloom (New York: Chelsea House Publishers, 1987), 149–50, 152

ANDREW FIELD

The outlines of Joyce's artistic development shadow down upon Barnes' own artistic strategies, and it is not too much to say that you must know something about Joyce to know certain things about Barnes.

The American poet Jack Hirschman touched upon some important specifics in the influence of Joyce upon Barnes in a doctoral thesis (Indiana, 1961). He first noted that the verbal intricacies and the imagery of *Ladies Almanack* are quite clearly influenced by the portion of *Work in Progress* that appeared in *transition* in 1927. The saint's life and calendar forms, too, may be attributed to Joyce's friendship with Barnes, for he was well known to be inclined to both. Some of the parallels found by Hirschman do not admit of any doubt whatsoever, as, for example, Barnes in *Ladies Almanack*: "And saying riddle me this, or meddle me that, contriving the Potion as ever you may, hiccup hic jacet," as contrasted with Joyce's passage in *Finnegans Wake*: "Latin me that, my trinity scholard, out of eure sanscreed into oure eryan. Hircus Civis Eblanensis!" Joyce read from the *Wake* for her. She laughed. He was delighted.

Above all it is in her extension of the limits of literary language that Djuna Barnes stands on common ground with Joyce. Joyce's earliest work was in Elizabethan form, and Elizabethan and Jacobean language is important in the work of both writers. Of the early twentieth-century English writers, few can be said to pay more persistent attention to layers of language and difficult historical allusion than Joyce, Eliot and Barnes. Joyce gave a new form to the novel. Eliot gave a new tone of voice to English poetry. Barnes was comparatively disadvantaged because her main narrative cargo was her rather singular family experience—a great and painful gift for her as a writer, to be sure, but a gift of less than universal appeal and currency—and also because she was a woman and a most unusual sort of woman at that.

The parallel development of Barnes and Joyce—she, of course, following shortly behind—is striking. Both have musical roots which fed their art. Both have a passion for the past and arcane language, which are applied to a present not very far removed. Both moved sharply from classically plain artistic expression to the invention of new mixed genres. The celebrated Joycean epiphanies, trivial moments of high emotion and significance, are matched by similar moments in the major early short stories by Barnes (though in her case the moments of intensity tend to be fixed at either the opening or the closing of the stories), many of which were written before it is likely that she would have been familiar with *Dubliners*. As Joyce moved from the early poems of *Chamber Music* to the short stories of *Dubliners*, so, too, Barnes moved from the poems of *The Book of Repulsive Women* to the short stories of *A Book*. Then both artists shift to the novel form, and the two "novels" of each writer both seeth with parody and travesty and wear the very term novel only with difficulty. Both writers play with drama left-handedly, and neither of them attaches much importance to narrative in the traditional sense. Hirschman goes too far, however, in suggesting that this entire period of Barnes' art is essentially imitative. There is to be sure a strong imitative current in her early art, but apart from certain places, such as her overly Beardsleyesque drawings before 1920, there is a much stronger vein of unmistakable originality in all that she did in her first decade as an artist.

After 1928 there follows nearly a decade of silence which ends with the appearance of her masterwork, *Nightwood*, in 1936. It is certainly true that that novel, though not without influences, speaks basically in its own unique voice. There is no shadow of Joyce. But it is equally true that the major Barnes work which followed after two decades of silence, the poetic drama *The Antiphon* (1958), is more Joycean than any other Barnes work for its apparently impenetrable density of language and intent. Both Djuna Barnes and James Joyce share a strong disposition to verbal encrustation. They both seek to conceal more than to reveal or "communicate," and in each writer one must learn to accept this manner if one is to be able to participate in the writer's poetic intensity. This important aspect of Djuna Barnes is natural to her and not the result of any influence.

—Andrew Field, *Djuna: The Formidable Miss Barnes* (Austin: University of Texas Press, 1985), 109–11

CHERYL J. PLUMB

Ladies Almanack, published in November 1928, is a deliberate answer, or companion, to *Ryder*, published in August 1928. In *Ladies Almanack*, Barnes uses the almanack form and notoriously ambiguous prose to serve multiple purposes. First, the humorous and explicit sexuality of *Ladies Almanack* continues Barnes's attack on middle-class sensibilities. Second, she satirizes lesbian love as sharing the same faults of heterosexual love. In this way she both legitimizes lesbian love and simultaneously demonstrates its limitations. Finally, Barnes is able to raise issues concerning spiritual well-being indirectly because the almanack tradition counterpoints seasonal time with the stages of human life. Thus, as in *Ryder*, Barnes contrasts the limitation of physical nature to the life of the superior sensibility represented by the artist.

Thematic considerations suggest that connections between *Ryder* and *Ladies Almanack* are conscious. In *Ryder*, "Three Great Moments of History" are told by Doctor O'Connor to one of Ryder's illegitimate sons who rejects his father's procreative philosophy. In *Ladies Almanack* the "Fourth Great Moment of History" is told to Evangeline Musset by Doll Furious who reminds Musset that she has undoubtedly heard the other three. Figuratively, the parallel suggests that Evangeline replaces the son.

This connection is strengthened by a conversation in *Ryder* between Wendell and his mother. Sophia dismisses Wendell's theory that his daughter Julie will be able to "get back" to him, meaning, presumably, be as he is. Sophia asserts instead that Julie will "go beyond" him. In *Ladies Almanack* Evangeline, figuratively the descendant of Ryder, does just that. Her messianic zeal in converting women to her creed parallels Ryder's espousal of his procreative philosophy, but because she advocates love of woman for woman, her actions parody his; therefore, she "goes beyond" him.

In addition, Evangeline surpasses Ryder in another way. She is identified with the Garden of Venus as opposed to the Camp of Nature, associated with heterosexual love, which Ryder represents. The image of the cultivated garden implies that lesbian love is to be preferred because it is "artificial," created, in contrast to what is "natural" and consequently base: heterosexual love. Such a reversal, reflecting the symbolist and decadent roots of Barnes's fiction, parodies middle-class sexual attitudes, which included the belief that forms of love other than heterosexual and procreative were perverse. However, the approval given to Evangeline Musset is undercut, though she is neither denied nor exactly condemned: the Garden of Venus, though cultivated and artificial, is yet subject to time and decay. ⟨. . .⟩

⟨. . . Although⟩ Ladies Almanack treats certain lesbian ideas humorously, for example, the argument for lesbian marriage advanced by Lady Buck-and-Balk and Tilly-Tweed-in-Blood, it is not a full-scale censure of lesbianism per se. However, the work is not limited to a celebration of lesbianism. The work explores not just lesbian or heterosexual love but the limitations of physical love as opposed to such characteristic virtues as wisdom and stoic indifference. Thus, the theme of Ladies Almanack unites Barnes's decadent interest in the perverse with her symbolist concern for individual consciousness and mortality. Furthermore, one can hardly speak of this work without considering the bawdiness of Barnes's humor, which, in itself, is a satiric attack on middle-class propriety and sexual reticence. Much of Barnes's salacious humor seems designed purely to outrage.

To challenge traditional sexual ideas, Barnes exploited the moral force of the saint's life as a witness to a faith, even though the faith Evangeline Musset advocates is a reversal of the traditional "martyrdom of the senses." The heroine Evangeline Musset is described as "one Grande Red Cross for the Pursuance, the Relief, and the Distraction, of such Girls as in their Hinder Parts, and their Fore Parts, and in whatsoever Parts did suffer them most, lamentably Cruelly. . . ." Red Cross undoubtedly recalls Spenser's Red Cross Knight in The Faerie Queen. Here, however, the Knight's traditional purity is parodied in Evangeline's mission to provide sexual relief for young women.

Introducing the theme of human passion and specifically, lesbian sexuality, the narrator mocks middle-class ideas of moral progress and human superiority. She implies humorously that passion rules human nature: ". . . from the day that we were indifferent Matter, to this wherein we are Imperial Personages of the divine human Race, no thing so solaces it as other Parts as inflamed, or with the Consolation every woman has at her Finger Tips, or at the very Hang of her Tongue?" (6)

Barnes's humor, building on puns, understatement, and circumlocutions, not only attacks middle-class ideas but is used to undermine readers' confidence in various characters. She thus continues the practice, demonstrated in *Ryder* and in various other early works, of introducing a character and then also questioning the values of that character. In *Ladies Almanack* Maisie Tuck-and-Frill and Patience Scalpel challenge Evangeline Musset's earthy creed. For example, Maisie Tuck-and-Frill is presented as one conscious of spiritual realities, yet the spoonerism of her name wittily undermines that seriousness of purpose. Readers are amused but tentative in responding to her character and ideas. Are Maisie's values to be trusted? Or those of Evangeline Musset? Barnes's humor achieves a distancing effect that is reinforced by the deliberate ambiguity of her prose.

—Cheryl J. Plumb, *Fancy's Craft: Art and Identity in the Early Works of Djuna Barnes* (Selinsgrove: Susquehanna University Press, 1986), 90–93

SANDRA M. GILBERT AND SUSAN GUBAR

Djuna Barnes provided what might be considered an anatomy of the destiny of transvestism in *Nightwood* (1936), a novel that focuses on the way in which salvation is possible only through the subversion preached and practiced by the invert, for *Nightwood* introduces us to the third-sexed figures of Robin Vote and Dr. O'Connor, who star in a novel that was introduced by T. S. Eliot himself. 〈. . .〉 A kind of witch doctor or medicine man, half Circe, half Ulysses, Dr. O'Connor lies in bed heavily painted with rouge and wearing a golden wig with long curls. As for Robin Vote, a girl who habitually dresses as a boy, she too may also have both unnerved and fascinated the creator of the hyacinth girl/boy, for Robin's gender identity is deeply blurred. Indeed, she is described as "outside the 'human type'—a wild thing caught in a woman's skin," whose first name connects her with nature and whose last name associates her with the triumphs of the women's movement and the votive powers of the sacred.

From baptismal basins described as "loosing their skirts of water in a ragged and flowing hem" (30), to rationalism which "dresses the unknowable in the garment of the known" (136), *Nightwood* is a clothing-obsessed book which asks "what is this love we have for the invert, boy or girl?" (136), as the male transvestite meditates on the passion the female cross-dresser creates in all who meet her. A "tall girl with the body of a boy" (46), Robin Vote initially wears men's clothes to gain a freedom from feminine constraints that allows her to wander through the streets at night like a libertine, a female Don Juan who enthralls all the women she meets. In addition, she rejects skirts because they allow women to be as easily violated as the "Tuppeny Uprights" Dr. O'Connor describes 〈. . . .〉

But, like ⟨artist⟩ Romaine Brooks's subjects and Radclyffe Hall's Stephen, Robin often seems to be victimized by the contradiction between her female anatomy and her metaphorically transsexual destiny. One of a kind, appearing from the first in male garb, she is described as sickly, solitary, half child, half criminal. When we first encounter her, she is asleep "in a jungle trapped in a drawing room" (35) where, to Dr. O'Connor, she looks like "a beast turning human" (37). Throughout the novel, moreover, she is characterized as a somnambulistic sexual wanderer who can neither remember her past nor fully awaken herself to her present. But the terrible dissonance between her transsexual desire and her biological reality is most vividly dramatized by her experience with pregnancy and childbirth, which drives her to murderous rage and to increasing efforts at intense self-obliteration. Denied interiority by the text, which never records her consciousness, Robin appears even to her lovers to be subhuman, though she seems to signal her aspiration to full humanity at least in part by dressing as a man. But she also is doomed to fall because she and Dr. O'Connor are misfits, neither masculine nor feminine, belonging nowhere. Like the ironically named Felix, a Jew who longs to be assimilated, these transvestites are "alone, apart and single" (10), objects of derision and marked scapegoats, as well as appropriate symbols of a confused culture where everyone feels, in Dr. O'Connor's words, as if he or she "turned up this time as I shouldn't have been" (91).

Yet the artifice of O'Connor's parodic persona, like the level of the beast to which Robin sinks, paradoxically functions to gain both these odd creatures potency in this novel which ultimately associates the transsexual with the transcendent. An apostle of darkness, Dr. O'Connor wears a nightgown, the "natural raiment of extremity," one character explains, because "What nation, what religion, what ghost, what dream, has not worn it—infants, angels, priests, the dead: why should not the doctor, in the grave dilemma of his alchemy, wear his dress?" (80). As a man who would be a prophet, this vatic transvestite who inhabits a nightwood far more empowering than Joyce's nighttown identifies himself with feminine insight and with visionary intuition. A gynecologist of sorts, Dr. O'Connor resembles the witch doctors, shamans, and *berdaches* of primitive cultures who have traditionally used women's garb, women's medicinal crafts, and even self-castration as a sign of their dedication to female powers.

—Sandra M. Gilbert and Susan Gubar, *No Man's Land: The Place of the Woman Writer in the Twentieth Century* (New Haven: Yale University Press, 1989), 358–61

SUSAN SNIADER LANSER

Ladies Almanack is ⟨. . .⟩ a linguistic and literary experiment, a dense and sometimes barely coherent discourse that spurns the conventions of realism, wanders far from the story it is supposed to tell, adopts and parodies a host of forms and norms, evokes a spectrum of times and texts. Its surface form is the monthly chronicle, a medium that Barnes used with some frequency, but the book resembles the picaresque fable in structure, the mock epic in tone; it uses or parodies the saint's life, the ode, the prayer, the lullaby, the allegory, the myth, as well as specific works from the Bible to *Finnegans Wake*. 〈. . .〉

The discourse of *Ladies Almanack*, similarly, is a dense and highly allusive prose through which almost nothing is made clear; the text speaks cryptically, figurally, and evasively. Sentences are winding, inverted, unfinished or impossibly long. Antecedents get misplaced, verbs dangle, pronouns lose their source. Key words are sometimes elided from sentences whose meanings remain forever indeterminate, as in "I came to it as other Women, and I never a Woman before nor since" (24). Archaisms are common—some as old as Chaucer, some barely obsolete; neologisms are frequent; grammatical forms are resurrected from the Renaissance or invented on the spot. There is a continual mingling of registers as well as lexicons: plain modern English coexists with fancy Elizabethan; obscure terms are juxtaposed with blunt Anglo-Saxon unpleasantries. Metaphors often make one strain desperately and still end up not quite making sense 〈. . . .〉 And enshrouding the whole are the Capital Letters: most nouns and a few adjectives and verbs are capitalized, so that the text seems at once Ancient and Fantastical.

The perspective and tone of *Ladies Almanack* are sometimes equally indeterminate, clouded by indirect discourse, rhetorical questions, oxymorons, and maxims of uncertain intent. Lesbian sexuality is called a "Distemper" and a "Beatitude" in the same paragraph; women who love women are like "a tree cut of life" yet they make "a Garden of Ecstasy" (12); "Love in Man is Fear of Fear," but "Love in Woman is Hope without Hope" (23). These contradictory and coded messages generate a narrative voice that is evasive, devious, playfully indirect. There are moments when the narrator does say or imply "I" and "we," but never in a context that commits her to a single, coherent textual identity. The result is "a Maze, nor will we have a way out of it" (58): a text that speaks in tongues.

At least three different modes of discourse combine to create this maze. First and most prominent are the narrative segments that tell the story of Dame Musset and her coterie of allegorically named characters (each with a historical counterpart). These narrative passages are the most ribald sections of the book and the most accessible. A second set of sequences fashions a fanciful amazonian lore, using song and poetry, illustration and myth, to turn patriarchal discourse to gynocentric ends 〈. . . .〉 The third and least common mode of discourse in *Ladies Almanack* is expository, pondering questions of a social and philosophical sort; perhaps because these passages cannot rely on fictional visions, they are the most ambiguous and ambivalent segments of the text, yielding much of its contradiction and its few moments of gloom. These three kinds of discourse are usually interwoven and interspersed rather than sequential and discrete: a myth about woman's Edenic origins slides into the story line as Eve becomes Daisy Downpour; Dame Musset's friends take on the philosopher's role and shift narrative to essay-in-dialogue; a single page juxtaposes poem and picaresque. Though each chapter is named for a month of the year and is headed by apt illustration, the segments vary in length, mode, and formal composition: some tell the story of Dame Musset; others are essays; several are composites of poetry, story, and inquiry.

This mélange of modes and media permits an exploration of lesbian culture and female experience from multiple points of view, each form or voice carrying another shade of difference, another piece of the prism that constitutes the book's elusive rhetorical stance. The interweaving of philosophic, mythic, and narrative modes, each with its particular tendencies of mood, creates a sense of motion in the text: not a beeline or a circle, but an uneven, irregular expedition, now meandering, now dashing, now turning back, like one of Dame Musset's romps through the Bois. Like all almanacs, this one allows time to be both cyclic and linear. (It is no accident that Barnes used the almanac form on several occasions: given her preoccupation with time, the almanac may have afforded her a way to mark its passage without despair.) As it progresses the text becomes at once more radical and more covert, until clarity is restored as narrative turns mythic in a climactic account of Dame Musset's death.

—Susan Sniader Lanser, "Speaking in Tongues: *Ladies Almanack* and the Discourse of Desire," *Silence and Power: A Reevaluation of Djuna Barnes*, ed. Mary Lynn Broe (Carbondale, IL: Southern Illinois University Press, 1991), 157–59

BIBLIOGRAPHY

The Book of Repulsive Women: 8 Rhythms and 5 Drawings. 1915.
Three from the Earth. 1919.
A Book. 1923.
Ladies Almanack. 1928.
Ryder. 1928.
A Night among the Horses. 1929.
Nightwood. 1936.

The Antiphon. 1958.
Selected Works. 1962.
Spillway. 1962.
Creatures in an Alphabet. 1982.
Smoke and Other Early Stories. 1982.
Interviews. 1985.

JANE BOWLES

1917-1973

JANE BOWLES was born Jane Sidney Auer in New York City on February 22, 1917, the only child of Sidney Auer and Claire Stajer Auer. The family moved to Woodmere, Long Island, in 1927. After her father's death in 1930, Jane and her mother returned to New York City and Jane entered a public high school. In 1931 she enrolled at Stoneleigh, a private girls' school in Massachusetts. Six months later, she fell from a horse and broke her leg; she then developed tuberculosis of the knee and entered a clinic in Leysin, Switzerland. In 1934, Jane returned to New York and, in 1936, completed a novel, *Le Phaeton Hypocrite*, but all copies of the manuscript were soon lost. The following year, Jane met the composer and poet Paul Bowles, whom she married on February 21, 1938.

After a honeymoon trip to Central America and Paris, Jane began writing *Two Serious Ladies*, which was published in 1943. While some critics (and her husband) recognized her talent, the book was not a popular success. Jane continued to write, publishing "A Guatemalan Idyll" the same year; "A Day in the Open" and *A Quarreling Pair* in 1945; and "Plain Pleasures" in 1946. The first act of *In the Summer House* was published in 1947.

On a trip to Mexico with Paul in 1940, Jane had met Helvetia Perkins, with whom she had an intimate relationship. She would have other relationships with women, but her marriage with Bowles remained intact. After publishing *In the Summer House*, Jane again traveled with Paul, and in Tangier she fell passionately in love with Cherifa, a young peasant woman who would take a prominent role in the rest of Jane's life. Her work continued, with "Camp Cataract" completed in 1948, followed the next year by "A Stick of Green Candy," a story about the breakdown of her belief in the imaginative world. In late 1948, Jane met Tennessee Williams, who would become a lifelong friend.

In January 1952, Jane returned to New York to oversee the production and final rewriting of *In the Summer House*. Although critically praised, it did not attract a large audience and closed in less than two months. Jane returned to Morocco, and in February 1957 "A Stick of Green Candy" was published in *Vogue*. That same year, at age 40, Jane suffered a stroke. Many Europeans and Moroccans in Tangier believed that Cherifa had poisoned her, but the various speculations have never

21

been proven. Jane's vision was damaged by the stroke, and she had severe difficulty reading and writing. After seeking therapy in England and New York, she returned to Tangier in 1958, but she would be plagued by small illnesses, depression, and an inability to write for the rest of her life.

Paul collected Jane's stories and submitted them to her publisher under the title *Plain Pleasures*. The volume was published in England, and *The Collected Works of Jane Bowles* was published in the United States in 1966. *Two Serious Ladies* was reissued, and her work was becoming increasingly popular. Suffering from depression, however, Jane entered a psychiatric hospital in Malaga in April 1967. She suffered more strokes and her physical health continued to deteriorate until her death on May 4, 1973.

CRITICAL EXTRACTS

EDITH H. WALTON

While it is not often that one comes across a novel which makes as little sense as ⟨*Two Serious Ladies*⟩, Jane Bowles has precedents and forerunners. In an elusive way—I make the comparison very gingerly—echoes of Firbank, Van Vechten and the lost days of Dada crop up now and again in *Two Serious Ladies*, plus an occasional reminiscence of Saroyan. To say, however, that the book is derivative would be clearly unfair. My feeling is that Mrs. Bowles has developed—and exploited—her own brand of lunacy and that she is, perhaps fortunately, unique. Certainly—to free her from the charge of plagiarism—she is nowhere near so witty as either Firbank or Van Vechten, nor do her characters, though eccentric, have the same decadent charm.

To attempt to unravel the plot of *Two Serious Ladies* would be to risk, I feel sure, one's own sanity. Obviously, however, I must identify this odd pair of heroines—one of whom is a wealthy spinster, Miss Goering, who suffers from obsessions; the other a feather-brained matron, Mrs. Copperfield. While the latter adventures down in Panama, acquiring a weird set of friends of very easy virtue, Miss Goering has her own startling experiences in her own austere home, where she is companioned by the sinister Miss Gamelon. Beyond the fact that they are casual acquaintances there is no visible connection between these two earnest ladies, nor do their deft stories dovetail in any important way.

What does, however, link both the *Two Serious Ladies* and the other characters in the book is their mad, their wayward, their bizarre aberrations, in which they indulge with so reasonable an air. Among their other eccentricities, more-over, is the naive bluntness and candor with which they all speak, the abrupt-ness with which they move inconsequentially from one topic to another. Their world, in short, is an almost frighteningly fantastic one—the more so because its outward lineaments are so natural and so normal, because their background is so soberly realistic. Belatedly one realizes that there is hardly a character in the book who could be called really sane, unless it is the charmingly wanton and amoral Pacifica.

Two Serious Ladies is intermittently funny and certainly original, but I also felt that it strains too hard to startle and to shock and that it all too often is just merely silly. Jane Bowles undoubtedly is a clever young writer with a good deal of talent, but I feel that she has written this book with her tongue in her cheek and that it is not as irresistible as she intended it to be.

—Edith H. Walton, "Fantastic Duo," New York Times Book Review (9 May 1943), excerpted in Twentieth-Century American Fiction, ed. Harold Bloom (New York: Chelsea House Publishers, 1986), 550

CHARLES THOMAS SAMUELS

Surrounding Mrs. Bowles's art is an effluvium of chic despair which will alien-ate many readers. On the other hand, her work can easily be overvalued since it combines proud idiosyncrasy with a rather startling prescience (her novel, Two Serious Ladies, published in 1943, forecast the current vogue of comic goth-icism). When that book first appeared here, reviewers could damn it with a clear conscience: modernism had not yet become an obligatory mass fashion. (On its first English appearance last year, the Times Literary Supplement, marching resolutely backward in its sensible shoes, still stomped it to bits.) Today in the United States, where the cultivated reader feels duty-bound to be affronted, Mrs. Bowles's controlled derision is likely to seem the definitive force of civi-lized disgust.

Surely her indictments have an easy inclusiveness. Like her husband, Paul, Mrs. Bowles writes tight little anecdotes about the pull of bestiality, an unex-pected form of self-fulfillment. Like her husband's stories, hers pit the weak against the strong, the righteous against the sensual, only to record a general rout. Though her tales lack his intellectual clarity, they have greater charm.

Two Serious Ladies follows the adventures of two wacky souls. Rich Christina Goering is one of those "fanatics who think of themselves as leaders without once having gained the respect of a single human being." Seeking salvation, she makes opportunities of other people; when her needle reaches its goal on the spiritual applause meter, her goodness abruptly stops. Fluttery Mrs. Copperfield, downtrodden by a selfish husband, nevertheless has one "sole object in life . . . to be happy, although people who had observed her behavior over a period of years would have been surprised to discover that this was all."

Out of strange charitable impulses, Christina takes a female companion, a succession of male lovers, and becomes a Samaritan of polite promiscuity. Mrs. Copperfield is dragged to Panama by her husband, where she discovers in herself a fund of willfulness to match Christina's. She installs herself in a disreputable hotel and takes up with a native prostitute. Ironically, Mrs. Copperfield gets what she has always wanted. To Christina's censorious concern in the book's last scene, she replies, with her fist meanly rapping on the table:

> "True enough . . . I have gone to pieces, which is a thing I've wanted to do for years. I know I am as guilty as I can be, but I have my happiness; which I guard like a wolf, and I have authority now and a certain amount of daring, which, if you remember correctly, I never had before."

Shocked, Christina confirms her chilling logic:

> "Certainly I am nearer to becoming a saint," reflected Miss Goering, "but is it possible that a part of me hidden from my sight is piling sin upon sin as fast as Mrs. Copperfield?" This latter possibility Miss Goering thought to be of considerable interest but of no great importance.

The book's final sentence reveals that glacial disregard for "significance" which makes *Two Serious Ladies* wonderfully self-possessed, but elusive. In a novel without recognizable motivation, whose characters do not so much communicate as collide, where all interstices of life and logic are effaced, the parallels in the stories of the two women are too slight to provide the structure and carry the meaning. Nor do the parallel situations support the scrutiny they seem to invite.

To be sure, there are hints of purpose scattered about. "One must allow," Christina suggests before a tryst, "that a certain amount of carelessness in one's nature often accomplishes what the will is incapable of doing." And, as Mrs. Copperfield casually asserts on another occasion, "No one among my friends speaks any longer of character . . . what interests us most . . . is finding out what we are like." But these hints never become more than hints. Too often, Mrs. Bowles is seduced by the bizarre behavior of her characters. And our wish to find life in her shadow play finally becomes mere nervous interest.

—Charles Thomas Samuels, "Serious Ladies," *New York Review of Books* (15 December 1966), excerpted in *Twentieth-Century American Fiction*, ed. Harold Bloom (New York: Chelsea House Publishers, 1986), 550–51

TRUMAN CAPOTE

I'm not all that keen on the theater: cannot sit through most plays once; nevertheless, I saw *In the Summer House* three times, and not out of loyalty to the author, but because it had a thorny wit, the flavor of a newly tasted, refreshingly bitter beverage—the same qualities that had initially attracted me to Mrs. Bowles' novel, *Two Serious Ladies*.

My only complaint against Mrs. Bowles is not that her work lacks quality, merely quantity. The volume in hand constitutes her entire shelf, so to say. And grateful as we are to have it, one could wish that there was more. Once, while discussing a colleague, someone more facile than either of us, Jane said: "But it's so easy for him. He has only to turn his hand. Just *turn* his hand." Actually, writing is never easy: in case anyone doesn't know, it's the hardest work around; and for Jane I think it is difficult to the point of true pain. And why not?—when both her language and her themes are sought after along tortured paths and in stony quarries: the never-realized relationships between her people, the mental and physical discomforts with which she surrounds and saturates them—every room an atrocity, every urban landscape a creation of neon-dourness. And yet, though the tragic view is central to her vision, Jane Bowles is a very funny writer, a humorist of sorts—but *not*, by the way, of the Black School. Black Comedy, as its perpetrators label it, is, when successful, all lovely artifice and lacking any hint of compassion. "Camp Cataract," to my mind the most complete of Mrs. Bowles' stories and the one most representative of her work, is a rendering sample of controlled compassion: a comic tale of doom that has at its heart, and *as* its heart, the subtlest comprehension of eccentricity and human apartness. This story alone would require that we accord Jane Bowles high esteem.

—Truman Capote, "Introduction" to *The Collected Works of Jane Bowles* (1966), excerpted in *Twentieth-Century American Fiction*, ed. Harold Bloom (New York: Chelsea House Publishers, 1986), 553

JOHN ASHBERY

Jane Bowles is a writer's writer's writer. Few surface literary reputations are as glamorous as the underground one she has enjoyed since her novel *Two Serious Ladies* was published in 1943. The extreme rarity of the book, once it went out of print, has augmented its legend. When a London publisher wanted to reprint it three years ago, even Mrs. Bowles was unable to supply him with a copy.

With the present publication of her "collected works," which comes with an introduction by Truman Capote and blurbs by Tennessee Williams ("my favorite book"), Alan Sillitoe ("a landmark in 20th-century American literature") and others, Jane Bowles has at last surfaced. It is to be hoped that she will now be recognized for what she is: one of the finest modern writers of fiction, in any language. At the same time it should be pointed out that she is not quite the sort of writer that her imposing list of Establishment admirers seems to suggest. Her work is unrelated to theirs, and in fact it stands alone in contemporary literature, though if one can imagine George Ade and Kafka collaborating on a modern version of Bunyan's *Pilgrim's Progress* one will have a faint idea of the qualities of *Two Serious Ladies*. ⟨. . .⟩

Mrs. Bowles's seemingly casual, colloquial prose is a constant miracle; every line rings as true as a line of poetry, though there is certainly nothing "poetic" about it, except insofar as the awkwardness of our everyday attempts at communication is poetic. This awkwardness can rise to comic heights, and in doing so evoke visions of a nutty America that we have to recognize as ours. An old man whom Christina questions about a certain cabaret in a place called Pig Snout's Hook replies:

" 'Yes . . . certain people do like that type of music and there are people who live together and eat at table together stark naked all the year long and there are others who we both know about'—he looked very mysterious—'but,' he continued, 'in my day money was worth a pound of sugar or butter or lard any time. When we went out we got what we paid for plus a dog jumpin' through burning hoops, and steaks you could rest your chin on.' "

In her later stories Mrs. Bowles has played down the picaresque local color she used to such effect in the novel. Especially in "A Stick of Green Candy," the story which ends the book and is apparently her most recent, she achieves a new austerity that is as impressive as anything she had done. As in all her work, it is impossible to deduce the end of a sentence from its beginning, or a paragraph from the one that preceded it, or how one of the characters will reply to another. And yet the whole flows marvelously and inexorably to its cruel, lucid end; it becomes itself as we watch it. No other contemporary writer can consistently produce surprise of this quality, the surprise that is the one essential ingredient of great art. Jane Bowles deals almost exclusively in this rare commodity.

—John Ashbery, "Up from the Underground," *New York Times Book Review* (29 January 1967), excerpted in *Twentieth-Century American Fiction*, ed. Harold Bloom (New York: Chelsea House Publishers, 1986), 553–54

ALFRED KAZIN

For many women writers in our day, the old novel of sensitiveness invites parody and counterstatement. And it is in this context that one can understand the strange, funny, perverse, calculatedly unacceptable fictions of Jane Bowles. In her (one) novel, *Two Serious Ladies*, the two heroines are unaccountably inno-

cent passersby through a totally depraved world. They are so closed off from
the rest of us by being so strange, offbeat and untouchably innocent that they
turn even the few male characters attending them—it is essentially a novel of
women and of their journeying into places beyond their ken—into versions of
singularity as strange as themselves.

In Jane Bowles all women characters become parallels to each other.
Everything is dialogue, but nothing advances by dialogue, there is no natural
exchange of experiences, only a mystified scratching by the characters themselves on the impenetrable surface of each other's personalities. This inability
to get below the surface is a mark of the cartoon-like queerness of the women
as central characters. They live in the world by not understanding it. And the
unwillingness to dig for any "deeper" reality is the mark of Jane Bowles herself,
who always worked with dialogue as if she were a Restoration dramatist fascinated not by the "hardness" of her characters but by their naturally closed-off
state. ⟨. . .⟩

Her characters are made original by characters that cannot open or communicate; they are total separates. Their gracious innocence in depraved joints
in Panama is Jane Bowles's joke, but it is not a joke on *them*; they become fond
of whores and pimps and obvious confidence men without knowing what
these strangers do. Their "innocence" is indeed what interests Jane Bowles in
her characters—their incommunicable queerness.

These *are* serious ladies, perhaps because the world is so plainly not serious that only the unconscious virtue of certain women can give it dignity.
They are first and last untouched souls, oddities, privacies, as the women in
Gertrude Stein's *Three Lives* are nothing but "characters." Although Jane Bowles's
women are closer to women than to men, they do not identify with anybody
at all. They are all remarkable children in literature: provisional guests in this
world. Things happen to them without modifying them—that is the comedy
of *Two Serious Ladies*. They just pass through the world. And such is the form of
their "seriousness," their unbreakable singularity, their sweet dim inexpressive-
ness, their obviously privileged position, that they turn the "world" into an
inconsequential background to themselves, a series of farcically tenuous stage
sets—islands, country estates, tropic bordellos. These are cities not on any
map, streets that do not lead into each other, islands that are *unaccountable*. The
prevailing strangeness and unconnectedness of these women makes each of
them a presence that just bulks over everything else. As there is no real trans-
action between them, so there is no action. The absurdity and intractability of
being nothing but an unresisting yet untouched single "character" is all ⟨. . . .⟩

Mrs. Bowles conceived of her fiction as an ironic extension of the old
insistence, in women's fiction, that woman is the heart of a heartless world.
The world in her altogether dry, vaguely jeering pages becomes even more

heartless than one could have imagined it. It is literally deaf, dumb, uncomprehending, made up of characters and situations which do not flow together in the slightest, which never interact. It is a world composed somehow of silence. Since women are the point of it, it dramatizes the heroine as farcically a force, the woman who to her own mind is so original that her personality is the only weight in the story, its dominating indecipherable presence. Woman is the idiosyncrasy around which this bizarre existence is composed.

—Alfred Kazin, "Cassandras," *Bright Book of Life* (1971), excerpted in *Twentieth-Century American Fiction*, ed. Harold Bloom (New York: Chelsea House Publishers, 1986), 551–52

MARK T. BASSETT

Jane Bowles' biographer, Millicent Dillon, notes that the short story "A Stick of Green Candy" concerns a "loss of belief in the imagination" ⟨*A Little Original Sin*, 1981, 183⟩. In this story, Bowles' protagonist—a young teenager named Mary—avoids other children, preferring an isolated clay pit to the crowded, noisy municipal grounds. Within her clay pit, Mary fancies there to be a regiment of soldiers, for whom she is the benevolent commander. One day her predictable, calm and orderly world is invaded by a strange boy named Franklin, whom Mary gradually realizes she loves. By the end of the story, Mary has betrayed her own value system and her men. As a result, she leaves the clay pit behind—along with the belief that a young girl can choose her role in society, or re-order society entirely, through the power of the imagination.

Bowles finished this story in March 1949, while in Taghit, Algeria, with her husband, Paul Bowles, author of *The Sheltering Sky*. In a letter to a couple of friends, she wrote about her stay in Algeria:

> Now I am in the Sahara desert. . . . The dunes are extremely high, and I shall not attempt to climb them again—well maybe I will—because it is so beautiful up there. Nothing but mountains and valleys of sand as far as the eye can see. And to know it stretches for literally hundreds of miles is a very strange feeling. . . . Anyway the rest is all rocks and rather terrifying. . . . There are just Paul and me, the Arab who runs the hotel, and the three soldiers in the fort, and the natives . . . Just *Paul* and *me*. And many empty rooms. The great sand desert begins just outside my window. I might almost stroke the first dune with my hand. ⟨*Out in the World*, 1985, 133⟩

In the oasis that marked the center of a beige funnel of Algerian sand dunes, Jane imagined herself to be alone with Paul. We wonder: Did the steep geography of these dunes inspire the faceless interior of Mary's conical clay pit? Were the barely acknowledged Taghit soldiers transfigured into Mary's obedient and loving regiment? Whatever Jane found terrifying in the desert rocks—was it symbolized by the cluttered, noisy adult world that Mary hopes to evade?

In her study of Jane Bowles, Millicent Dillon discusses several other biographical features of the story. She remarks that Mary's stern father, exhorting her to play at the municipal park "with the other children," mirrors Jane's own father. Sidney Majer Auer, who died when Jane was thirteen, had always frowned upon her dramatizing and had continually urged her to accept the facts of everyday life. Dillon also comments that, because "A Stick of Green Candy" was Bowles' last finished work, the story's theme is doubly intriguing: Jane's central concern for the rest of her life was the fear of losing imaginative control of her work.

—Mark T. Bassett, "Imagination, Control and Betrayal in Jane Bowles' 'A Stick of Green Candy,'" *Studies in Short Fiction* 24, no. 1 (Winter 1987): 25–26

MILLICENT DILLON

⟨*Two Serious Ladies*⟩ is a novel about sex and about religion and about being in the world and falling out of the world. The tone of the novel is startlingly innovative and difficult to pin down. The point of view is continually shifting and the tone itself suddenly shifts from wry humor to tragic vision—sometimes in a paragraph, sometimes within one sentence. The authorial voice is always at a distance from the reader, and it also holds itself at a distance from the characters. Reading, one feels that the relationship between oneself and the writer is constantly shifting. Yet one soon begins to know the sound of a Jane Bowles sentence, its odd jumps, the way in which it continuously confounds expectations, the way in which secrets are withheld and as suddenly revealed.

In the narrative, too, there are sudden shifts. Plot, instead of being an enveloping form, seems to be at the mercy of the tyrannical impulses of the women. Miss Goering and Mrs. Copperfield, each of whom is the shadow of the other, are mired in feminine quandaries: the desire for one's own destiny against the need to care for others, the desire for stability against the need for change, the desire for submission against the need for assertion, the love of men as against the love of women as against the love of self.

The rhythms of the book as a whole are odd, dense, and compacted. As the power of the authorial voice is not a stable one, power itself within the novel comes to be seen in a strange light. Power is imposed, shared, abdicated, inflated then deflated. A character at one instant is menacing, at the next instant pitiable. The alternations that take place from section to section, from paragraph to paragraph and even within sentences are amusing, startling, and disturbing. ⟨. . .⟩

⟨"Camp Cataract"⟩, which has brilliant comic moments alternating with the darknesses, shares many themes with *Two Serious Ladies*, in particular the desire for stability against the need to change and the desire to pursue one's own destiny against the need to care for others. In "Camp Cataract," however, the contrast between the two women is more fixed than the novel. One is cared for, the other does the caring, one feels the need to change, the other wants things to stay as they are. Plot falls into a more conventional mode than in the novel. Yet within the individual paragraphs and sentences one finds the sudden turns and twists and the confounding of expectations so characteristic of Jane Bowles. That secretiveness still remains hidden at the core of the work is apparent in the description of Sadie as she realizes that she is going to make the trip to Camp Cataract:

> She often made important decisions this way, as if some prearranged plot were being suddenly revealed to her, a plot which had immediately to be concealed from the eyes of others, because for Sadie, if there was any problem implicit in making a decision, it lay, not in the difficulty of choosing, but in the concealment of her choice. To her, secrecy was the real absolution from guilt. . . . (365)

"Camp Cataract" is, I believe, a work that cuts closer to the bone than *Two Serious Ladies*. It risks more. The authorial voice allows itself to become closer to Sadie. In surrendering distance from the characters, it also surrenders distance from the readers. Sadie's dread of going out into the world and the agony of that voyage reflect a darkening in Jane Bowles's personality at the time she was writing. Her seven-year affair with Helvetia Perkins was coming to an end. She was, as she told Paul, different from the person she had been before she had started it. She was now, she said, far more uncertain. Yet the exploration of the rupture between two women in fictional form led her to a certainty of conviction, the necessity for the rupture, which was the equivalent of going out into the world. The fictional consequences of this rupture, the death of one of the women, was to have its own reverberations in Jane Bowles's life and in her later fiction.

—Millicent Dillon, "Jane Bowles: Experiment as Character," *Breaking the Sequence: Women's Experimental Fiction*, ed. Ellen G. Friedman and Miriam Fuchs (Princeton: Princeton University Press, 1989), 141–44

EDOUARD RODITI

In her novel, her play, her stories, and the few fragments of her unfinished fiction salvaged and published since her death, all the major characters are women whose behavior is often odd, if not somewhat hysterical or clearly psychopathic. The readiness with which Christina Goering, in *Two Serious Ladies*, yields in turn to the sexual advances of Arnold, Arnold's father, Andy, and ultimately Ben too might well be that of a nymphomaniac, but actually reveals Christina's total lack of interest in men and her desire to mortify herself in order to achieve her own spiritual salvation through what she believes to be sin. Heretical doctrines of salvation through sin have been preached at various times by Christian mystics, by the false messiah Shebtai Zvi in Judaism, and in Islam by a number of Sufi mystics, but Jane seems to have remained unaware of all this. Again in *Two Serious Ladies*, Mrs. Copperfield is at first quite unconscious of the attraction exerted on her by women rather than by her very conventional husband, but soon abandons him to live with Pacifica, an exotic prostitute whose physical appearance, way of life, and company become her obsession while she rapidly succumbs also to alcoholism.

Although Miss Gamelon, Mrs. Quill, and most of the male characters of *Two Serious Ladies* are likewise rather odd or lead a somewhat marginal or purposeless life with what is generally known as "a one-track mind," the oddness of their behavior consists mainly in such minor peculiarities as alcoholism, Arnold's obsession with food, Toby's attempts to convince Mrs. Quill to run her hotel in Panama on a more conventionally profitable basis, or the utterly desultory pattern of Andy's life. Alcoholism appears also to be one of the weaknesses of Christina Goering and Mrs. Quill. Like Mrs. Copperfield, they both have recourse to great quantities of gin in moments of indecision or of stress, much as Jane too had recourse to alcohol in real life.

In describing the odd behavior of Christina Goering and Mrs. Copperfield in particular, Jane seems to have reified in fiction her own fears of becoming sexually indifferent to men, or an alcoholic and emotionally too dependent, as she indeed became some years later in Tangier, on as exotic and in many ways unsatisfactory a female companion as Pacifica. Charifa, the Arab woman with whom I found Jane living, had certainly exerted on her, at least in the first few years of their relationship, a fascination very similar to Pacifica's on Mrs. Copperfield.

In Jane's play *In the Summer House*, Gertrude Eastman Cuevas is likewise a fictional reification of a type of rigidly authoritarian older woman who was destined to play an important part in Jane's emotional life. ⟨. . .⟩

In *In the Summer House*, both Gertrude's daughter Molly and Vivian Constable seem to be reified self-portraits of Jane, each of them betraying in turn Jane's own fears of becoming either as manic as Vivian or as depressed as Molly, who is indifferent to men, even to Lionel, whom she finally marries. The intimate connection between Vivian's manic exaltation and Molly's depressive inaction is revealed when Molly is presumably roused to murder Vivian as her rival in her otherwise quite insignificant relationship with Lionel, a very colorless young man whom she then marries only out of fear of being left alone when her mother decides to marry the wealthy but vulgar Señor Solares for very obviously material reasons.

Jane's almost constant preoccupation with hysteria, epilepsy, or insanity is even more clearly illustrated in "Camp Cataract," which is widely recognized as her best story. Here each one of three sisters reveals in turn her own particular obsession. Like Christina Goering who declared, in the last paragraph of *Two Serious Ladies*, that "Certainly I'm nearer to becoming a saint," Harriet is here obscurely concerned with her own spiritual salvation. She plans to achieve it by escaping from her stiflingly mediocre family life at home with her two sisters and her totally uninteresting brother-in-law Bert Hoffer. Everything in the story leads one moreover to suspect that Harriet may well be subject to spells of hysteria or epilepsy and is allowed to go alone to Camp Cataract in order to recuperate from these, far from her family and in healthier natural surroundings.

—Edouard Roditi, "The Fiction of Jane Bowles as a Form of Self-Exorcism," *The Review of Contemporary Fiction* 12, no. 2 (Summer 1992): 188–89

BIBLIOGRAPHY

Two Serious Ladies. 1943.
A Quarreling Pair. 1945.
In the Summer House. 1947.
Plain Pleasures. 1966.
The Collected Works of Jane Bowles. 1966.
Feminine Wiles. 1976.
My Sister's Hand in Mine. 1978.

KAY BOYLE

1902-1992

KAY BOYLE was born on February 19, 1902, in Saint Paul, Minnesota, the youngest of two daughters of Katherine Evans Boyle and Howard Peterson Boyle. A wealthy family, the Boyles lived in Atlantic City, Washington, and Bryn Mawr before settling in Cincinnati after the ruin of the family business. Seemingly prey to every childhood disease and ultimately refusing to attend school at all, Kay had little formal education. Her mother, convinced that Kay was a genius, encouraged her to write and exposed Kay and her sister, Janet, to the works of modern writers and artists; Gertrude Stein's *Tender Buttons* was a favorite book often read aloud.

In 1922, Kay moved to New York, where she worked at the magazine *Broom*, wrote book reviews for *The Dial*, and studied creative writing at Columbia University. A published poet at the age of 21, Boyle left New York for France and married Richard Brault. By 1926, however, she had left Brault and was living with Irish-American poet and editor Ernest Walsh. Boyle's work was published frequently in Walsh's *This Quarter* and Eugene Jolas's *transition*. Walsh died of consumption the year Boyle joined him, and six months after his death, their daughter was born.

Living in England in 1927, Boyle published 10 poems, the first part of *Plagued by the Nightingale*, five short stories, and a review. Increasingly, she was the central figure in her poetry and prose. Although impoverished and alone in Paris in 1928, Boyle became popular among the expatriates and numbered among her friends Harry and Caresse Crosby, James Joyce, Marcel Duchamp, Constantin Brancusi, Hart Crane, and Robert McAlmon. She knew Gertrude Stein and Robert Duncan, the brother of dancer Isadora, whose "simple life movement" was an important influence. Harry Crosby published Boyle's first book, *Short Stories*, in 1929.

In Paris, Boyle married the painter and surrealist Laurence Vail and continued to write stories, poems, the rest of *Plagued by the Nightingale* (1931), and the novels *Year Before Last* (1932), *Gentlemen, I Address You Privately* (1933), *My Next Bride* (1934), and the disturbingly pro-Fascist *Death of a Man* (1936). In 1936, she left Vail for the anti-Fascist Austrian baron Joseph Franckenstein and returned to the United States for the duration of the war.

By 1941, Boyle was one of the foremost women writers of her generation. She won the O. Henry prize for two of her short stories and a Guggenheim Fellowship, in 1934. She returned to Paris after the war as a foreign correspondent for *The New Yorker* (1946–1953) and continued to publish for the next four decades.

In her own 60s during the 1960s, Boyle took an increasingly direct approach to political causes in her work. *The Underground Woman*, published in 1975, concerns a woman's spiritual awakening during the Vietnam War. Other works include *Fifty Stories* (1980); the autobiographical *Being Geniuses Together: 1920–1930* (1968); *Testament for My Students* (1970); and *Words That Must Somehow Be Said: The Selected Essays of Kay Boyle 1927–1984* (1985). When she was nearly 90, she organized a chapter of Amnesty International.

Kay Boyle received honorary degrees from Columbia University and Skidmore College and was a member of the American Academy of Arts and Letters. She died in Mill Valley, California, in 1992.

CRITICAL EXTRACTS

GERALD SYKES

Anyone with an ear for new verbal harmonies will appreciate that Miss Boyle is a stylist of unusual taste and sensibility. It is time, therefore, to cease to regard her as a mere lower-case *révoltée* and to begin to accept her for what she is: more enterprising, more scrupulous, potentially more valuable than nine-tenths of our best-known women authors.

She is potentially valuable because it is possible—as it is so rarely possible—that she may write something that has not been written before. When we have read these few brief stories we realize that they sprang from a genuine inner necessity, that the author was helplessly obliged to communicate them with that blind honesty which is the best augury for the future. We also realize that she has an original gift. This gift is a sexual one. With the first sentence of the first story—"the horses . . . stamping and lashing themselves with fury because she passed by them"—we are thrust into the presence of feelings which could have been generated in no other place than a woman's body. And those pages which come to life prove almost invariably to have been written either by or about desire. This is a difficult subject to handle. Miss Boyle's solution, which for the most part is mischievous, not only stakes out a new field for herself but gives the clearest evidence of her integrity. For although she has allowed herself absolute freedom on one of the most delicate of all subjects she has not written an offensive line. In fact, she has put to shame nearly every other emancipated woman writer who has attempted to deal with this subject: she is by comparison so simple, so honest, so pure. It is probable that the two stories in which she has given comic treatment to sexual themes, "Episode in the Life of an Ancestor" and "Summer," mark the highest stage of her development.

In view of her virtues it is all the more unfortunate that her work abounds in mannerisms, that it lacks a face of its own, that it bears so continually the stamp of fashionable influences. It is unfortunate that she has expended so much of her freedom in exile toward the development of an impeccability of style which is after all but the testimony of her admiration for Hemingway, Cocteau, and others. The result of her smartness is that even her best work has its roots in nothing, being nourished by the repetition of a repetition. Surely we must all be aware by this time that we cannot hope to grow orchids in America until we have had our hardy perennials. One wonders if Miss Boyle is aware that she has only to look within herself to find strong and deep roots for her art. Does she know that she is much better when she describes a lover's kiss—"his mustache tasting of snow"—than when she repeats the jumbled password of the advance guard?

—Gerald Sykes, "Too Good to Be Smart," *Nation* (24 December 1930), excerpted in *Twentieth-Century American Literature*, ed. Harold Bloom (New York: Chelsea House Publishers, 1986), 561

KATHERINE ANNE PORTER

Miss Kay Boyle's way of thinking and writing stems from sources still new in the sense that they have not been supplanted. She is young enough to regard them as in the category of things past, a sign I suppose, that she is working in a tradition and not in a school. Gertrude Stein and James Joyce were and are the glories of their time and some very portentous talents have emerged from their shadows. Miss Boyle, one of the newest, I believe to be among the strongest. At present she is identified as one of the *Transition* group, but these two books just published should put an end to that. What is a group, anyhow? In this one were included—as associate editors and contributors to *Transition*— many Americans: Harry Crosby, William Carlos Williams, Hart Crane, Matthew Josephson, Isidor Schneider, Josephine Herbst, Murray Godwin, Malcolm Cowley, John Herrman, Laura Riding—how many others?—and Miss Boyle herself. They wrote in every style under heaven and they spent quite a lot of time fighting with each other. Not one but would have resented, and rightly, the notion of discipleship or of interdependence. They were all vigorous not so much in revolt as in assertion, and most of them had admirably subversive ideas. Three magazines sustained them and were sustained by them: *Transition*, Ernest Walsh's *This Quarter* and *Broom*. The tremendous presences of Gertrude Stein and James Joyce were everywhere about them, and so far as Miss Boyle is concerned, it comes to this: that she is a part of the most important literary movement of her time.

She sums up the salient qualities of that movement: a fighting spirit, freshness of feeling, curiosity, the courage of her own attitude and idiom, a violently dedicated search for the meanings and methods of art. In these short stories and this novel (*Wedding Day* and *Plagued by the Nightingale*) there are further positive virtues of the individual temperament: health of mind, wit and the sense of glory. All these are qualities in which the novel marks an advance over the stories, as it does, too, in command of method.

The stories have a range of motive and feeling as wide as the technical virtuosity employed to carry it. Not all of them are successful. In some of the shorter ones, a straining of the emotional situation leads to stridency and incoherence. In others, where this strain is employed as a deliberate device, it is sometimes very successful—as notably in "Vacation Time," an episode in which an obsessional grief distorts and makes tragic a present situation not tragic of itself; the reality is masked by drunkenness, evaded by hysteria, and it is all most beautifully done. "On the Run" is a bitter story of youth in literal flight from death, which gains on it steadily; but the theme deserved better treatment.

In such stories as "Episode in the Life of an Ancestor" and "Uncle Anne," there are the beginnings of objectiveness, a soberer, richer style; and the sense of comedy, which is like acid sometimes, is here gayer and more direct. In "Portrait" and "Polar Bears and Others," Miss Boyle writes of love not as if it were a disease, or a menace, or a soothing syrup to vanity, or something to be peered at through a microscope, or the fruit of original sin, or a battle between the sexes, or a bawdy pastime. She writes as one who believes in love and romance—not the "faded flower in a buttonhole," but love so fresh and clear it comes to the reader almost as a rediscovery in literature. It was high time someone rediscovered it. There are other stories, however—"Spring Morning," "Letters of a Lady," "Episode in the Life of an Ancestor"—in which an adult intelligence plays with destructive humor on the themes of sexual superstition and pretenses between men and women. "Madame Tout Petit," "Summer," "Theme" and "Bitte Nehmen Sie die Blumen" are entirely admirable, each one a subtle feat in unraveling a complicated predicament of the human heart. "Wedding Day," the title story, is the least satisfactory, displaying the weakness of Miss Boyle's strength in a lyricism that is not quite poetry.

The novel, *Plagued by the Nightingale*, has the same germinal intensity as the shorter works, but it is sustained from the first word to the last by a sure purpose and a steadier command of resources. The form, structure and theme are comfortably familiar. The freshness and brilliancy lie in the use of the words and the point of view.

—Katherine Anne Porter, "Kay Boyle: Example to the Young," *New Republic* (22 April 1931), excerpted in *Twentieth-Century American Literature*, ed. Harold Bloom (New York: Chelsea House Publishers, 1986), 564

GLADYS GRAHAM

In this, her fourth volume [*The First Lover and Other Stories*], Kay Boyle has returned to the form with which she first attracted attention to herself and which has since brought her such wide recognition and acclaim. To call this form by the blanket name "short story" is to come very far from giving any idea of the carefully wrought, life and character enclosing sketches which may cover nominally only a few hours but which run into the depths of the past of each situation, into the promise or threat of the future. In Miss Boyle's first two volumes the arcs of her plots were short, tenuous, delicate. They were often perfect in themselves, strong-sinewed beneath their fragile technique, but in their brevity there was no assurance that the author could sustain her effects under stress of greater length. With her first novel, the year before last, Kay Boyle demonstrated that her prose medium was entirely at her command. The vibrant quality, the moving suspense, the characters held firmly in their nervous orbit, all these that gave the particular and personal tone to the short sketches came out as successfully in her distinguished novel of death on the Riviera.

In the story that gives the title to the present volume Miss Boyle has achieved an unusual and difficult effect. She has presented, by some magic, three sisters as one person in their simple, loving, hoping response to life. We are shown them only for the brief, bright lunch hour at their Monte Carlo pension, but we know they have been there a month; their soft conversations have run on into midnights; they have laughed away mornings and afternoons; but the years before this careless, well-fed month press upon them separately, narrowed with abstinence, dark with denial. They are all love for their father, he has saved this month for them. A young Englishman enters the dining-room. He will be their first lover. He is good, he is happy, he has never known want; they can bring him back to their father; he will be a lover for life, a husband. The thoughts of one stir in the minds of the others as the gentle breathing of one disturbs the soft hair of the others close-standing at the window to watch the desired Englishman. The lunch hour passes, the Englishman leaves unguessing, the years lie ahead with only emptiness for the father.

"Lydia and the Ring-doves" strikes a different note. This Lydia with her copper hair, her forty years, has come to England to be with dead men. Her titled ancestry lies here. That documents exist proving these great dead to have left no issue disconcert Lydia not at all. The ring-doves of the village cry outside her window, "Ah, God, ah, God, ah, God." The young vegetable man comes to her door. She sees his shining kindliness. Soft-nosed goats follow for his cabbage leaves, the doves cling with naked feet along the edges of his cart. He comes each day until the great winds sweep across the village, beating down the flowers and leaving doves broken-winged and helpless in the hedges. Lydia gathers them up each morning and carries them to the vegetable man for succor. One day she comes at dinner time, she sees the browned forms upon the platter.

There are other stories in the volume much less successful than these. Miss Boyle has set herself too high a standard for continuous realization. But if the best stories from "Plagued by the Nightingale," "Wedding Day and Other Stories," and "The First Lover" were collected in a single volume it would not be easy to find another to place beside it. In each of Miss Boyle's later books she has included an historical reconstruction or two. For them a strange, definitely looking backward technique has been used. The characters and events are clear, but they are seen distant, minute, as through the wrong end of an opera glass. These sketches, while interesting, lack the warmth of her contemporary recitals. It is obvious that Miss Boyle is a workman as well as an artist. One sees her growth from book to book in the lesser sketches—the best, from first to last, show the same ordered finality.

—Gladys Graham, "Artistic Fiction," *Saturday Review of Literature* 25 (March 1933): 501

EDMUND WILSON

I have heard Miss Boyle praised as a stylist, but, though there are in *Avalanche* a few fine images and gray and white mountain landscapes, I cannot see how a writer with a really sound sense of style could have produced this book even as a potboiler. One recognizes the idiom of a feminized Hemingway: "There was one winter when the blizzard got us part way up. . . . If you looked in the direction the wind was coming from, your breath stopped suddenly as if someone took you by the throat;" and a sobbing Irish lilt: "He touches my hand as if it were a child's hand, and his promise of love is given to a woman. To him it is nothing to walk into a mountain refuge and find me, and to me it's the three years without him that have stopped crying their hearts out at last." And, for the rest, there are several tricks that Miss Boyle overworks with exasperating effect. She is always giving possessives to inanimate objects, so that you have "the weather's break," "the balcony's rail," and "the mitten's pattern" all within a space of sixteen lines; and there is a formula that recurs so often in the passages of conversation that one can almost say the whole book is built of it: " 'They're fiercer, more relentless,' he said, and the sound of threat was there;" " 'And there is de Vaudois,' he said, and he put the mittens on;" " 'You're French, partly French,' he said, and his eyes were asking the promise of her"— these are quoted from a space of less than two pages. Sometimes you get both these refrains together: " 'What is the story of that?' said de Vaudois, and his eyes went suddenly shrewd beneath his hat's crisp brim."

Miss Boyle has indulged herself, also, in the bad romantic habit of making foreign conversation sound translated. It is perhaps a part of her Hemingway heritage. A Spaniard, Arturo Barea, has sought to show, in the English review *Horizon*, that the dialogue of *For Whom the Bell Tolls* is not really a translation of Spanish but a language of Hemingway's own. So Miss Boyle—to take her at her simplest, where there is no question of special eloquence involved—will have her characters make speeches like the following:

> "And Bastineau? What of Bastineau?"
> "One by one they've gone from us."
> "A friend come back from America is here."

Now this is certainly not colloquial English; but when you try putting it into French, you have:

> "Et Bastineau? Quoi de Bastineau?"
> "L'un après l'autre, ils s'en sont allés de nous."
> "Une amie revenue de l'Amérique est ici."

—which is even more impossible as French. My best guess at the kind of thing you would get if the last of these thoughts, for example, were naturally expressed in French would be "*Voici une amie revenue de l'Amérique*"—of which the natural English would be "Here's a friend of ours who's come back from America." But Miss Boyle needs the false solemnity, the slow-motion portentousness, that this Never Never language gives to carry off her absurd story.

It is easy to be funny about *Avalanche*, but it has its depressing aspect. I have not read much else by Kay Boyle since her very early work, so that I do not have a definite opinion about the value of her writing as a whole; but I know from those early stories, written when she lived abroad and printed in the "little" magazines of the American *émigrés*, that she was at least making an effort at that time to produce something of serious interest. Today she is back at home, and *Avalanche* was written for the *Saturday Evening Post*, I did not see it there, but I have been haunted since I read it by a vision of *Saturday Evening Post* illustrations, in which the ideal physical types of the skin-lotion and shaving-soap ads are seen posing on snowy slopes. Nor do I doubt that this novel was constructed with an eye to the demands of Hollywood, that intractable magnetic mountain which has been twisting our fiction askew and on which so many writers have been flattened.

—Edmund Wilson, "Kay Boyle and the *Saturday Evening Post*," *New Yorker* (15 January 1944), excerpted in *Twentieth-Century American Literature*, ed. Harold Bloom (New York: Chelsea House Publishers, 1986), 561–62

MAXWELL GEISMAR

What *Nothing Ever Breaks Except the Heart* proves, in short, is that Kay Boyle has at last become a major short-story writer, or a major writer in contemporary American fiction, after three decades of elusiveness, sometimes of anonymity, almost of literary "classlessness," while she has pursued and has finally discovered her true metier. It is a joy to discover such an event: not a new talent, which is rare enough, but an established and mature talent which has developed and perfected itself—and particularly in an epoch when so many false talents are proclaimed every year.

Unlike her earlier collection of *Thirty Stories*, which was arranged chronologically—and that earlier volume is fascinating now to read over and to compare with the present one—*Nothing Ever Breaks Except the Heart* is arranged topically: "Peace," "War Years" and "Military Occupation." And perhaps one should add, in the selfish concern of pure art, that nothing better could have happened for Kay Boyle than World War II and the periods of military occupation, by the German and then the Allied forces. For even in the present volume, the first section, "Peace," is less effective than the remainder of the book—and still Kay Boyle is less effective about the American than she is about the European scene. When it comes to a story like "Anschluss," dealing with a world-weary Parisian fashion-writer and a marvelously gay brother and sister in a dying Austria, she is superb.

Here, as in so many of her earlier stories and novels, her satiric strain works unrelentingly upon the German character and physique. Here, more convincingly than in earlier books, her romantic lovers are destroyed by the dissolution of a society; and here, just as in her work of the early forties, she dramatizes the pageantry of a dissolute and amoral social scene over and above the sensibilities of her characters. ⟨. . .⟩

Indeed, in *Nothing Ever Breaks Except the Heart*, it is a toss-up as to who the true villains are, Germans or Americans or just plain Occupiers—while the heroes, to Miss Boyle, are those who have been conquered and occupied, those who have resisted, those who have put to the acid test their property, their career and their lives. To her earlier version of sensibility, she has added what every first-rate writer must have, a standard of human morality—and the fact that human morality is usually, if not always, related to a specific social or historical context.

It is this familiar concept, missing in so much current and "new" American fiction, that is embodied in the magnificent stories of her maturity. (For conversely, it is of no use to an artist to have a perfect sense of morality without an adequate art form to project it.) The title story of the present collection is another beauty: a Hemingway tale, so to speak, (about a pilot who is finished) but produced by an intensely feminine talent, and with an anti-Hemingway moral. (By this I mean anti-late-Hemingway, when all that remained in him was the killer pitted against a hostile menacing universe.) What is so remarkable in these late tales of Kay Boyle, by contrast, is the increased sense of sympathy in them for all the losers, all the defeated persons and peoples of contemporary history.

Here again, an earlier sense of nostalgia in her work has become an intense sense of compassion. I don't pretend to know the secrets of this fine craftsman, but I do realize how many of these stories leave you on the brink of tears. And a world in tears; since Kay Boyle has become the American writer to express the texture of European life after Chamberlain and Daladier and Munich.

There is still a final phase of writing in *Nothing Ever Breaks Except the Heart*, still another epoch of our modern history: the period of the Occupation, the black market and the reappearance of the same old people, asking for privilege and power and "deals" all over again, after the heroism, the gallantry, the selflessness of the liberation battle. No wonder that the last one of these stories describes an American State Department official returning to a McCarthyite America— ironic sequel to the war for European freedom. And no wonder that the last of these beautiful tales describes an American mother, who agrees with "a terrified race"—the French peasants of the atomic age. " 'I am American,' she said to that unseen presence of people in the silent room, 'and the wrong voices have spoken out for me, and spoken loudly, and I too, I too, am terribly afraid.' "

> —Maxwell Geismar, "Aristocrat of the Short Story," *New York Times Book Review* (10 July 1964), excerpted in *Twentieth-Century American Literature*, ed. Harold Bloom (New York: Chelsea House Publishers, 1986), 563

HARRY T. MOORE

From the time of her first book in 1929, *Wedding Day And Other Stories*, ⟨Kay Boyle's⟩ fate has been occasional high praise and an occasional succès d'estime. Meanwhile, writers far less gifted have been overrated by public and critics alike. At present there are only a few books of Kay Boyle's in print; these fortunately include a hardbound edition of her novel *Monday Night* and paperbacks of *Thirty Stories* and *Three Short Novels* (the last containing one of the masterpieces of this genre in our time, *The Crazy Hunter*). Of her first novel, *Plagued by the Nightingale*, it is safe to say that it is the finest portrait of a French family by a writer from this side of the Atlantic since Henry James fixed his attention upon the Bellegardes in *The American*. Nor is it out of place to mention James here, for Kay Boyle is an important later practitioner in the area in which he worked—"the international theme." Since James, no American except Kay Boyle has concentrated so thoroughly upon that theme. ⟨. . .⟩

⟨The Germany of *Generation Without Farewell*⟩ is haunted alike by its Gothic and Nazi past and its American present. Most of the Americans in the story, whether well meaning or not, are essentially childlike. They include an army colonel who brings in his wife and college-girl daughter; a post-exchange manager whose Italian ancestry seems to offend the colonel; a sycophantic lieutenant; a marmotlike intelligence officer; and an *Amerika Haus* director named Honerkamp, whose nonconformist thinking is "dangerous"—a man who has hanging behind his office door the *Totentanz* figure of a skeleton found buried in the ruins.

The central consciousness in the story is that of a young German newspaperman, Jaeger, who has been a prisoner of war in the United States. And several of the other characters are Germans, including a young groom who watches over the white Lippizaner horses which (as in Kay Boyle's notable short story, "The White Horses of Vienna") suggest the aristocratic splendor of the past. There is also the battered young actor who presents the Wolfgang Borchert play from whose words this novel takes its title: "We are the generation without farewell. . . . We have many encounters, encounters without duration and without farewell." This applies to most of the relationships in the book, particularly to that of Jaeger and the colonel's wife. He falls in love with her and she responds, but she is abruptly sent away with her daughter, who in her quiet way has also been drawn into Germanic involvements. The colonel hustles his women off before they have a chance for farewells.

This Colonel Roberts, who is suggestively identified with the boar that is rumored to be raiding villages at night, shares a triumph with the intelligence officer when, at the end of the story, the *Amerika Haus* liberal is given dismissal orders. All such events have their parallels in the dark conflicts that take place in the forest where the colonel leads patrol parties by night to track down (ostensibly at least) the illegal hunters reported to be prowling the area in a jeep with covered-over license plates. There are violence and bloodshed in this forest but, since this is among other things a symbolist novel, the meaning of it all is not spelled out so facilely as in a popular type of book such as *The Ugly American*. Many of the same meanings that book drives toward are ultimately to be found here, however, particularly American incompetence in dealing with other nations. Colonel Roberts in this story is the embodiment of the military mind, essentially uneducated and incapable of growth, that has so often damaged America by mixing in government, for which it is untrained and temperamentally unsuited.

These points come to mind because this book is—for all its symbolic bestiary of boar, fox, and Lippizaner horse—also a political story, with politics and symbolism blending in an unusually successful way. For example, the terrible symbol of the buried man, which has a certain kinship with Honerkamp's office skeleton, is political. This "underground" man, accidentally dislodged from the ruined house where he has been immured for three years (a place stocked with food), is seen by Jaeger as he emerges.

> It moved like a spider caught in its own web, like a broken crab,
> clawing its way up through rusted girders and disjointed stones. . . .
> The rags of a *Wehrmacht* uniform clung to the figure's bones, the
> sleeves, the trousers hanging in shreds, slashed back and forth and up
> and down by outraged time.

Several men had been similarly unearthed in different parts of Germany, but to see one is a new experience for Jaeger who, in writing about the event for his paper, says that every German now "must claw his way out of the depths of what he was, letting the faded, filth-encrusted insignia fall from him, and the medals for military valor drop away." But a defeated chauvinism has been taken over by new chauvinists, and the military mind of the conquerors has no tolerance for the Jaegers or the Honerkamps, who at the last are either frustrated or defeated.

This book is not one of narrow-visioned propaganda; rather it is a later and richer chapter in Kay Boyle's continuing involvement with the international theme, which in our time has new phases. And perhaps this novel will bring her some of the recognition she deserves and will help to place her among the fine women authors of our time who do not write like men (as, say, Willa Cather does), but operate through a distinctly feminine vision (as Dorothy Richardson does), to capture and project experience in a unique and important way.

—Harry T. Moore, "Kay Boyle's Fiction," *Age of the Modern and Other Literary Essays* (1971), excerpted in *Twentieth-Century American Literature*, ed. Harold Bloom (New York: Chelsea House Publishers, 1986), 565–66

MARGARET ATWOOD

Kay Boyle's writing has sometimes been spoken of as approaching the surreal, but there is nothing of the ant-covered clock about it. What it approaches instead is the hallucinatory, or rather the moment of visionary realism when sensation heightens and time for an instant fixes and stops. If one were to pick a painter who corresponds to Boyle, it would not be Salvador Dali. One thinks rather of Brueghel, a landscape clearly and vividly rendered, everything in its ordinary order, while Icarus falls to his death, scarcely noticed, off to the side.

But to concentrate entirely on quality of vision or sureness of craft would be to miss the point entirely about Kay Boyle. It is only in North America that critics can indulge in the luxury of separating craft and politics into watertight boxes; Kay Boyle, although in many ways quintessentially American, belongs also to a wide tradition. Central to her fiction is the issue of moral choice, an issue that is as present in the family drama of "The Crazy Hunter" as it is in the much more obviously political "Decision."

"He will make his own decision," says the naïve American narrator in "Decision." She has access to papers that will save a man from the police.

"No," replies another character. "You are either every third man who is taken out and shot, or else you are not, but one is not permitted a decision. There is no choice that he can make, except the profounder choice which lies between good and evil, and that choice Jerónimo has made."

Victims of fate and circumstance Boyle's characters may be, but not entirely. Some of their destiny still rests with themselves. Although none of these stories has a resolution that suggests happiness for the protagonists, Boyle's universe is neither absurd nor hopeless. Love and its opposite, hatred, loyalty and therefore betrayal, heroism and cowardice, are all still possible within it. The *nada* that is supposed to be so central to the twentieth-century sensibility is not at its core.

"Defiance" is a word that recurs in these stories. For Boyle, it is a defiance not only of the powers ranged against the protagonists but also of easy literary fashionability. Reading Kay Boyle, one recalls Flannery O'Connor saying that novels are not written by people without hope.

—Margaret Atwood, "Introduction" to *Three Short Novels* (1982), excerpted in *Twentieth-Century American Literature*, ed. Harold Bloom (New York: Chelsea House Publishers, 1986), 560–61

SANDRA WHIPPLE SPANIER

Kay Boyle's first four novels express a Romantic's concern for freedom of action and imagination, but a cynic's view of the possibility for attaining it. The individual in her world is trapped by nature, for one thing: three of the four books feature an "unwanted pregnancy," and in *Plagued by the Nightingale*, *Year Before Last*, and *My Next Bride*, the protagonist's loved one either is stalked by death or actually dies. Love is the only reprieve in such an ultimately futile existence, yet too often it is tragically lost or was never found. The material of these novels is idiosyncratic, a direct outgrowth of the author's private experiences as an expatriate in France in the twenties. Her concern with the lonely, isolated individual in search of an identity and a meaningful context in which to live may well have its roots in her own proud and painful exile.

The focus of these novels is the individual struggle, but they also provide a forum for Kay Boyle's social and political positions, which she feels are implicit in nearly everything she has written ⟨. . . .⟩ Beginning in the thirties much of Kay Boyle's work would become overtly political. Yet it is important to remember that even in her earliest fiction she was concerned not only with "personal love" but with "the love of humanity which is expressed in political protest."

In these four novels, Kay Boyle was engaged in a Revolution of the Word as well as one of the individual and collective spirit. As in her short stories of the same period, she was not writing for the plain reader. Yet while they show her continuing experimentation with language, her novels are not as icono-clastic in style as some of her short stories. Kay Boyle's loyalties were begin-ning to divide between the avant-garde literary revolution and her concern for humanity, between her sense of language as a statement of rebellion and her sense of it as a "fervent prayer" offered up "for the salvation of man, for the defense of his high spirit, for the celebration of his integrity," as she would say decades later. In time her need to communicate with her fellow men and women would outweigh her desire to merely express herself.

—Sandra Whipple Spanier, *Kay Boyle, Artist and Activist* (Carbondale, IL: Southern Illinois University Press, 1986), 90–91

MARILYN ELKINS

Boyle ⟨redefines traditional gender roles⟩ with characters who, on the narra-tive's surface, appear to follow the more traditional romance quest, but each of Boyle's early female protagonists challenges both its purpose and goal. ⟨. . . The⟩ heroines of *Plagued by the Nightingale* (1931), *Year Before Last* (1932), and *My Next Bride* (1934), attempt to alter the patriarchy's existing models. In these early novels Boyle produces narratives that adopt and adapt the male quest pattern while she destroys most of that myth's traditional assumptions. Like the male artist portrayed by Joyce, Lawrence, Forster, Hemingway, and other male modernists, the Boyle heroine sets out to define the self through her explorations of the world around her. And like many of these protagonists, she finds a member of the opposite sex who helps her in this goal. Also like her male counterparts, Boyle's sensual heroine does not limit her emotional attach-ments to members of the opposite sex. She inevitably has close friends and mentors of the same sex. As is true of her male counterpart, Boyle's heroine discovers that finding self does not require that she remain either chaste or unmarried.

This independent, creative, heterosexual heroine sets Boyle's work apart from ⟨. . .⟩ most of the women modernists whose work is currently receiving reclamation. For Boyle's women seek a balance between their conflicting needs for autonomy and heterosexual relatedness. These novels' heterosexual relationships, both inside marriage and outside it, challenge the conventions of gender within such partnerships. But they also dispute the theory that heterosexual marriage is not a viable option for a strong, independent woman.

In addition Kay Boyle's young American heroines contest the traditional definition of autonomy, the separation of public and private spheres. They offer a new, female version of autonomy that does not automatically reject family and motherhood. And while the characteristics of these women change somewhat with their age and that of their author's at the time of their creation, they all share certain basic characteristics. They insist on their art, their sexuality, and their politics. They are assertive in their efforts to obtain these rights. But they do not insist on their rights to the exclusion of the rights of others. Nor do they pursue these rights alone, preferring to find a male partner who can value their active, assertive personalities. In many respects these women's most appealing and important characteristic—and the innovation for which Boyle should be most highly commended—is their ability to remain autonomous within a sexual, familial, and communal context. ⟨. . .⟩

⟨. . .⟩ Creating unusual heroes who participate fully within the private worlds of marriage and family, particularly in their ability to nourish others, Boyle ⟨also⟩ challenges the assumption that only women nurture.

⟨In⟩ works revolving around cross-gendered character behavior, Boyle also presents two cautionary tales that delineate the dangers involved when people become too interested in either the private or public worlds: overemphasizing one component results in a damaged psyche and an individual who cannot function. In *Death of a Man* (1936), Pendennis follows the typical romance plot, ignoring everything except her focus on "her man," but Boyle uses this narrative to point out its pitfalls. Pendennis' emptiness and its attendant horror demonstrate the importance of having something of one's own that is independent from others. And in the novella, *The Crazy Hunter*, Mrs. Lombe's rejection of her husband for her embrace of the mundane forces outside their marriage delineates the inherent failure in taking the extreme opposite position.

—Marilyn Elkins, *Metamorphosizing the Novel: Kay Boyle's Narrative Innovations* (New York: Peter Lang, 1993), 11–13

BIBLIOGRAPHY

Short Stories. 1929.

Wedding Day and Other Stories. 1930.

Landscape for Wyn Henderson. 1931.

Plagued by the Nightingale. 1931.

Year Before Last. 1932.

The First Lover and Other Stories. 1933.

Gentlemen, I Address You Privately. 1933.

My Next Bride. 1934.

Death of a Man. 1936.

The White Horses of Vienna. 1936.

Monday Night. 1938.

The Crazy Hunter: Three Short Novels. 1940.

Primer for Combat. 1942.

Avalanche. 1944.

A Frenchman Must Die. 1946.

Thirty Stories. 1946.

1939: A Novel. 1948.

His Human Majesty. 1949.

The Smoking Mountain: Stories of Postwar Germany. 1951.

The Seagull on the Step. 1955.

The Youngest Camel. 1959.

Generation Without Farewell. 1960.

Breaking the Silence: Why a Mother Tells Her Son about the Nazi Era. 1962.

Collected Poems. 1962.

Nothing Ever Breaks Except the Heart. 1966.

Being Geniuses Together: 1920–1930. 1968.

Testament for My Students. 1970.

The Underground Woman. 1975.

Fifty Stories. 1980.

Words That Must Somehow Be Said. 1985.

PEARL S. BUCK
1892-1973

PEARL SYDENSTRICKER was born on June 26, 1892, in Hillsboro, West Virginia. The daughter of Presbyterian ministers in China, she received her early education in Shanghai and graduated from Randolph Macon Woman's College in 1914. She returned to China, became a university professor in Nanking, and married a missionary, John Lossing Buck, in 1917. Her only daughter was born mentally retarded, and she took full financial responsibility for the child's care and education.

In 1925, Buck brought her daughter to the United States for treatment and the next year earned a master's degree in English literature at Cornell University. At the same time, her articles about contemporary issues and Chinese life were appearing in *Atlantic Monthly*, *Forum*, and *The Nation*. She returned to China in 1926, and five years later, she had her first novel published. *The Good Earth* (1931), which became one of the most famous best-sellers in American fiction, was translated into over 30 languages and would help earn Buck the Nobel Prize for Literature in 1938. In 1935, it was published as part of a trilogy, *House of Earth*, that also included *Sons* (1932) and *A House Divided* (1935).

Divorced in 1934, Pearl Buck moved permanently to the United States. The following year, she married Richard J. Walsh, a New York publisher. Buck continued to write, publishing articles and a collection of short stories, *The First Wife and Other Stories*. *The Exile*, published in 1936, was in fact Buck's first book. Written after her mother's death in 1921, the story is a biography of a missionary wife, written as a memorial; *Fighting Angel* (1936) is a portrait of her father. She was elected to The National Institute of Arts and Letters in 1936.

Pearl Buck was as much a humanitarian as an author. The struggle against racial prejudice, the care and education of Amerasian children, and the needs of the mentally retarded were among her many concerns. In 1941, she founded the East and West Association to promote cultural understanding through literature and the arts. Before and during World War II, Buck was an active member of a group that brought food and medical supplies to China.

During this period, Buck continued to write about and be involved in China. *Dragon Seed* (1942) depicts the horror felt by Chinese farmers caught in the Japanese invasion and their subsequent resistance movement. In her autobiography, *My Several Worlds* (1954),

48

Buck speculates that, if she had been a young Chinese who had experienced the wars, concessions, and treaties that white men brought to China, she too may have wanted to drive them out of the country. In all her writing she consistently stressed the idea of humanity above other concerns. In 1949, she and her husband founded Welcome House, an adoption agency for Amerasian children.

At this point in her career, Pearl Buck had been labeled a writer about China. To overcome this limitation among American readers, she published five novels under the pseudonym John Sedges, the best of which is *The Townsman* (1945). Although meticulously researched and competently written, these novels lack the vitality of her stories about China. In *Pavilion of Women* (1946), written during the same period and under her own name, Buck returned to China and to themes of humanitarianism and self-sacrifice, focusing upon two generations of Chinese women; the book proved to be one of her most popular. Refusing to adopt more modern novelistic techniques, Pearl Buck remained a writer in the tradition of Chinese storytelling. "I am always in love with great ends," she has said.

In 1964, the Pearl S. Buck Foundation was established to provide medical care, clothing, counseling, and educational opportunities to Amerasian children. In 1967 Buck gave most of her earnings, over $7 million, to the foundation. Pearl Buck died on March 6, 1973, in Danby, Vermont.

CRITICAL EXTRACTS

PHYLLIS BENTLEY

In that delicious story by Henry James, "The Figure in the Carpet," it will be remembered that a famous novelist is perpetually ruffled because all his reviewers without exception, whether they offer him praise or blame, miss the point, the significance, of all his work, the string, as he says, on which he threads all his pearls, the figure which, repeated and diversified, forms the pattern in his literary carpet. It is now time for us to seek the figure in Mrs. Buck's carpet, the theme on which she threads her pearls.

Is it her deep intention to present China to the West? Yes, I suppose it is; and she succeeds in it to admiration. But I do not feel that this is the only figure in the carpet; indeed, at times I feel that China makes the colors of her design rather than the pattern. If this is going too far, and perhaps it is, I would say at least that there is another figure which springs out of this one and is intertwined with it.

Is it her aim to present China in contact with Western civilization, China in revolution, the transition, in a word, from the old China to the new? Yes, I suppose it is; though personally I do not feel this to be the most successful part of her work. In *East Wind: West Wind*, and still more in *A House Divided*, some of her truest art is lacking. *A House Divided* is an extremely interesting contemporary record of a transition period in Chinese history; but it is not a work of art. This is so because the incidents are not, I believe, viewed in true perspective. In part this perspective cannot yet be achieved; for we do not yet know which of these manifestations of revolutionary spirit are significant and lasting, and which ephemeral; only time can tell us that. ⟨. . .⟩

For my part I consider that the figure in Mrs. Buck's carpet, her true theme, is the continuity of life.

One aspect of this continuity is beautifully revealed in that miniature masterpiece, *The Mother*. All the characters in this novel remain anonymous, it will be remembered. The mother, the man, the old woman, the girl, the townsman, the younger lad—they have only these general names, and though they belong to a particular nation and have strongly individual personalities, they are also all mothers, all townsmen, all old women, all brothers and sisters; what they say and do is deeply true to all human motive, so that we sympathize and understand. This again is a hallmark of quality in a novelist; for those only tell the truth who make us feel the biological certainty that all men are made of the same elements, differently arranged.

Another aspect of this continuity is the one most generally recognized in Mrs. Buck's work—the passing of life on from generation to generation. The sense of this continuity is strongly present in every detail of our author's work ⟨. . . .⟩ It is especially strong in the *Good Earth* trilogy, and is summed up for us in *Sons*, where Wang the Tiger is riding to his father's funeral. "Riding thus at the head of his cavalcade," writes Mrs. Buck, "his women and his children, Wang the Tiger took his place in the generations . . . . he felt his place in the long line of life."

An even deeper sense of continuity, which takes in not only the human species but the fruitful earth itself and all the life it nourishes, is revealed in this fine passage, which occurs after the burial of Wang Lung on his own land:

> Thus were the fields upon which Wang Lung had spent his whole life
> divided and the land belonged now to his sons and no more to him,
> except that small part where he lay, and this was all he owned. Yet
> out of this small secret place the clay of his blood and bones melted
> and flowed out to join with all the depths of his land; his sons did as
> they pleased with the surface of the earth but he lay deep within it
> and he had his portion still and no one could take it from him.

Whether any novelist can be in the very first flight who depicts a civilization other than his own, I do not know; I am not quite sure whether the local, in such a case, does not inevitably at times override the universal. But we may say at least that for the interest of her chosen material, the sustained high level of her technical skill, and the frequent universality of her conceptions, Mrs. Buck is entitled to take rank as a considerable artist. To read her novels is to gain not merely knowledge of China but wisdom about life.

—Phyllis Bentley, "The Art of Pearl S. Buck," *The English Journal* 24, no. 10 (December 1935): 798–800

DOROTHY CANFIELD FISHER

Dear, dear Pearl:

How you and I always feel the impulse to put our heads together, to clasp hands closely, to share what is in our hearts, in grave moments of crisis! ⟨. . .⟩

⟨. . . There⟩ is so much to say, dear Pearl, that I should never put it all down, in the rich complication of detail as it is brought to me sweepingly from one of our terrifically complicated, nervously tense, angry, frightened modern world. So I'll set a little of it down with short-hand brevity. I used always, when I heard you criticized, to spring quickly to contradict, to defend you. Now I don't always, because I want to hear exactly *what* it is felt by the people who resent your attitude (so very few, *never forget that*, in comparison to the astoundingly large number whose hearts are reached by your every word).

They seem to feel (I think I've written you this before) that your protests against racial prejudice, against the idiotic assumption of the superiority of the white race, oversimplify a situation, by leaving out of it the myriad complexities of the economic and political aspects of the matter.

They feel that you do this because you are primarily a splendid writer of fiction, who really does not understand the economic elements in the international situation. Suspect in fact, so little about them, that you are not even aware of their prime importance, and so are quite sincere and single-hearted (but none the less over-simplifyingly mistaken) in putting into the foreground in an exaggeratedly important position, the matter of racial relations. Remember I am only reporting as accurately as I can what I gather your critics—the honest ones—feel. These are no opinions of mine.

They feel—here the historic difference of opinion between "the gradualists" and the "revolutionaries" of ideas comes acridly to the fore, as so many times in the last two centuries—that your approach to the question is dangerous, because (whether you say or only imply this) your readers get from your expression of opinions a terrific impact of "immediacy" (if there is such a word!). They gather that what you think should be done is instantly to sever ties and connections which, having lasted a century or so, have grown into organic connections and hence, should be (will have to be they think) untangled slowly; like a good surgeon performing an operation who patiently lifts one nerve after another, separating one muscle from another, compared to the hasty one who slashes straight through, causing mortal danger of "shock" to his patient. Here again *I* think that the urgency of the hour should be taken into account. There may not be time for the gradual untangling of fibres. In the fact that there is *not* time, (perhaps) we are paying the deadly price for not having begun earlier to do the untangling. It takes perhaps just such clear compelling voices as yours to make people *begin* to untangle.

The people of the United States were profoundly shocked, in the real medical meaning of the word, by the horror of the Civil War, and the awful price that was paid for the settling by the sword of a matter that should have been (as in England in 1833 by the Emancipation Act) settled without bloodshed. The hundred million dollars (wasn't it something like that?) which was the price to the British of a non-violent, non-bloody political and sociological solution of a matter settled in our country by violence, was infinitesimal compared to the dreadful moral wounds and scars left in the U.S.A. by an abrupt ending of a wrong, known to be evil by all decently civilized men and women. I think (I've never heard anybody else say this, it comes just from the long, passionately intent meditation on our national history by an old American woman) that deep in the American sub-conscious mind, there is now a dread of such quick endings to ancient wrongs.

All this is only such an explanation as my observation brings to me, of the reasons underlying the resistance to your anti-imperialist thesis (to which in theory every decently civilized man and woman assents) on the part of some of the better-grade responsible, fairly well-informed Americans. Of the others, the Jew-hating, Negro-baiting ignorant mob, I say nothing, because they are primitive "nativism" unqualified by any intelligent thought at all—such members of the mob were supporters of Hitler, exist alas! in all nations and are only kept from power by the concerted efforts of more civilized people.

—Dorothy Canfield Fisher, [26 August 1943 letter to Pearl Buck], *Keeping Fires Night and Day: Selected Letters of Dorothy Canfield Fisher*, ed. Mark J. Madigan (Columbia, MO: University of Missouri Press, 1993), 226–28.

AMI HENCHOZ

The first thing to be noticed is that Pearl Buck takes a delight in transplanting favourite characters to different climates in order to see their reactions to the new surroundings; she is a specialist in transplantation.

The work in which this method appears at its best is the first novel *East Wind, West Wind*. It is the simple story of the son and daughter of an old

Chinese family. The daughter is married to the man to whom she was promised even before her birth, but her husband is modern and has studied in America; the son, on the other hand, goes to America without his parents' consent and there he marries an American girl. Such are the causes of the arising conflict; when we have all the elements of the problem, skilfully presented, Pearl Buck successively examines, as one would do in mathematics, every possible solution; in other words, the whole book might have been written in dialogues, on the stage, presenting each actor in conversation with all the others. ⟨. . .⟩

⟨. . . In subsequent books, when⟩ the author placed her characters in eastern countries, the landscapes and the contrasting customs had their share in the transplantation. ⟨When⟩ she deals with American people, this background disappears and the personages are purely conventional; they are mere puppets, existing to give shape to, we dare not even say to embody, the author's ideas. And we have the impression that Pearl Buck feels herself a foreigner in her own country. Many readers, therefore, will have been relieved to see that in her latest novel, *Dragon Seed*, Pearl Buck has returned to Eastern civilization.

And yet it may be that some of these readers were a bit deceived: for the first time indeed, the author is less neutral and less impartial, and she uses such words as "hatred" and "vengeance", to which we were not accustomed before. The space devoted to the cruelties committed by the conquering soldiers seems exaggerated, too. But if we allow for changed circumstances and do not take the matter of the book into serious account, we realize that, on a purely mechanical plane, the story is well built and perfectly balanced; all the members of a family are suddenly transplanted from a peaceful life to a state of war and destruction. Pearl Buck insists on the fact that these people were deeply attached to their soil and the word 'seed' in its different meanings, appears many times in the first chapters of the book, without mentioning the title: *Dragon Seed* . . . But the conquest is so violent at first, that the transplantation is complete, as the farmer says himself, page 288: "He was taken out of this little valley and set into the world, and he felt it." Expressions such as: "these are new times, it is a strange day", are numerous; the soil no longer belongs to the peasants, who are strangers in their own fields. After the first wave of conquest they all begin to resist the invader, each in his private way. From the son-in-law, who, as a merchant, yields to the enemy to save his shop, down to the third cousin who tries to get freedom and oblivion in opium, they all suffer; according to their ability in adapting themselves to new ideals, they offer various degrees of resistance: the mother, who is old-fashioned, does not understand and remains stubborn and silently hostile. The father reluctantly kills some soldiers but he is soon disgusted and gives it up. The first son wages guerilla warfare and occasionally kills an enemy. The second undertakes the obscure and perilous task of carrying messages from occupied areas to the free lands of the western hills. The third son, an extremist, becomes a leader of rebels and is happy only in action and killing. Now that every member has his definite position, Pearl Buck opposes them to one another and they realize that they are so changed that they can no longer understand each other; the first conflict, therefore, has brought another, more terrible than the first; the sufferings they had before are nothing compared with what they now endure; the whole family is disorganized, confidence and good will disappear; the father is forced to confess, page 191, "even wife and husband are strangers." As for his third son, he does not know him any longer, for (251) "the son stepped forward and raised his hand against his father, and he said in a bitter voice: 'these are other times! you may not strike me! I can kill you as well as another!'". The father understands with sadness that his sons have gone beyond him and that "the young have cut themselves from the old" (266). The unity of the book resides in the second son and his modern wife; they are the central hinges on which the whole thing turns and develops. His mind is half-way between old doctrines and new ideals and this enables him to be the peace-maker among his relatives. "Between his brothers in the hills and the ones at home, he was a messenger, too, and more than a messenger, because he kept them patient with each other" (300). Once this internal conflict has been presented under all its aspects, the right solution is given in the fact that each of the three sons gets the very wife that suits his mind, and if it is not "All's well that ends well", for this family at least one part of its sufferings is over and they can wait and hope.

Now, this way of cutting to pieces beautiful stories, however interesting it may seem, is yet a dry and barren method. Is there only this in Pearl Buck's writings? A mere transplantation in order to enjoy the contrast? If such were the case, Pearl Buck would be like those real or imaginary travellers who think they have done enough simply by placing their readers in different countries; the contrasts would be nothing but admirable dilemmas, the triumphs of an infallible reasoning. But the change here is deeper; it is a part of the author's life and experience, and experience means pain, sacrifice, an innocent victim. These three themes, constantly repeated throughout her works, give them their human and eternal value. Whether it is a conflict caused by the creative impulse of a gifted woman, or the poignant story of the love between a man and a foreign woman, everywhere a heart or a mind suffers. Because each civilization is ignorant of its neighbour, men do not understand one another, and this total incomprehension engenders misery. Those who, like Pearl Buck, belong to both sides by their feelings, have the greatest share of pain.

—Ami Henchoz, "A Permanent Element in Pearl Buck's Novels," *English Studies: A Journal of English Letters and Philology* 25, nos. 1–6 (1943): 97, 100–1

PAUL A. DOYLE

The style of *The Good Earth* is one of the novel's most impressive characteristics. This style is based on the manner of the old Chinese narrative sagas related and written down by storytellers and on the mellifluous prose of the King James version of the Bible. At certain times Buck declared that her style was Chinese rather than biblical. She explained that she learned to speak Chinese and used Chinese idioms. Therefore, when she wrote about Chinese subject matter, the narrative formed itself mentally into the Chinese language, and she then translated this material into English. She asserted that her prose was based on idiomatic Chinese and that she was often uncertain about the English qualities of the style. At other times she admitted, however, the combined influences of the old Chinese sagas and the King James version. Many similarities exist between the two forms, ranging from the use of parallelism to an old-fashioned, even archaic, form of expression. The King James version of the Bible was often studied and read aloud in Pearl Buck's childhood home, and much of its phraseology remained in the young girl's mind, both consciously and subconsciously, and became a part of her stylistic forms and patterns. This double influence of the Chinese saga and the Bible, then, explains most accurately her stylistic mannerisms.

Pearl Buck's writing in *The Good Earth* is characterized by simplicity, concreteness, a stress on long serpentine sentences, parallelism, balance, and repetition of words. Although the majority of the sentences are lengthy, they break into shorter, sometimes choppy, segments of thought which undulate in movement. The style, generally slow-paced, evinces a quiet stateliness and seriousness. It does not at all rival the color or richness of the biblical imagery, principally because it follows the simplicity of word choice of the Chinese saga rather than the more imaginative and exotic coloring of the Old and New Testaments. At certain times Buck's style achieves poetical suggestion, but never is the imbalance between the normal and the more poetic so pronounced as to produce isolated "purple passages," as was the case in *East Wind: West Wind.* ⟨. . .⟩

Mention should be made of the haze of romanticism that hovers over and about the novel. Buck has wisely avoided the artificial romanticism and the obvious sentimentalism that marred *East Wind: West Wind.* Yet the story of *The Good Earth,* although it maintains a convincing realism, takes on a certain exotic remoteness which lends additional charm to its episodes. The strange is made familiar, and the familiar is made pleasantly strange. Indeed, certain sections of Wordsworth's preface to the *Lyrical Ballads* apply perfectly here: "The principal object . . . was to choose incidents and situations from common life . . . to throw over them a certain coloring of imagination, whereby ordinary things should be presented to the mind in an unusual aspect; and further, and above all, to make these incidents and situations interesting by tracing in them, truly though not ostentatiously, the primary laws of our nature." The faraway coloring of *The Good Earth* lights the familiar elements with new freshness and appeal. Realism and romanticism blend in just the right proportions. Life is given the glow of legend, and legend is given the aura of life.

The motto opposite the book's first page taken from Proust's *Swann's Way* alludes to the phrase from Vinteuil's sonata which had so affected Swann with truth, love, and deep feelings for humanity. This motto relates that the musician Vinteuil refused to add his own subjective feelings and emotions to the composition. He had captured life and truth in the music, and he did not wish to distort the music with his personal attitudes. This motto thus heralds the objectivity of *The Good Earth*. Buck claims that she is not inventing; she is simply transposing life to paper. 〈. . .〉 So objective and impersonal is the novel that it almost seems to exist apart from authorial composition.

Other than proclaiming the eternal cycle of birth and death, growth and decay, and continual change, the "message" of *The Good Earth* has to be inferred since it is never explicitly stated. The novel does suggest that diligent toil may achieve some satisfaction but that luxury may corrupt and ruin "the spiritual meaning of life." Certainly, too, *The Good Earth* does champion "the old American belief in hard work, thrift, ceaseless enterprise and the value of living close to the land." But, while such a "message" may be extracted from the book, such a theme is not presented as a didactic preachment. The "message" exists simply as a corollary of the movement of life itself. Even where a moral or lesson can be drawn, for example, in Wang Lung's contempt for the common people, once he himself achieves wealth and position, no exhortation or sermon is attempted. There rings in our mind only universal truth: this is the way life is; the way people are.

Life's successes, failures, passions, devotions, high points of joy, distressing moments of sadness, constant variety and change, in short the great adventure that is life—these aspects of existence pass continually in review. The novel is didactic only in the sense that life can be so. By watching *The Good Earth*'s pageant of living move before us, we come to know not only ourselves more deeply, but life itself more fully and more comprehensively.

—Paul A. Doyle, *Pearl S. Buck* (New York: Twayne Publishers, 1980), 33–34, 37–38

PRADYUMNA S. CHAUHAN

To take Pearl S. Buck's true measure, it may be necessary to recall that an average English novel tends to fasten itself on a particular scene, attend to a set of characters, and see them through a course of action by the time the curtain is ready to come down. When we are done with the novel, if we remember it at all, what we turn over in our mind is some traits of a character, the nature of a locality, or the social and psychological issue from which the story evolved. Not so with *The Good Earth*, however. What we are left with is a feeling of immensity, the sensation of having watched from space the life of earthlings, embroiled in a struggle for existence—ploughing, fighting, mating, dying— while the earth keeps turning and turning, sometimes parched by the sun, sometimes swept by floods, at times invaded by locusts and pestilence. Like Tennyson's gods looking down upon the Lotos land, then we watch from high

> Blight and famine, plague and earthquake, roaring deeps and fiery
> sands
> Clanging fights, and flaming towns, and sinking ships, and praying
> hands. ⟨. . .⟩

Now such a capacity in the writing to wrest from the obscuring flux of life sharp patterns of human existence and to project their ceaseless cavalcade through tumbling seasons of the earth is a rare gift indeed. And it is the gift, generally, of an epic writer, of one endowed with a macroscopic vision, of a writer who sees life and sees it whole. That hers was such a vision is borne out by passage after passage in *The Good Earth*. We are told what Wang Lung and O-lan encountered working in their field: "Sometimes they turned up a bit of brick, a splinter of wood. It was nothing. Some time, in some age, bodies of men and women had been buried there, houses had stood there, had fallen, and gone back into the earth. So would also their house, some time, return into the earth, their bodies also. Each had his turn at this earth" ⟨33–34⟩. After reading this, the earth appears no strange place, nor death a terror. This couple but rehearses what generations of human ancestors have perpetually gone through.

Ezra Pound, summing up Henry James's achievement, remarked upon the latter's epic talent, which, according to him, consisted in James's capacity to "show race against race; immutable; the essential Americanness, or Englishness, or Frenchness" ⟨"Henry James," 1918⟩. Buck's powerful narrative conveys to the reader not only the Chineseness of her characters, but also a feel of what it must have been like to be living in the era between the old dynasty and the modern state.

It conveys something else, too: the recurring scheme of life on the planet, caught amid the cycles of seasons and the alternating pattern of plenty and scarcity. Equipped, like an epic writer, with a prophet's vision that can not only see, but also reveal to others, the patterns that are embedded in human lives and Nature's kingdom, Buck brings all this to her readers, and without leaving them with any sense of despondence either. When we are told that "the woman and the child were as brown as the soil and they sat there like figures made of earth [and] there was dust of the fields upon the woman's hair and upon the child's soft black head" (44), we find there is nothing for tears in their plight. Eternal like the earth, they are possessed of its strength. There is such vitality in their motion that nothing, it seems, can stop this fountain of life. If we begin Buck's novel with some curiosity, we end it with wisdom.

Now such an effect is rarely achieved by a realistic novel, which special-izes in compiling a record of each fact like a police diary. Its chronicle can, at best, show us the root and branches of some trees, but never the shape of the entire wood. The latter effect is achieved by works like Homer's *Odyssey*, or a novel like Tolstoy's *War and Peace*, where the entire social fabric is rendered for our contemplation. The only two American novels that come close to this stature are Melville's *Moby Dick* (1851) and Steinbeck's *The Grapes of Wrath* (1939). What makes Buck's achievement all the more remarkable is the fact that her novel arrived nine years before Steinbeck's and might well have served as a model for his work.

> —Pradyumna S. Chauhan, "Pearl S. Buck's *The Good Earth*: The Novel As Epic," *The Several Worlds of Pearl S. Buck: Essays Presented at a Centennial Symposium, Randolph Macon Woman's College, March 26–28, 1992*, ed. Elizabeth J. Lipscomb, Frances E. Webb, and Peter Conn (Westport, CT: Greenwood Press, 1994), 120–22

PETER CONN

⟨Pearl Buck⟩ thought of herself as a writer working in both the Chinese and the Western traditions. She was using what she took to be the narrative devices and conventions she had learned from Chinese literature to represent Asian subjects for her English-speaking audience. Her preference for episodic plots over complex structures, her relative indifference to psychological analy-sis, her taste for time-honored phrases, all were rooted in her years of absorp-tion in the classic Chinese novels. In short, what her critics dismissed as defects, she robustly defended as methodical choices.

Pearl Buck believed that her Chinese material was itself part of the reason for her vexed relationship with American literary opinion. She felt victimized by the literary nationalism that emerged as such a potent force in the 1930s and 1940s. To put it bluntly, Americans simply had trouble taking her distant subjects seriously. Academics and lay persons alike saw Asia through Orientalizing lenses: the East remained exotic, inscrutable, irreducibly Other.

At the same time, she wanted to write on American subjects, not to sat-isfy her critics, but to prove her own versatility. ⟨. . .⟩

⟨. . .⟩ In May of 1945 she published a long novel, *The Townsman*, under the pseudonym John Sedges. The pen name gave her a measure of artistic freedom—and the chance to test her talent in the marketplace as an unknown writer. The name itself was the result of Buck's calculations about the sexual politics of American letters: "I chose the name of John Sedges, a simple one, and masculine because men have fewer handicaps in our society than women have, in writing as well as in other professions." (She had also used a male pseudonym when she submitted her M.A. thesis at Cornell in 1925; as "David Barnes," she won the Messenger Prize. She believed that as "Pearl S. Buck," she would have won nothing at all.)

Buck could be relatively satisfied with her experiment in pseudonymity: *The Townsman* was widely and favorably reviewed, it was a Literary Guild selection, and it sold tens of thousands of copies.

Pearl Buck was always a careful student of literary fashions; in *The Townsman* she deliberately made use of several of the chief formulas and conventions that characterized American popular fiction in the 1930s and 1940s. The book is a historical romance, set on the Kansas frontier in the late nineteenth and early twentieth century. Most importantly, *The Townsman* is a novel of the land: like so many of the best-selling stories of the troubled Depression decade and early forties—*God's Little Acre, The Grapes of Wrath*, Pearl Buck's own *The Good Earth*, above all *Gone with the Wind*, which Buck regarded with envious contempt—*The Townsman* celebrates the American soil and the durable people who live on it. ⟨. . .⟩

Pearl Buck's allegorically named hero, Jonathan Goodliffe, comes to America from his native England with his parents in their search for New World opportunity. The novel patiently records Jonathan's long and useful life in the town of Median, Kansas. Jonathan's ambitions are at once modest and exalted: to build a functioning, self-sufficient community on the formidable landscape of the great plains. He opens the first school in his part of the state, plans the town's growth from a cluster of sod huts to a prosperous county seat of six thousand, and finds his fulfillment in the tasks of settlement and civilization.

As this summary suggests, Pearl Buck did not simply use literary formulas; she transformed them to serve her thematic purposes. She could rarely resist preaching in her fiction, especially on the subjects of racial and sexual equality. Beneath its frontier trappings, *The Townsman* teaches an extended lesson in civic virtue. To begin with, Jonathan Goodliffe is not the typical hard-riding sheriff (or outlaw) of most Western fables. Instead, as Buck herself described him ⟨in the Foreword to *American Triptych*⟩, he is a rather ordinary fellow, "who refuses to ride wild horses, be a cowboy, shoot pistols into the air, kill his enemies, find gold in any hills, destroy Indians, or even get drunk. He is content merely to become the solid founder of a city." In short, Pearl Buck used her main male character to embody a new notion of American heroism. Jonathan exemplifies productive domesticity rather than flamboyant adventuring, and to that extent he represents the sort of masculinity Buck called for in *Of Men and Women* (1941), her spirited inquiry into America's gender roles.

—Peter Conn, "Pearl S. Buck and American Literary Culture," *The Several Worlds of Pearl S. Buck: Essays Presented at a Centennial Symposium, Randolph Macon Woman's College, March 26–28, 1992,* ed. Elizabeth J. Lipscomb, Frances E. Webb, and Peter Conn (Westport, CT: Greenwood Press, 1994), 112–13, 115

JANE M. RABB

Like traditional Chinese novelists, ⟨Pearl Buck⟩ wrote to engage ordinary readers, who made her one of the world's most widely translated authors. Buck apparently decided to become a great woman rather than a great writer, a brilliant educator rather than a brilliant artist. This choice brought continuing universal regard and reputation, as well as the necessary financial support for her family and projects. But it killed what remained of her reputation among the literary establishment, who assumed she had "sold out." So although her books, given their large circulation, continued to be reviewed in the popular press, they ceased to be taken seriously by most intellectuals, no matter what their subject.

Scholarly neglect of her writing probably had still other causes. Teachers (who are often influential literary critics and book reviewers) could not have found Buck's lucid prose susceptible to any of the methods of literary analysis that have prevailed since *The Good Earth*. For example, in the 1930s they would have found it difficult to apply the predominant historical approach to a Buck work. How could scholars properly place the works of an American working within the tradition of the Chinese novel (about which they knew little or nothing), yet also influenced by Victorians like Dickens (then out of favor and little studied), as well as her American contemporaries, Theodore Dreiser and Sinclair Lewis (whose stature had not yet been determined)? After the Second World War, literary scholars favored the New Criticism, a close analysis of texts independent of history and biography, an approach no more suited to Buck's writing than its convoluted successors, Structuralism and Deconstructionism. ⟨. . .⟩

⟨. . .⟩ If this process is not soon reversed, Buck's writings—and therefore Buck herself—will be totally forgotten in scholarly circles, however widely translated and read they remain around the world.

Buck's omission from postwar university courses may explain why contemporary feminists never mention her. She should have been one of their heroines, and not only because she was the first American female Nobel Prize winner in Literature. As a woman, Buck was one of the few in her era to apparently "have it all"—fame, fortune, marriage, and children, whom her earnings largely supported. Yet hers was no sheltered life. Buck had survived many life-threatening episodes, experienced heartbreak over her child's retardation, agonized over her divorce, endured the stresses of adoptive and foster mothering, as well as widowhood, and shared these experiences in her writings with an appreciative audience. Indeed, her example has facilitated our present-day discussions of these formerly taboo subjects.

The insights of her public writings and the example of her private choices still anticipate the insights and choices of the leading feminists. Long before Betty Friedan, Buck, in her 1941 collection of essays, *Of Men and Women*, lamented at length and in detail the waste of women's gifts in American society. ⟨. . .⟩

Literary feminists, like other scholars, instead focus on the writings of Austen, Brontë, Wharton, and Woolf, who wrote fewer works; addressed a smaller readership, usually about private issues rather than public affairs; and led narrower lives—two were spinsters and none had children. Not surprisingly, these are precisely the women writers most literary students studied in colleges and graduate schools in the 1960s and 1970s. They all deserve their distinguished status, but Buck does not deserve her present obscurity.

—Jane M. Rabb, "Who's Afraid of Pearl S. Buck?" *The Several Worlds of Pearl S. Buck: Essays Presented at a Centennial Symposium, Randolph Macon Woman's College, March 26–28, 1992*, ed. Elizabeth J. Lipscomb, Frances E. Webb, and Peter Conn (Westport, CT: Greenwood Press, 1994), 105–8

BIBLIOGRAPHY

East Wind, West Wind. 1930.
The Good Earth. 1931.
The Young Revolutionist. 1931.
Sons. 1932.
The First Wife and Other Stories. 1933.
The Mother. 1934.
A House Divided. 1935.
House of Earth. 1935.
The Exile. 1936.
Fighting Angel. 1936.
This Proud Heart. 1938.
The Chinese Novel. 1939.

The Patriot. 1939.
Stories for Little Children. 1940.
Other Gods. 1940.
Men and Women. 1941.
Today and Forever. 1941.
American Unity and Asia. 1942.
The Chinese Children Next Door. 1942.
Dragon Seed. 1942.
The Promise. 1943.
What America Means to Me. 1943.
The Water Buffalo Children. 1943.
The Promise. 1943.
The Dragon Fish. 1944.
Tell the People. 1945.
The Townsmen. 1945.
Yu-lan, Flying Boy of China. 1945.
Portrait of a Marriage. 1945.
Talk about Russia. 1945.
How It Happens. 1946.
Pavilion of Women. 1946.
Far and Near. 1947.
The Big Wave. 1948.
Peony. 1948.
American Argument. 1949.
Kinfolk. 1949.
The Child Who Never Grew. 1950.
One Bright Day. 1950.
God's Men. 1950.
The Hidden Flower. 1952.
Come, My Beloved. 1953.
My Several Worlds. 1954.
The Beech Tree. 1955.
Imperial Woman. 1956.
Letter from Peking. 1957.
Christmas Miniature. 1957.
American Triptych. 1958.
Friend to Friend. 1958.
Command the Morning. 1959.
Christmas Miniature. 1959.

The Christmas Ghost. 1960.
Fourteen Stories. 1961.
A Bridge for Passing. 1962.
Hearts Come Home. 1962.
Satan Never Sleeps. 1962.
The Living Reed. 1963.
Welcome Child. 1964.
Children for Adoption. 1965.
My Mother's House. 1965.
The Big Fight. 1965.
Death in the Castle. 1965.
The Little Fox in the Middle. 1966.
The Time Is Noon. 1967.
The New Year. 1968.

WILLA CATHER

1873-1947

WILLA CATHER was born in Gore, Virginia, on December 7, 1873. She was the first of seven children of Charles Fectigue and Mary Virgina Boak Cather. From stories of both sides of the Civil War recounted by relatives, Cather developed a lifelong distrust of causes, preferring to put her faith in individuals. Her family moved to Nebraska when she was nine years old, the last part of the journey being made in a farm wagon. Cather recounts her first impression of the prairie in the words of Jim Burden in *My Ántonia*: "There seemed nothing to see; no fences, no creeks or trees, no hills or fields. . . not a country at all, but the material out of which countries are made."

She received a B.A. from the University of Nebraska in 1895 and accepted the editorship of a new magazine, *Home Monthly*, in Pittsburgh. She never again lived in Nebraska, although she returned to visit her parents. She went on to become drama critic and telegraph editor for the Pittsburgh *Daily Reader* and then for five years was a high school English teacher. During the latter period, her first books were published: a volume of poetry, *April Twilights*, and a collection of stories, *The Troll Garden*. On the strength of these, in 1906 she was hired as managing editor for *McClure's Magazine* in New York. There she would remain until 1912, when her first novel, *Alexander's Bridge*, was published.

It was *O Pioneers!* (1913) that brought Cather her first success. Based on her childhood memories of Nebraska, the book was written in the evocative, "unfurnished" prose that became her trademark. She returned to Nebraska in *My Ántonia* (1918), which was hailed by critics as a work of greatness. Her next novel was a departure: *One of Ours* (1922) was a bitter story of World War I that won Cather a Pulitzer Prize and best-seller status, although it received mixed reviews. Critics were more enthusiastic about *A Lost Lady* (1923), which continued in the vein of *My Ántonia*. Her next novels were set in the Southwest, a bleak landscape that suited the depression she felt throughout the 1920s. This phase culminated in *Death Comes for the Archbishop* (1927), based on the story of the first bishop of New Mexico. Her next book was also historically based: *Shadows on the Rock* (1931) was a tale of 17th-century Quebec. Her last novel, *Sapphira and the Slave Girl* (1940), was set in pre–Civil War Virginia.

In addition to her novels, Cather produced dozens of short stories, several books of essays, and many poems. Her awards included the William Dean Howells Medal, the Prix Femina Americain, and the National Institute of Arts and Letters Gold Medal. She received honorary doctorates from Yale, Princeton, Smith, Columbia, the University of Michigan, the University of Nebraska, and the University of California at Berkeley. Willa Cather died in New York City on April 24, 1947.

CRITICAL EXTRACTS

WILLA CATHER

There is a popular superstition that "realism" asserts itself in the cataloguing of a great number of material objects, in explaining mechanical processes, the methods of operating manufactories and trades, and in minutely and unsparingly describing physical sensations. But is not realism, more than it is anything else, an attitude of mind on the part of the writer toward his material, a vague indication of the sympathy and candour with which he accepts, rather than chooses, his theme? ⟨. . .⟩

If the novel is a form of imaginative art, it cannot be at the same time a vivid and brilliant form of journalism. Out of the teeming, gleaming stream of the present it must select the eternal material of art. There are hopeful signs that some of the younger writers are trying to break away from mere verisimilitude, and, following the development of modern painting, to interpret imaginatively the material and social investiture of their characters; to present their scene by suggestion rather than by enumeration. The higher processes of art are all processes of simplification. The novelist must learn to write, and then he must unlearn it; just as the modern painter learns to draw, and then learns when utterly to disregard his accomplishment, when to subordinate it to a higher and truer effect. In this direction only, it seems to me, can the novel develop into anything more varied and perfect than all the many novels that have gone before.

One of the very earliest American romances might well serve as a suggestion to later writers. In *The Scarlet Letter* how truly in the spirit of art is the mise-en-scène presented. That drudge, the theme-writing high-school student, could scarcely be sent there for information regarding the manners and dress and interiors of Puritan society. The material investiture of the story is presented as if unconsciously; by the reserved, fastidious hand of an artist, not by the gaudy fingers of a showman or the mechanical industry of a department-store window-dresser. As I remember it, in the twilight melancholy of that book, in its consistent mood, one can scarcely see the actual surroundings of the people; one feels them, rather, in the dusk.

Whatever is felt upon the page without being specifically named there—that, one might say, is created. It is the inexplicable presence of the thing not named, of the overtone divined by the ear but not heard by it, the verbal mood, the emotional aura of the fact or the thing or the deed, that gives high quality to the novel or the drama, as well as to poetry itself.

Literalness, when applied to the presenting of mental reactions and of physical sensations, seems to be no more effective than when it is applied to material things. A novel crowded with physical sensations is no less a catalogue than one crowded with furniture. A book like *The Rainbow* by D. H. Lawrence sharply reminds one how vast a distance lies between emotion and mere sensory reactions. Characters can be almost dehumanized by a laboratory study of the behaviour of their bodily organs under sensory stimuli—can be reduced, indeed, to mere animal pulp. Can one imagine anything more terrible than the story of *Romeo and Juliet* rewritten in prose by D. H. Lawrence?

How wonderful it would be if we could throw all the furniture out of the window; and along with it, all the meaningless reiterations concerning physical sensations, all the tiresome old patterns, and leave the room as bare as the stage of a Greek theatre, or as that house into which the glory of Pentecost descended; leave the scene bare for the play of emotions, great and little—for the nursery tale, no less than the tragedy, is killed by tasteless amplitude. The elder Dumas enunciated a great principle when he said that to make a drama, a man needed one passion, and four walls.

—Willa Cather, "The Novel Démeublé" (1922), *On Writing* (1949), excerpted in *Twentieth-Century American Literature*, ed. Harold Bloom (New York: Chelsea House Publishers, 1986), 692

LLOYD MORRIS

From *Alexander's Bridge* to *A Lost Lady* Miss Cather's books reveal her explicit concentration upon a single theme. That theme is the effort of the individual to overcome the obstacles offered by circumstance and to control or dominate environment. She has been chiefly concerned with pioneers and with artists who, as she conceives them, bring to this effort similar propensities toward action and similar attitudes toward life. Both types, as Miss Cather has portrayed them, are driven forward by a spontaneous energy which they exercise without clearly understanding; they are passionate rather than intelligent, feeling life deeply, though seldom reflecting upon it profoundly; they are superbly self-confident though spiritually isolated; their abundant vitality nourishes the stubborn will which secures for them the prizes of intelligence in the absence of its possession. In a group of her novels, Miss Cather has dealt with the effort of the individual to subdue his physical environment to his own uses, revealing the warping contest between primitive human nature and the defiant soil of the frontier. Out of them arises her now considerable gallery of portraits of pioneers; the characters of *O Pioneers!* and *My Ántonia*, the elder generation of *One of Ours*, Captain Forrester and several of his lightly sketched associates in *A Lost Lady*. These are figures in the sunset of an epoch, and almost before the accomplishment of their purposes they become picturesque survivors in a new order. The recalcitrant soil is finally tamed, the empty spaces of the frontier fill up, the era of rapid communication and mechanical agriculture sets in, and there are no frontiers left to conquer. There are none, at least, on the land.

The new frontier, Miss Cather suggests, occurs within the imagination. In the arts there are always unbroken lands open for settlement, and her pioneers of yesterday become the artists of today, turning from the conquest of the land to a fresh contest with an equally obdurate spiritual environment. In default, perhaps, of any ideal sufficiently comprehensive to claim an undivided loyalty, the undisciplined and unemployed spiritual energy of the race is pushing forward its discoveries in the creative life of the arts. Perceiving this, Miss Cather has chronicled the inception of a new age of pioneering in her portraits of artists; the figures who move through her stories in *Youth and the Bright Medusa*, Thea Kronborg in *The Song of the Lark*, the violinist in *One of Ours*.

Although Miss Cather responds vigorously to the heroism called forth by these two aspects of individual experience and indispensable to success in either, there is seldom absent from her work a recognition of its accompanying pathos. She reveals the beauty of wide horizons and open spaces and untamed solitude, but she does not fail to indicate that her prairies are more propitious to the ripening of wheat than to that of the human spirit. A group of characters intervenes between her pioneers and her artists, those who, unable to dominate their environment, have succumbed to it and are thereby defeated. ⟨. . .⟩

⟨. . .⟩ The total absence from Miss Cather's work of an epic outlook upon American life is nowhere more strikingly revealed than in the concluding section of *One of Ours*. It is perhaps not without significance that Miss Cather, who is among the most thoughtful of our contemporary novelists, has failed to isolate in our national life any ideal faith or noble purpose deserving the allegiance that awaits its discovery. So remote is she from that discovery that she intimates the futility of the quest.

—Lloyd Morris, "Willa Cather," *National Review* (April 1924), excerpted in *Twentieth-Century American Literature*, ed. Harold Bloom (New York: Chelsea House Publishers, 1986), 693

REBECCA WEST

The most sensuous of writers, Willa Cather builds her imagined world almost as solidly as our five senses build the universe around us. This account ⟨in *Death Comes for the Archbishop*⟩ of the activities of a French priest who was given a diocese in the southwest during the late 'forties, impresses one first of all by its amazing sensory achievements. She has within herself a sensitivity that constantly presents her with a body of material which would overwhelm most of us, so that we would give up all idea of transmitting it and would sink into a state of passivity; and she has also a quality of mountain-pony sturdiness that makes her push on unfatigued under her load and give an accurate account of every part of it. So it is that one is not quite sure whether it is one of the earlier pages in *Death Comes for the Archbishop* or a desert in central New Mexico, that is heaped up with small conical hills, red as brick-dust, a landscape of which the human aspect is thirst and confusion of the retina at seeing the earth itself veritably presenting such reduplications of an image as one could conceive only as consequences of a visual disorder. When the young bishop on his mule finds this thirst smouldering up to flame in his throat and his confusion whirling faster and faster into vertigo, he blots out his own pain in meditating on the Passion of our Lord; he does not deny to consciousness that it is in a state of suffering, but leads it inward from the surface of being where it feebly feels itself contending with innumerable purposeless irritations to a place within the heart where suffering is held to have been proved of greater value than anything else in the world, the one coin sufficient to buy man's salvation; this, perhaps the most delicate legerdemain man has ever practised on his senses, falls into our comprehension as lightly as a snowflake into the hand, because of her complete mastery of every phase of the process. But she becomes committed to no degree of complication as her special field. A page later she writes of the moment when the priest and his horses come on water, in language simple as if she were writing a book for boys, in language exquisitely appropriate for the expression of a joy that must have been intensest in the youth of races.

    —Rebecca West, "The Classic Artist," *The Strange Necessity* (1928), excerpted in *Twentieth-Century American Literature*, ed. Harold Bloom (New York: Chelsea House Publishers, 1986), 698–99

BERNARD BAUM

Chronologically older than the writers usually classed as "Waste Landers," Cather at her most significant level, nevertheless, belongs thematically with T. S. Eliot, D. H. Lawrence, Aldous Huxley, Evelyn Waugh, the elder F. Scott

Fitzgerald, John Crowe Ransom, and those poets, including MacLeish, Tate, and Bishop, who largely under Eliot's influence inhabited for a time what Edmund Wilson described as "exclusively barren beaches, cactus-grown deserts, and dusty attics over-run with rats." All these writers had in common a profoundly disturbing sense of modern civilization as bankrupt morally and intellectually—a desert of the spirit inhabited by hollow men. This is the atmosphere of Eliot's poetry from "Prufrock" and "Gerontion" and "Sweeney" in crescendo to *The Waste Land* and "The Hollow Men." Haunting the literature of the Waste Land is a sense not only of desolation but of complete loss of meaningful living through secularization of the primary areas of human experience: love, art, and all the shared values that make for an integrated society. 〈. . .〉

Cather's relation to the literature of the Waste Land is not peripheral. The Waste-Land motif provides the unifying principle in several of her best novels and helps to set the tone and to give a certain solidity to much of her work that otherwise suffers from thin characterization, episodic structure, and stylistic lapse. There is, moreover, a remarkably close similarity of ideological web in her most significant fiction and Eliot's poetry. *One of Ours* was published the same year as *The Waste Land* (1922) without anyone observing, so far as I know, that Cather's novel contained the record of a "Death by Water." Claude Wheeler's death in battle in the First World War was, for his creator, the most meaningful thing that could have happened to him in the modern Waste Land. He redeemed himself thereby as a spiritual entity. It was not death but a birth, albeit a hard one: "Hard and bitter agony for us, like Death, our death." Thus a Magus in one of Eliot's later poems of redemption. Cather's alter ego in *One of Ours* had once thought:

> Claude would become one of those dead people that moved about
> the streets of Frankfort; everything that was Claude would perish, and
> the shell of him would come and go and eat and sleep for fifty years.

But Claude, unlike the Magi, did not have to return plaintively to the world of hollow men and women—to the Babbittry of Bayliss and the anemic piety of Enid: "the old dispensation,/With an alien people clutching their gods." It should be recognized that the term "Waste-Land theme" involves both death and rebirth concepts as integrally related. There is obvious continuity from Eliot's earlier through his later poetry. . . .

In *Death Comes for the Archbishop* as in *The Professor's House* it is the Waste-Land theme that provides a basic unity to a segmented narrative. The series of anecdotes, historical sketches, Indian and saints' legends have all an articulation with the meaning of the basic situation: Father Latour and Father Vaillant pouring forth the waters of spiritual life in the desert. Ironically, it is in the desert, not in Ohio, that Father Latour finds life even in its humbler aspects touched by a natural artistic sensitivity. We have already observed that, to Cather, art was an aspect of the life-giving power. The priest's adobe house has everywhere the evidence of the craftsman's hand in communion with his material. Father Latour's sympathetic response to Indian culture, including its pagan vestiges, is a means by which the unifying theme is strengthened. In the Indian legends and ritual he recognizes and respects the life-nurturing mythos, the impelling need to poetize life to the level of religious significance. "Father Latour remarked that their veneration for old customs was a quality he liked in the Indians, and that it played a great part in his own religion."

The struggle of the two French priests to bring the rain of the spirit to a parched land has its counterpart in the age-old heroic struggle of the natives to make this dry country yield life. Father Vaillant was fired with a desire to go out to the people added to the diocese by the Gadsden Purchase. "There are hundreds of poor families down there who have never seen a priest," he says. "They are full of devotion and faith, and it has nothing to feed upon but the most mistaken superstitions. . . . They are like seeds, full of germination but with no moisture." The contrast running through the novel is between those who, like the bishop and his vicar, fructify and those who do not; between those who strive to make the Waste Land yield life and those who neglect or destroy life. In Eusabio and Jacinto, Cather has tried to portray Indians as the inheritors of a disciplined, life-yielding past. Theirs is essentially the fertile spirit; they live by a humanizing code. Even the reprobate Mexican priests, Martínez and Lucero, are "men enough to be damned," and that is more than Cather can say for many of the Americans settling the area later in the century.

The spiritual and physical symbolism is readily blended in the novel as in Eliot's poem. Father Latour demonstrates in relation to the earth itself the presence of his creative spiritual force. Both in Santa Fe and in the villa outside the city, which he bought for the years of his retirement, he painstakingly planted and watered. He brought seeds and bulbs and tree cuttings to make the parched land produce.

> He grew such fruit as was hardly to be found even in the old
> orchards of California: cherries and apricots, apples and quinces, and
> the peerless pears of France—even the most delicate varieties. He
> urged the new priests to plant fruit trees wherever they went, and to
> encourage the Mexicans to add fruit to their starchy diet. Wherever
> there was a French priest, there should be a garden of fruit trees and
> vegetables and flowers.

In Colorado of the Gold Rush period, however, Father Vaillant found a Waste Land indeed. "Nobody in Colorado planted gardens . . . ; nobody would stick a shovel into the earth for anything less than gold."

—Bernard Baum, "Willa Cather's Waste Land," *The South Atlantic Quarterly* (Autumn 1949), excerpted in *Twentieth-Century American Literature*, ed. Harold Bloom (New York: Chelsea House Publishers, 1986), 713–14

MORTON DAUWEN ZABEL

The interesting thing about Miss Cather's career is that it started in protest against and flight from the very world she ended by idealizing and mourning. It recapitulates a characteristic American pattern of rebellion and return, censure and surrender. The prairie and small town, the Western hinterland and the neighborly community, as she presented them in her best early stories— "A Wagner Matinee," "Paul's Case," "The Sculptor's Funeral," "A Death in the Desert"—were objects of a moral reproach and castigation as severe as anything she later directed against the vulgarizing influences of the modern world. She was, indeed, a pioneer in the twentieth-century "revolt from the village," and she spared no scorn in describing the provincial spirit. It had created the life of a "dunghill," of petty existences, of "little people" and a small humanity, of stingy hates and warping avarice that made generous spirits shrivel and ardent natures die. The savagery of her indictment was perhaps the strongest passion she ever summoned in any of her works. Her frontier in those days was not the West; it was the East and the world of art, with desire the goad of her heroes and heroines and the running theme of her stories, as much as it was of Dreiser's.

It was in young artists—the dreaming, headstrong, fractious, or unstable young, fated to defeat or bad ends by the materialism and ugliness of their surroundings—that she first envisaged the heroic ideal. Paul, Katharine Gaylord, Harvey Merrick, and Don Hedger are the defeated or dishonored "cases" that foreshadow the triumphant lives of Alexandra Bergson, Thea Kronborg, Ántonia Shimerda, Archbishop Machebeuf, and Nancy Till, and that lend their note of desire or vision to the middle terms of Miss Cather's argument— the inspired spirits who do not succeed but who, by some force of character or apartness of nature, lend significance to the faceless anonymity around them. These characters—the "lost lady" Marian Forrester, Myra Henshawe, Tom Outland, Professor St. Peter, even the slighter Lucy Gayheart in a later novel—are the most persuasive of Miss Cather's creations, her nearest claims to skill in a field where she was admittedly and obviously incompetent—complex and credible psychology. But somehow she could never bring her opposites into full play in a novel. They remained irreconcilably differentiated, dramatically hostile, morally and socially incapable of true complexity.

The full-bodied and heavily documented novel was never congenial to Miss Cather; she rightly understood her art to be one of elimination and selection, which eventually meant that it was an art of simplification and didactic idealization. *The Song of the Lark* and *One of Ours* drag with detail. *My Ántonia* and *A Lost Lady* are her finest successes because there her selection defines, suggests, and evokes without falsely idealizing. When she seized a theme of genuine social and moral potentiality in *The Professor's House* or *My Mortal Enemy*, she pared away its substance until she produced what must always be, to her admirers, disappointingly frugal and bodiless sketches of two of the most interesting subjects in the America of her time. And when she decided to model *Death Comes for the Archbishop* on the pallid two-dimensional murals of Puvis de Chavannes, she prepared the way for the disembodied idealization, making for inertness and passivity, that overtook her in *Shadows on the Rock*, weakest of her books and portent of the thinness of her final volumes.

What overtook her plots and characters is the same thing that overtook her version of American life and history. She could not bring her early criticism into effective combination with her later nostalgic sentiment. She represents a case analogous to that of Van Wyck Brooks, who started by vigorously but disproportionately castigating American literature, and has ended in a sentimentalization equally unbalanced and simplistic. So Miss Cather, having never mastered the problem of desire in its full social and moral conditioning, passed from her tales of ambitious artists and defeated dreamers, worsted by provincial mediocrity or careerism, to versions of American idealism and its defeat that never come to satisfactory grips with the conditions of society and personal morality. As her lovers, her artists, her pioneers, and her visionary Titans become disembodied of complex emotion or thought, so her America itself became disembodied of its principles of growth, conflict, and historical maturity. There obviously worked in her nature that "poetic romanticism" to which Lionel Trilling has referred her case: what Parrington called "the inferiority complex of the frontier mind before the old and established"; the pioneer's fear of failure but greater fear of the success which comes "when an idea becomes an actuality"; the doctrine of American individualism to which F. J. Turner credited the pioneer's failure to "understand the richness and complexity of life as a whole." So to Willa Cather's early veneration for the distant goals and shining trophies of desire, ambition, and art, there succeeded a veneration for lost or distant sanctities which gradually spelled her diminution as a dramatic and poetic craftsman. The village, the prairie, the West, the New Mexican missions thus became in time abstractions as unworkable, in any critical or moral sense, as her simplified understanding of Mann's Joseph cycle.

Art itself, in her versions of Flaubert, Gogol, Mann, or Katherine Mansfield, took on a remote ideality and aesthetic pathos that do much to explain her distaste for Dostoevsky or Chekhov. And the Church, to which she finally appealed as a human and historical constant, became in her unimplicated and inexperienced view of it the most abstract of all her conceptions, a cultural symbol, not a human or historical actuality, and the least real of any of the standards she invoked in her judgments and criticism of the modern world.

—Morton Dauwen Zabel, "Willa Cather: The Tone of Time," *Craft and Character in Fiction* (1957), excerpted in *Twentieth-Century American Literature*, ed. Harold Bloom (New York: Chelsea House Publishers, 1986), 696

JOHN H. RANDALL III

My Ántonia has an interesting and rather peculiar introduction or prologue. In it Willa Cather pretends to have met Jim Burden, the fictitious narrator of the tale, on a train and has them agree that each one of them shall set down on paper his impressions of Ántonia, a mutual friend of their childhood. After months go by they meet again to find that Jim is the only one who has written anything; the rest of the book purports to be his manuscript. Thereafter Willa Cather herself drops out of the story as a separate character. The book that follows really consists of the parallel stories of Ántonia and Jim. The narrator points this out to us while explaining what he has written. "I simply wrote down what of herself and myself and other people Ántonia's name recalls to me. I suppose it hasn't any form. It hasn't any title either." Then he clinches the fact that this is to be the story of a relationship rather than of an individual by changing the wording on the front of the manuscript from "Ántonia" to "My Ántonia."

My Ántonia is usually called a novel with a single protagonist—the heroine—and the narrator has been considered relatively unimportant. I would like to suggest a different interpretation, because the role played by Jim Burden seems to me far too important to be merely that of a first-person onlooker who is relating someone else's story. He enters into the action too much, for one thing. In the early part of the book the Burden family is continually trudging over to their neighbors the Shimerdas to see if they can help them out. Later on there is a long section in which Jim attends the University of Nebraska and flirts with Lena Lingard; here Ántonia scarcely even appears. Even in the parts of the book where Ántonia and Jim appear together, Jim's reactions to events are at least as important as hers. If Willa Cather wanted her heroine to hold the undisputed center of the stage, she should have focused less attention on her narrator. As it is, the center of interest shifts back and forth between Jim and Ántonia, and the result is best understood as the story of parallel lives.

In her later novels Willa Cather often has a double protagonist such as this, one of whom resembles herself and the other someone who is not herself but whom she admires. One of these usually stands for the contemplative life, the other for the life of action. The use of a double protagonist has certain advantages: it allows one character to be an actor and the other a spectator; one can be youth which performs and accomplishes unthinkingly, the other middle age which can interpret the significance of action in others but itself has lost the capacity to act. In *My Ántonia* this double protagonist consists of Jim Burden and Ántonia, who, true to the best traditions of the romantic movement, stand for head and heart, respectively. It is as if Ántonia actually lives life, while Jim merely records it, or at best lives vicariously through her. When he is with her, Jim is a complete personality and reaches his highest development as a human being, but his personal life falls apart when he leaves her, however successful he may be in his professional role. Later in the book when he returns to visit Nebraska after a twenty years' absence, he finds out just how far Ántonia has forged ahead of him during that time. He is generous enough to rejoice in her good fortune, but it merely underlines his own lack of progress, and even regression, during that same interval. The more she tells him about her successful present, the more his mind wanders back to thoughts of their childhood together. Together he and the friend of his youth make a complete personality, but it is Janus-faced, one of them looking forward and the other back. Ántonia has the whole future for her domain; Jim Burden has only the past. ⟨. . .⟩

Although the two lives run parallel and are given almost equally extensive treatment, no doubt is left in the reader's mind that Ántonia is the one who has achieved the real success. Willa Cather loads the story in Ántonia's favor, not only by emphasizing Jim's obvious admiration for her, but by making all the significant action take place in Nebraska; Jim Burden's marriage and Eastern career are mentioned merely in passing. Accordingly, the early years on the plains are heavily stressed. This is not surprising, since the two main characters see relatively little of each other after childhood. But it does contribute mightily to the mood of nostalgia which is so strong an ingredient in Jim Burden's personality and which swells toward the end of the book into a hymn of praise for the past which Willa Cather aptly sums up in a line quoted from Vergil: *"Optima dies . . . prima fugit"* (*Georgics*, III, 66–67).

—John H. Randall III, "Ántonia and Jim: The Contrasting Life Cycles," The Landscape and the Looking Glass (1960), excerpted in *Twentieth-Century American Literature*, ed. Harold Bloom (New York: Chelsea House Publishers, 1986), 696–97

BLANCHE H. GELFANT

Jim Burden belongs to a remarkable gallery of characters for whom Cather consistently invalidates sex. Her priests, pioneers, and artists invest all energy elsewhere. Her idealistic young men die prematurely; her bachelors, children, and old folk remain "neutral" observers. Since she wrote within a prohibitive genteel tradition, this reluctance to portray sexuality is hardly surprising. What should intrigue us is the strange involuted nature of her avoidance. She masks sexual ambivalence by certainty of manner, and displays sexual disturbance, even the macabre, with peculiar insouciance. Though the tenor of her writing is normality, normal sex stands barred from her fictional world. Her characters avoid sexual union with significant and sometimes bizarre ingenuity, or achieve it only in dreams. Alexandra Bergson, the heroine of O Pioneers!, finds in recurrent reveries the strong transporting arms of a lover; and Jim Burden in My Ántonia allows a half-nude woman to smother him with kisses only in unguarded moments of fantasy. Their dreams suggest the typical solipsism of Cather's heroes, who yield to a lover when they are most solitary, most inverted, encaptured by their own imaginations. As Alexandra dispels such reveries by a brisk cold shower, their inferential meaning becomes almost comically clear. Whenever sex enters the real world (as for Emil and Marie in O Pioneers!), it becomes destructive, leading almost axiomatically to death. No wonder, then, that Cather's heroes have a strong intuitive aversion to sex which they reveal furtively through enigmatic gestures. ⟨. . .⟩

In My Ántonia, Jim Burden grows up with an intuitive fear of sex, never acknowledged, and in fact, denied: yet it is a determining force in his story. By deflecting attention from himself to Ántonia, of whom he can speak with utter assurance, he manages to conceal his muddied sexual attitudes. His narrative voice, reinforced by Cather's, emerges firm and certain; and it convinces. We tend to believe with Jim that his authoritative recitation of childhood memories validates the past and gives meaning to the present even though his mature years stream before him emptied of love, intimacy, and purpose. Memory transports him to richer and happier days spent with Ántonia, the young Bohemian girl who signifies *"the country, the conditions, the whole adventure . . . childhood."* Because a changing landscape brilliantly illumines his childhood— with copper-red prairies transformed to rich wheatfields and corn—his personal story seems to epitomize this larger historical drama. Jim uses the coincidence of his life-span with a historical era to imply that as the country changed and grew, so did he, and moreover, as his memoirs contained historical facts, so did they hold the truth about himself. Critics support Jim's bid for validity, pointing out that "*My Ántonia* exemplifies superbly [Frederick Jackson] Turner's concept of the recurring cultural evolution on the frontier."

Jim's account of both history and himself seems to me disingenuous, indeed, suspect; yet it is for this very reason highly pertinent to an understanding of our own uses of the past. ⟨. . .⟩ Ultimately, Jim forgets as much as he remembers, as his mind sifts through the years to retrieve what he most needs—a purified past in which he can find safety from sex and disorder. Of "a romantic disposition," Jim substitutes wish for reality in celebrating the past. His flight from sexuality parallels a flight from historical truth, and in this respect, he becomes an emblematic American figure, like Jay Gatsby and Clyde Griffiths.

—Blanche H. Gelfant, "The Forgotten Reaping-Hook: Sex in *My Ántonia*," *American Literature* 43, no. 1 (March 1971), reprinted in *Modern Critical Views: Willa Cather*, ed. Harold Bloom (New York: Chelsea House Publishers, 1985), 104–5

EUDORA WELTY

Willa Cather saw her broad land in a sweep, but she saw selectively too—the detail that made all the difference. She never lost sight of the particular in the panorama. Her eye was on the human being. In her continuous, acutely conscious and responsible act of bringing human value into focus, it was her accomplishment to bring her gaze from that wide horizon, across the stretches of both space and time, to the intimacy and immediacy of the lives of a handful of human beings.

People she saw slowly, with care, in their differences: her chosen characters. They stood up out of their soil and against their sky, making, each of them and one by one, a figure to reckon with.

"For the first time, perhaps, since that land emerged from waters of geologic ages," she says of Alexandra in that memorable passage of *O Pioneers!*, "a human face was set toward it with love and yearning. It seemed beautiful to her, rich and strong and glorious. Her eyes drank in the breadth of it, until her tears blinded her. Then the Genius of the Divide, the great, free spirit which breathes across it, must have bent lower than it ever bent to a human will before. The history of every country begins in the heart of a man or a woman."

And the farther and wider she could see when she started out, the closer it brought her, we feel, full circle—to the thing she wanted, the living, uncopyable *identity* of it that all her working life she wrote in order to meet, to face, to give us as well as she knew it in stories and novels.

The lack of middle distance may have something to do with the way the characters in the foreground cast such long, backreaching shadows. In that lonely stretch of empty and waiting space, they take on heroic stature. And so,

Jim Burden tells us—and this has been earned; we have almost reached the end of her novel: "Ántonia had always been one to leave images in the mind that did not fade—that grew stronger with time. . . . She lent herself to immemorial human attitudes which we recognize by instinct as universal and true. She was a battered woman now, not a lovely girl; but she still had that something which fires the imagination, could still stop one's breath for a moment by a look or gesture that somehow revealed the meaning in common things. She had only to stand in the orchard, to put her hand on a little crab tree and look up at the apples, to make you feel the goodness of planting and tending and harvesting at last. All the strong things of her heart came out in her body . . . . She was a rich mine of life, like the founders of early races."

A writer uses what he's been given. The work of William Faulkner— another writer of Southern origin, who was destined himself to live in the thick of his background and who had his own abiding sense of place and time and history—is packed most densely of all at the middle distance. The generations clustered just behind where the present-day characters are in action are in fact the tallest—and the most heavily burdened with that past. Faulkner's ancient peoples, his Indians, whose land was taken away by unjust treaty, who were expelled from their own, their race dispersed and brought to nothing, have made the land inimical to the white man. The slave has cursed him again. History for Faulkner is directly inherited; it has come down to the present with the taint of blood and the shame of wrongdoing a part of it. Along with the qualities of nobility and courage and endurance, there were for him corresponding qualities of guilt; there is torment in history and in Faulkner's wrestling with it, in his interpretation of it. Willa Cather's history was not thus bonded to the present; it did not imprison the present, but instructed it, passed on a meaning. It was pure, remained pure, and in its purity could come and go in crystal air. It had the character and something of the import of a vision. The spirit, and not the blood, received it.

In the world of her novels, history lies in persistence in the memory, in lost hidden places that wait to be found and to be known for what they are. Such history is barely accessible, the shell of it is only frailly held together, it will be loseable again. But the continuity is *there*.

Where does the continuity lie, then? It is made possible, it is carried out, is lived through, by the pioneer. And it is perceived by the artist. And even more profoundly, it exists, for Willa Cather, as a potential in the artist himself; it is his life's best meaning, his own personal, and responsible, connection with the world.

—Eudora Welty, "The House of Willa Cather," in *The Art of Willa Cather* (Lincoln: University of Nebraska Press, 1974), reprinted in *Modern Critical Views: Willa Cather*, ed. Harold Bloom (New York: Chelsea House Publishers, 1985), 147–49

PHILIP GERBER

Superficially the story of Ántonia Shimerda seems cut from a quite different piece of cloth than its predecessors. A Bohemian girl, she is trapped in the worst possible conditions on the Nebraska Divide: indentured to a town family, uneducated, bereft of special talents, so trusting as to be easy prey to a glib scoundrel. Yet, maintaining a steellike equanimity, she becomes a farmer's wife, mother to a houseful of happy children. Hers is the rarest of Cather's lives—a joyous one.

For Ántonia, no iron bridges span obedient rivers, no spread of prairie transforms into pasture and cornfield, and no audiences pay homage to a perfect aria. The professional career underlying previous stories is entirely removed, allowing Cather to show "just the other side of the rug, the pattern that is supposed not to count in a story." Celebration of professional fulfillment broadens to a struggle for personal identity. Ántonia's instinct plunges her always into life's mainstream, disregarding money, position, possessions, or career. To live merely for the rich experience of living itself is the "career" she labors at with as much diligence as Kronborg ever practiced her scales. One thinks of Thoreau withdrawing to Walden purposely to confront life, drive it into a corner, and derive its essential quality—all to determine whether it be mean or fine and finally to be able to say that he had lived. So armed with a fierce necessity to breathe and act, Ántonia rises relatively unscathed from ordeals that might ruin a lesser spirit. Lacking any "talent," she possesses the gift of a warm heart, a buoyant sense of humor, and an infinite capacity for enthusiasm.

This pursuit of life—not to achieve any lofty aim but merely to go with the tides, to exist fully, passionately—was foreign to Cather's nature. But the more she came to understand the toll exacted by a career, the more attractive seemed the life given over wholly to immediate experiences, and the more she came to admire—almost to envy—those equipped to approach their lives in this seemingly easy fashion. Cather could never truly comprehend such persons, the Ántonias of the world. The Thea Kronborgs, the Alexandra Bergsons she knew intimately, for they were so nearly surrogates for herself. In contrast, Ántonia Shimerda required not analysis but worship. She was to be marveled at, something like a Sequoia that stands forever in contradiction of all one's experience.

Thus Cather needed to contemplate her heroine from a safe distance in order to protect herself (as author) from an involvement so intimate that it might reveal her inability to project the girl's personality firsthand. When Cather was writing *The Song of the Lark*, her delight at and fascination with the creative process had allowed her to crawl temporarily inside the skin of another individual. But this was not possible with Ántonia; she and the

Bohemian girl had too little in common. Cather's solution was to tell the story through the viewpoint of a relatively detached narrator. It was a relatively common device, much used by Henry James, that Cather's knowledge of painters and their methods would seem to have suggested. Elizabeth Sergeant remembers a discussion of artistic form and technique that occurred in the spring of 1916, when Willa Cather was beginning *My Ántonia*. Cather leaned forward suddenly, took a Sicilian apothecary jar filled with orange-brown flowers, and placed it alone on an antique table. For a moment she might have been a painter setting up a still-life arrangement. "I want my new heroine to be like this," she said, "like a rare object in the middle of a table, which one may examine from all sides. I want her to stand out—like this—because she *is* the story."

The narrator whom Cather selected, Jim Burden, allows for Ántonia to be examined in this manner and the various "sides" from which she is seen correspond to the different ages at which Jim knows (of) her—as a child, as an adolescent, as a maiden in full bloom, and finally as a mature woman. Because Jim Burden himself grows older as the story progresses and because his experiences alter him as Ántonia's experiences alter her, each successive view or "side" from which she is observed is more complex and more interesting. At the same time, the adoption of Jim's point-of-view not only explains but actually mandates the episodic structure of the novel. In the introductory chapter Jim is shown as he emphasizes the personal nature of his memoir: "He . . . wrote on the pinkish face of the portfolio the word, 'Ántonia.' He frowned at this a moment, then prefixed another word, making it 'My Ántonia.' That seemed to satisfy him." The most effective way for Jim to create the really strong impressions that will make the manuscript-Ántonia *his* and not another's is to see or hear of her at widely scattered but fairly regular intervals— above all at moments of significance in her life. This, of course, is the manner in which the novel proceeds ⟨. . . .⟩

—Philip Gerber, "The Bright Challenge," *Willa Cather* (1975), excerpted in *Twentieth-Century American Literature*, ed. Harold Bloom (New York: Chelsea House Publishers, 1986), 697–98

Patricia Raub

The farm and pioneer novels ⟨of the 1930s and 1940s⟩ permitted social conservatives to turn their backs upon a potentially troubling present and return to a "golden age" of gender relationships. In pioneer novels, this "golden age" is separated from the present by time, while in farm novels it is space which isolates the characters from the lives of a majority of the books' readers. While some women novelists use the farm and pioneer genres to introduce female protagonists whose actions redefine women's traditional place in society, more often women writers of farm and pioneer novels feature heroines who conform to conventional standards of female behavior, seldom questioning the gender roles which society has assigned them. Interestingly enough, both those women writers of the Twenties and Thirties who set out to demonstrate that women had the ability and strength to stand alone and those who attempted to show that women belonged in more subordinate roles relied on prototypes provided by Willa Cather.

In *O Pioneers!* (1913) Cather constructed one of the strongest woman characters yet to appear in American fiction. Alexandra Bergson, daughter of a Swedish immigrant who has struggled for eleven years to become a successful farmer on the Nebraska prairie, is left in charge of family and farm by her dying father. Alexandra proves to be worthy of her father's confidence. The next few years are hard, but, though many of the Bergsons' neighbors begin to despair of ever taming the land and her own brothers are ready to admit failure and sell out, Alexandra retains her faith in the prairie. Unlike male pioneers who perceive themselves to be fighting against the frontier, ruthlessly bending it to their will, Alexandra has a more empathetic relationship with her environment. Because Alexandra turns toward the land "with love and yearning," the prairie responds by bending "lower than it ever bent to a human will before" (65). Under Alexandra's hands, as Cather's section titles indicate, the "Wild Land" becomes "Neighboring Fields."

Alexandra Bergson is certainly unlike most previous fictional heroines ⟨in being autonomous and not defined by her relationship to men⟩. Although the novel ends with Alexandra's marriage, this event is hardly the climax of the story. Alexandra and Carl's union is a union of friends, not of lovers. Carl is aware that Alexandra's first love is still the land: " 'You belong to the land,' Carl murmured, 'as you have always said. Now more than ever' " (307).

If Alexandra "belongs" to the land, Antonia Shimerda, the subject of Cather's other great pioneer novel, *My Antonia* (1918), "belongs" to other people. Even the narrator of the story of this Bohemian immigrant feels entitled to write about "my" Antonia. As a girl, she plows the fields, not because of her love for the land but because she takes pride in helping her family survive. As the Harlings' hired girl, the narrator tells us (with a tinge of jealousy) she is "fairly panting with eagerness to please" her employers' son Charlie (155). Eventually Antonia marries fellow Bohemian Anton Cuzak. The two buy a farm and raise a large family, and Antonia lavishes her considerable store of love upon husband and children.

Narrator Jim Burden grew up with Antonia on the Nebraska prairie. When he leaves Nebraska to study law in New York, he realizes that it is Antonia's face that he means "always to carry with me; the closest, realest face, under all the shadows of women's faces, at the very bottom of my memory" (322).

Antonia has become all women to Jim. By the time Jim finally returns to the prairie and to Antonia, twenty years have passed. On the first night of his visit to Antonia and her family, Jim lies awake on his blankets in the barn, thinking of Antonia. It is her ability to bring forth life that impresses Jim:

> She had only to stand in the orchard, to put her hand on a little crab tree and look up at the apples, to make you feel the goodness of planting and tending and harvesting at last. All the strong things of her heart came out in her body, that had been so tireless in serving generous emotions.
>
> It was no wonder that her sons stood tall and straight. She was a rich mine of life, like the founders of early races. (353)

While Alexandra is a strong and independent goddess of the land, Antonia is a mother-figure, who brings forth a race of pioneers to till the soil. Many later novelists ⟨. . .⟩ will model their heroines on one of these two prototypes, sometimes emphasizing the competence and self-reliance of their protagonists and sometimes stressing their fecundity and maternal devotion.

—Patricia Raub, *Yesterday's Stories: Popular Women's Novels of the Twenties and Thirties* (Westport, CT: Greenwood Press, 1994), 61–63

BIBLIOGRAPHY

April Twilights. 1903.
Alexander's Bridge. 1912.
O Pioneers! 1913.
Samuel Sidney McClure, My Autobiography (ghostwriter). 1914.
The Song of the Lark. 1915.
My Ántonia. 1918.
Youth and the Bright Medusa. 1920.
One of Ours. 1922.
April Twilights and Other Poems. 1923.
A Lost Lady. 1923.
The Professor's House. 1925.
My Mortal Enemy. 1926.
Death Comes for the Archbishop. 1927.
Shadows on the Rock. 1931.
Obscure Destinies. 1932.
Lucy Gayheart. 1935.

Sapphira and the Slave Girl. 1940.
The Old Beauty and Others. 1948.
On Writing. 1949.
Writings from Willa Cather's Campus Years. 1950.
Willa Cather in Europe: Her Own Story of the First Journey. 1956.
Early Stories. 1957.
A Lost Day. 1961.
Willa Cather's Collected Short Fiction. 1965.

JESSIE REDMON FAUSET

1882-1961

JESSIE REDMON FAUSET was born on April 26, 1882, in Fredericksville, New Jersey, the seventh child of the Reverend Redmon Fauset and Anna Seamon Fauset. The Fausets were a prosperous, middle-class family. Jessie's mother died when she was very young, and her father married Belle Huff shortly thereafter. Upon graduating from the Philadelphia Girls' School in 1900, Fauset was denied admission to a local teachers' college. She applied to Bryn Mawr College, but the school delayed acceptance, urging her instead to take a scholarship offered by Cornell University. Fauset subsequently graduated from Cornell in 1905, Phi Beta Kappa and the school's first black alumna.

Fauset had planned to become a teacher but was denied a position in the Philadelphia school system. Instead, she taught in Baltimore for a year before going to Washington, D.C., where she taught French for 14 years at the M Street (later Dunbar) High School, an institution devoted exclusively to the preparation of black students for college.

In 1912, Fauset began contributing articles to the journal *Crisis*. Some of her poetry, written in French, came to the attention of editor W. E. B. Du Bois, who in 1919 urged her to move to New York and become the journal's literary editor. That same year, Fauset received a master's degree in French from the University of Pennsylvania. Fauset seemed to some a paradox: as an editor, she encouraged novels and poems about ghetto life, and her essays communicated both an enthusiasm and an anger that attracted young militant readers; as a novelist, however, she wrote only about the genteel life she knew best.

A member of the movement that became known as the Harlem Renaissance, Fauset was one of its most prolific writers of the genteel school. All four of her novels are concerned with racial prejudice and the position of the black middle class in a white society. *There Is Confusion* (1924), Fauset's first novel, is a prescient story about the struggle for equality by the rising black middle class in the early 20th century. The restricted vocational choices of all women of that period is one of its themes. *Plum Bun* (1929) is a novel about a black woman who "passes" as white and in so doing becomes estranged from her darker-skinned sister. *The Chinaberry Tree* (1931) describes the love affair of a freed slave and her white master. In *Comedy: American Style* (1933), Fauset again focuses upon the alienating effects of passing as white. Although Fauset's novels met with mixed critical reviews and were ignored after her death, interest in her "novels of manners" has increased in recent years. She is also gaining recognition as an early black feminist.

Fauset's later life was spent outside black intellectual circles. In 1927, she began teaching French at De Witt Clinton High School in New York City. Two years later, she married Herbert E. Harris, and in 1939 they moved to Montclair, New Jersey. Fauset retired from teaching in 1944, having long since stopped writing. Jessie Redmon Fauset died on May 2, 1961.

CRITICAL EXTRACTS

MONTGOMERY GREGORY

⟨There Is Confusion⟩ is a sincere effort to view the life of the race artistically—objectively. Heretofore we have either imbibed the depreciatory estimates of our enemies or gulped down the uncritical praise of our friends. We have not dared to see ourselves as we really are nor have our artists treated our life as material to be objectively moulded into creations of beauty. Our writers of the younger school have been the first to catch this sound point of view and upon their strict adherence to it in the future depends the successful development of Negro art and literature. Even Miss Fauset occasionally errs in this respect and diverts the reader's interest from her story into bypaths of special pleading against race prejudice.

Technically There Is Confusion more than reaches the level of the better class of contemporary American fiction. The romance of Peter Bye and Joanna Marshall, etched on the interesting background of the family life of the cultured Negroes of Philadelphia and New York, is well conceived and skillfully executed. The plot holds the interest of the reader unflaggingly to the end. There are fewer faults of construction than might be expected in a "first" novel. It may be said, however, that the latter part of the story is the least convincing. ⟨. . .⟩ The characters are cleverly drawn, especially that of Maggie Ellersley who, like Brutus, although not intended to be the leading figure in the story, certainly appeals to the reviewer as the finest achievement of the author. On the other hand, the white Byes, young Meriweather Bye and his grandfather seem to make their entrance on the stage as supernumeraries and to add little to the value of the novel.

—Montgomery Gregory, "The Spirit of Phyllis Wheatley," Opportunity 2, no. 6 (June 1924), excerpted in Black American Women Fiction Writers, ed. Harold Bloom (New York: Chelsea House Publishers, 1995), 31

GWENDOLYN BENNETT

Many there will be who will quibble over Miss Fauset's fortunate choice of incident by which all her characters and happenings are brought together ⟨in *Plum Bun*⟩. This will not be altogether fair since "Truth is stranger than Fiction." I'll wager that Miss Fauset could match every incident in her book with one from real life. I imagine this book will be even less convincing to members of the white race. They still conjecture over the possibility of a Negro's completely submerging himself in their group without a shadow of detection. But here again Miss Fauset can smile benignly up her writing sleeve and know whereof she speaks.

The author of this story does not seem concerned to a great extent with the inner workings of her characters. In this day of over-emphasis on the mental musings of people and things this may be called a fault but I feel that the author was wise in not delving into the mental recesses of people to whom so much was happening. This is a task for a master psychologist. Who can tell how the minds of white Negroes work? Is it not a problem to stump the best of us that they who are so obviously white should feel a "something" that eventually draws them from the luxury and ease of a life as a white person back to the burden of being a Negro? Miss Fauset tells her story, packed as it is with the drama and happenings of a life of passing for white. It is better for the story that Miss Fauset avoided too much of a metaphysical turn.

—Gwendolyn Bennett, [Review of *Plum Bun*,] *Opportunity* 7, no. 9 (September 1929), excerpted in *Black American Women Fiction Writers*, ed. Harold Bloom (New York: Chelsea House Publishers, 1995), 32

GERALD SYKES

The greater portion of *The Chinaberry Tree* is devoted to the love affair of two colored high-school students who do not know that they are brother and sister. This dramatic theme, singularly enough, is the least exciting part of the story. We learn most about Miss Fauset's book as a whole not through Melissa and Malory, or their narrowly averted incestuous marriage; but through Laurentine, the beautiful apricot-colored dressmaker who is the book's real heroine and symbol of the world it depicts; Laurentine, who sat as a child under the Chinaberry Tree and wondered why other children, either white or black, wouldn't play with her. ⟨. . .⟩

⟨Laurentine⟩ is brought up in comparative luxury, but is a double outcast. And the passion which animates her is closely allied to the passion which animates the book. What does the illegitimate mulatto grow up to want? Respectability. Once she cries: "Oh God, you know all I want is a chance to show them how decent I am." This might serve as the motto for *The Chinaberry Tree*. It is so much the book's real theme that once recognized it helps to explain the striking gentility of certain passages, as well as the exceptional importance attached to small material comforts that most white people would take for granted. ⟨. . .⟩ The book attempts to idealize this polite colored world in terms of the white standards that it has adopted. And here lies the root of Miss Fauset's artistic errors. When she parades the possessions of her upper classes and when she puts her lovers through their Fauntleroy courtesies, she is not only stressing the white standards that they have adopted; she is definitely minimizing the colored blood in them. This is a decided weakness, for it steals truth and life from the book. Is not the most precious part of a Negro work of art that which is specifically Negroid, which none but a Negro could contribute?

We need not look far for the reason for Miss Fauset's idealization. It is pride, the pride of a genuine aristocrat. And it is pride also that makes her such a remarkable psychologist. However many her artistic errors, Miss Fauset has a rare understanding of people and their motives. ⟨. . .⟩ Every great psychologist has been a thin-skinned aristocrat. Considering the position of a sensitive, educated Negro in America, it is no wonder then that an aristocrat like Miss Fauset has idealized her little world, has made it over-elegant! Inspired by the religious motive which so many Negro writers seem to feel, she has simply been trying to justify her world to the world at large. Her mistake has consisted in trying to do this in terms of the white standard.

—Gerald Sykes, "Amber-Tinted Elegance," *Nation* (27 July 1932), excerpted in *Black American Women Fiction Writers*, ed. Harold Bloom (New York: Chelsea House Publishers, 1995), 33–34

WILLIAM STANLEY BRAITHWAITE

I daresay, as a novelist Miss Fauset would be credited with many a virtue by certain eminent critics, if she were but obliging enough to ignore the *conventional* ideals and triumphs of the emerged group of the Race. She has been infinitely more honest with her characters than her critics have cared to acknowledge, indeed, to have even suspected. After all, her purpose, whether conscious or unconscious, has been to create in the pages of fiction a society which outside the Race simply did not and preferably, in accordance with granted assumption, could not be allowed to exist. The spirit, the consciousness of pride, dignity, a new quality of moral idealism, was breathed into this darker body of human nature by her passionate sympathy and understanding of its ironic position in the flimsy web of American civilization. Only recently a review of Miss Fauset's latest novel, *Comedy: American Style*, in one of the leading Negro papers, resented what the reviewer charged was a lack of climax and philosophy in the recital of Olivia Cary's color obsession and the pain it brought her family. The philosophy in this latest novel, as in the three earlier ones, is not, and never was intended to be, an imposed thesis upon the surface of the story. Miss Fauset is too good an artist to argue the point; to engrave a doctrine upon so intangible an element as Truth, or to array with a misfitting apparel of rhetoric the logic which like a pagan grace or a Christian virtue should run naked as the wind through the implications that color and shape the lives of her characters and their destinies. I am afraid that Negro critical eyes as well as white critical eyes have quite often failed to discern these implications in which are contained the philosophy of a tremendous conflict; the magnificent Shakespearean conflict of *will* and *passion* in the great tragedies from *Titus Andronicus* to *Coriolanus*; for in this Negro society which Miss Fauset has created imaginatively from the realities, there is the *will*, the confused but burning *will*, to master the *passion* of the organized body of lusty American prejudice.

—William Stanley Braithwaite, "The Novels of Jessie Fauset," *Opportunity* 12, no. 1 (January 1934), excerpted in *Black American Women Fiction Writers*, ed. Harold Bloom (New York: Chelsea House Publishers, 1995), 35

DEBORAH E. MCDOWELL

To be sure, ⟨Fauset⟩ was traditional to some extent, both in form and content, but as Gary de Cordova Wintz rightly observes, "in spite of her conservative, almost Victorian literary habits," Fauset "introduced several subjects into her novels that were hardly typical drawing room conversation topics in the mid-1920s. Promiscuity, exploitative sexual affairs, miscegenation, even incest appear in her novels. In fact prim and proper Jessie Fauset included a far greater range of sexual activity than did most of Du Bois's debauched tenth."

When attention is given Fauset's introduction of these challenging themes, it becomes possible to regard her "novels of manners" less as an indication of her literary "backwardness" and more as a self-conscious artistic stratagem pressed to the service of her central fictional preoccupations. Since many of Fauset's concerns were unpalatable to the average reader of her day and hence unmarketable in the publishing area, the convention of the novel of manners can be seen as protective mimicry, a kind of deflecting mask for her more challenging concerns. ⟨. . .⟩

In addition to the protective coloration which the conventional medium afforded, the novel of manners suited Fauset's works in that the tradition "is primarily concerned with social conventions as they impinge upon character." Both social convention and character—particularly the black female character—jointly form the nucleus of Fauset's literary concerns. The protagonists of all of her novels are black women, and she makes clear in each novel that social conventions have not sided well with them but, rather, have been antagonistic.

Without polemicizing, Fauset examines that antagonism, criticizing the American society which has institutionalized prejudice, safeguarded it by law and public attitude, and in general, denied the freedom of development, the right to well-being, and the pursuit of happiness to the black woman. In short, Fauset explores the black woman's struggle for democratic ideals in a society whose sexist conventions assiduously work to thwart that struggle. Critics have usually ignored this important theme which even a cursory reading of her novels reveals. This concern with exploring female consciousness is, in a loose sense, feminist in impulse, placing Fauset squarely among the early black feminists in Afro-American literary history. ⟨. . .⟩ A curious problem in Fauset's treatment of feminist issues, however, is her patent ambivalence. She is alternately forthright and cagey, alternately "radical" and conservative on the "woman question." On the one hand, she appeals for women's right to challenge socially sanctioned modes of feminine behavior, but on the other, she frequently retreats to the safety of traditional attitudes about women in traditional roles. At best, then, we can grant that Fauset was a quiet rebel, a pioneer black literary feminist, and that her characters were harbingers of the movement for women's liberation from the constrictions of cultural conditioning.

—Deborah E. McDowell, "The Neglected Dimension of Jessie Redmon Fauset," *Conjuring: Black Women, Fiction, and Literary Tradition*, ed. Marjorie Pryse and Hortense J. Spillers (Bloomington: Indiana University Press, 1985), excerpted in *Black American Women Fiction Writers*, ed. Harold Bloom (New York: Chelsea House Publishers, 1995), 37–38

MARY JANE LUPTON

As a woman writer writing *as* a woman, if not *for* women, Fauset was likely to notice the aesthetic relationship between skin and clothing. This kind of thing is important in the daily lives of most middle-class women and, I would guess, of many middle-class men. By including chestnut hair and puff sleeves in her fictional world ⟨of *Comedy: American Style*⟩, Fauset is only being true to the tradition of American realism. But these concerns are not merely gratuitous. ⟨. . .⟩ Fauset uses clothing as a way to articulate not only the racial differences between mother and daughter but also the hierarchy of class/race which she then addresses throughout the novel: the desperate, white-identified mother; the middle-class daughter caught between her mother's notion of "a cruder race" and her own desire to be like her peers; the Black-identified Marise in her "glowing, gay colors"; the naturally gifted, light-skinned Phebe, who is already accumulating capital.

Fauset also captures ⟨. . .⟩ the excitement of adolescent anticipation, the thrill of choosing for oneself what one is to wear and not to wear. Thus Teresa is transformed, through clothing, from "mouse" to warm, young Black woman. As she puts her "nice narrow feet" into "bronze slippers," she becomes reminiscent of Cinderella on her way to the ball—in this case a neighborhood party. It is in fact Teresa's crowning moment. For later she meets a young Black man, falls in love, and is humiliated by her mother, who forces her into a disastrous marriage. The Cinderella Line has reversed itself irrevocably.

Near the end of the novel Olivia visits her daughter: "She found Teresa silent, pale, subdued, the ghost of her former self, still wearing dresses taken from the wardrobe which her mother had chosen and bought for her during her last year of college. The dresses had been turned, darned, cleaned, and made over, combined in new and bizarre fashions. Their only merit was that they were quite large enough. Certainly Teresa had put on no weight." ⟨. . .⟩ Teresa's "former self" has become a "ghost." She is colorless, as are the dresses of unnamed hue. Literally, Teresa has lost her color, her racial identity. As Phebe had once made Teresa the beautiful party dress, so now Teresa makes over and mends the dress of her past. This recreation of identity, however, operates within the closed system of passing or death.

In dismantling the Cinderella Line, Fauset leaves as an alternative a more feminist bourgeois hope in the person of Phebe the dressmaker. Through hard work and through affirmation of her Blackness, Phebe manages to rise from shopgirl to highly paid fashion designer. Her marriage to Teresa's brother, Christopher, is part of the bargain.

—Mary Jane Lupton, "Clothes and Closure in Three Novels by Black Women," *Black American Literature Forum* 20, no. 4 (Winter 1986), excerpted in *Black American Women Fiction Writers*, ed. Harold Bloom (New York: Chelsea House Publishers, 1995), 38–39

HAZEL V. CARBY

Deborah McDowell, in her introduction to the new edition of Fauset's *Plum Bun*, pleads for a sympathetic consideration for the progressive aspects of Fauset's novels, especially in relation to her implicit critique of the structures of women's romance. However, I would argue that ultimately the conservatism of Fauset's ideology dominates her texts. In *The Chinaberry Tree*, for example, which focused on two women, the movement of the text is away from the figures of isolated unmarried mothers and daughters supporting themselves through their own labor, toward the articulation of a new morality and community in which black women were lifted from the abyss of scandal and gossip, which threatened to overwhelm them, by professional black men who reinserted them into a newly formed and respectable community as dependent wives. The individual and collective pasts of the female characters led them to flounder in the waters of misdirected desires; their history was anarchic and self-destructive. The future, within which the women could survive, was secured when they were grounded, protected, and wrapped around by decent men. In order to represent a new, emergent social group, Fauset by necessity had to sever ties with the past; the characteristics of the new class were those of individual success and triumph over ties to and previous interpretations of history. ⟨. . .⟩ ⟨In⟩ *The Chinaberry Tree*, Fauset constructed a chaotic and irrelevant history to which the heroes, not the heroines, brought a new order and meaning. The new middle class both emerged from and changed previous history and its interpretations; the forces of previous history alone could not provide a basis for its future. Fauset adapted but did not transcend the form of the romance. It is important that her work did reveal many of the contradictory aspects of romantic conventions of womanhood, but her imaginary resolutions to what were social contradictions confirmed that women ultimately had to be saved from the consequences of their independence and become wives.

> —Hazel V. Carby, *Reconstructing Womanhood: The Emergence of the Afro-American Woman Novelist* (New York: Oxford University Press, 1987), excerpted in *Black American Women Fiction Writers*, ed. Harold Bloom (New York: Chelsea House Publishers, 1995), 39–40

VASHTI CRUTCHER LEWIS

Fauset does not give Laurentine much racial consciousness ⟨in *The Chinaberry Tree*⟩; however, she is the vehicle through which the reader experiences culture of the Harlem Renaissance. Fauset, a 1920s resident of Harlem, allows Laurentine and the reader to become acquainted with the famed Lafayette Theatre, notable restaurants, and nightclubs of the era. Laurentine's uneasiness with an animated black folk culture in Harlem cabarets indicates Fauset's own rejection of it, as well as that of Du Bois, her mentor. Fauset provides Laurentine with thoughts that mirror some of the reasons why Du Bois was critical of Harlem Renaissance writers who depicted what he considered the exotic in African-American culture. Laurentine is puzzled over reasons why anyone would frequent clubs where a "drunken black woman . . . slapped a handsome yellow girl," and "where a dark, sinuous dancer, singing . . . making movements . . . postured . . ." ⟨. . .⟩

Fauset's portrayals of African-American women who are overly class- and color-conscious must be assessed against the stereotypical images that bordered on the caricature that white writers were using to depict men and women of African descent at the turn of the twentieth century and later. It is not difficult to understand her desire to reverse those images and to write with sympathy and understanding about an educated African-American middle/upper class to which she belonged. The real paradox of so much interest in class-conscious mulattoes is, as suggested earlier, that they depict a select group who have never been representative in number or lifestyle of African-American women. And just as important, the highly class-conscious mulatto has served to perpetuate a divisiveness within African-American culture since the genesis of a mulatto caste in the era of American slavery. Certainly the very images of black female arrogance so often depicted in Fauset's novels are ones that have caused "other Blacks to look at mulattoes as Greeks whose gifts should always bear watching."

—Vashti Crutcher Lewis, "Mulatto Hegemony in the Novels of Jessie Redmon Fauset," *CLA Journal* 35, no. 4 (June 1992), excerpted in *Black American Women Fiction Writers*, ed. Harold Bloom (New York: Chelsea House Publishers, 1995), 42

MARCY JANE KNOPF

Scholars and critics typically perceive Jessie Fauset to be outside modernist literary circles. Instead they describe her as a regionalist or sentimentalist. On the one hand, the dichotomy at work in the academy that privileges white modernists over Harlem Renaissance writers and many times male (read "experimental") over female (read "sentimental") modernists contributes to Fauset's exclusion. On the other hand, despite the "traditional" stylistic modes that she used in her fiction, Fauset presents powerful critiques of race, class, and gender hierarchies in American society, critiques that manifest what might usefully be considered a modernist sensibility. Furthermore, although the Harlem Renaissance defined a cultural moment that is particular to African-American history, the movement in the most general sense was "modernist," for it represented a radical new phase of group consciousness and artistic production that consciously broke from African-American past. New Negro writers continued to interrogate and revise both the historical and literary constructions of slavery, striving to "make new" the conventions grounded in slave narratives and other abolitionist texts. Similarly, some black modernists—such as Langston Hughes, Sterling Brown, and Zora Neale Hurston—use language as a way to dissociate black art from Western or "white" literary aesthetics. ⟨. . .⟩

⟨. . .⟩ Jessie Fauset (as well as other African-American women writers) establishes her own form of African-American modernism by incorporating sentimental conventions in her texts. Fauset's writing also manifests her particular debt to the sentimental tradition in American history, for she, like other black women authors, uses a wide range of sentimental conventions. What is so strikingly new about her adaptation of these conventions, however, is the extent to which they provide the framework for the sophisticated political work that Fauset does in her writing as she explores, from the perspective of the 1920s, the new freedoms specific to first- and second-generation emancipated African-American women. Like her literary foremother, Pauline Hopkins, Fauset focuses on the unique plight of middle-class black women. Even more thoroughly than Hopkins, however, Fauset masters the conventions of the sentimental novel only to disrupt them by her incisive, at times pointedly ambiguous, considerations of African-American women's experiences at the intersection of race, sex, and class.

A highly educated member of Du Bois' "Talented Tenth" and a Phi Beta Kappa graduate of Cornell University, Fauset was well read in British, French, and African-American literature and history. Drawing upon her studies, Fauset engages and re-works many strategies from mainstream literary traditions such as Greek mythology and Shakespearean drama. In this sense, Fauset appropriates conventions used by U.S. and European writers for her own African-American political purposes. ⟨Houston⟩ Baker contends that this kind of black discursive modernism is rooted in the relationship between what he calls "mastery of form" and "deformation of mastery." Fauset "masters" past literary canons such as the nineteenth-century sentimental novel or Greek tragedy and "deforms" or modifies them as she generates her own version of "modern" black culture. ⟨. . .⟩

By writing novels that many readers and/or critics perceive to be sentimental, Fauset masks her revolutionary, and modernist, consideration of miscegenation and black female independence. In this way Fauset resembles other female "modernists"—both inside and outside of the canon—who take bold new steps in exploring sexuality, women such as Nella Larsen, Virginia Woolf, Mina Loy, Zora Neale Hurston, H. D., Djuna Barnes, Angelina Weld Grimké, and Gertrude Stein.

> —Marcy Jane Knopf, "Foreword to the 1995 Edition," The Chinaberry Tree: A Novel of American Life *and* Selected Writings, by Jessie Redmon Fauset (Boston: Northeastern University Press, 1995), ix–xi, xiii

BIBLIOGRAPHY

There Is Confusion. 1924.
Plum Bun: A Novel Without a Moral. 1929.
The Chinaberry Tree: A Novel of American Life. 1931.
Comedy: American Style. 1933.

EDNA FERBER

1885-1968

EDNA FERBER was born in Kalamazoo, Michigan, on August 15, 1885, the younger of two daughters of Jacob and Julia Neumann Ferber, Hungarian immigrants. The family moved to Appleton, Wisconsin, where she worked as a cub reporter for the Appleton *Daily Crescent*. From 1905 until 1910, Ferber was a reporter for the *Milwaukee Journal*, where she encountered the former reporter Zona Gale, whom she later called an early influence.

From her newspaper work Ferber developed an astute journalistic sense that shaped her stories and her feminist convictions. Her first novel, *Dawn O'Hara, The Girl Who Laughed*, was published in 1911. Although Ferber herself thought the novel too sentimental, it was favorably reviewed and would continue to gain in popularity over the years. *Emma McChesney and Co.* (1915) had been published as a series of stories from 1911 to 1915 in *American* and *Cosmopolitan* magazines. Published in two additional volumes as *Personality Plus* and *Roast Beef Medium*, the stories brought Ferber national recognition; President Theodore Roosevelt was one of the stories' devoted readers. Through her character Emma, Ferber championed the independent woman seeking adventure, stimulation, and income. In *Cheerful, by Request* (1918), another collection of short stories, Ferber continued her portrayals of energetic female characters who could be seen as representatives for the modern woman.

The publication of *So Big* in 1924 marked the beginning of Ferber's career as a best-selling novelist; the book sold well in America and Europe and received the 1924 Pulitzer Prize. The novel *Show Boat* (1926) became the basis for the classic musical that opened in 1927, coinciding with the Broadway success of *The Royal Family*, the first of five plays Ferber wrote in collaboration with George S. Kaufman. By the time her novel *Cimarron* appeared in 1930, Ferber had achieved extraordinary success and had become a leading figure in New York social circles. *Cimarron* was adapted to film in 1931 and again in 1960. Ferber enjoyed two further Broadway successes with Kaufman, *Dinner At Eight* (1932) and *Stage Door* (1936).

In 1931, Rudyard Kipling enthusiastically described Ferber as a "historical painter" of American experience. She was militantly pro-American in her depiction of life in various sections of the country— and a meticulous researcher. After the publication of *American Beauty*

(1931), *Come and Get It* (1935), and *Saratoga Trunk* (1941), Billy Rose wrote of Ferber's novels that "every one [was] a thank-you hymn to the land which welcomed her emigrant parents." Her most notable postwar novels are *Giant* (1952), a story about three generations of a Texas family, and *Ice Palace* (1958), set in Alaska. The many films based on her fiction provided starring roles for such actors as Ingrid Bergman, Gary Cooper, James Dean, Irene Dunne, Rock Hudson, Elizabeth Taylor, and Jane Wyman.

Ferber wrote two volumes of autobiography, *A Peculiar Treasure* (1939) and *A Kind of Magic* (1963), which was her last publication. Although a best-selling author, her standing with literary critics was less secure, and she is little read today. Edna Ferber died on April 16, 1968.

CRITICAL EXTRACTS

LOUIS KRONENBERGER

At a time when realism is all but monopolizing literature, one experiences a sensation of delighted relief in encountering *Show Boat*. It is gorgeously romantic—not in the flamboyant and artificial manner of the historical romance which twenty-five years ago, under the titles of *Janice Meredith* and *Richard Carvel*, came definitely labeled before the American public; not staggering beneath a weight of costume and local color. *Show Boat* comes as a spirited, full-breasted, tireless story, romantic because it is too alive to be what the realists call real; because it bears within itself a spirit of life which we seek rather than have; because it makes a period and mode of existence live again, not actually different from what they were, but more alluring than they could have been. *Show Boat* is romantic not because its people and events violate any principle of possibility, but because they express a principle of selection. Miss Ferber has chosen the brightest colors and let the dull ones go. She has avoided the contrasts by which the brightness would fade into the common light of day. *Show Boat* is dominated by one tone as Hergesheimer's *Balisand* is dominated by another.

After the days of Mark Twain, the Mississippi holds small place in American literature. Now it reclaims its place, happily as the scene of later days than Mark Twain's. ⟨. . .⟩

All art is a luxury in the sense that it fills a place beyond the physical necessities of life, but some art there is which is entirely ornamental, which does not reveal life, or probe character, or feed the soul. *Show Boat* is such a piece of writing—a gorgeous thing to read for the reading's sake alone. Some, perhaps, will conscientiously refer to it as a document which reanimates a part of the American scene that once existed and does no more. But this writer can- not believe it is that; rather it is a glorification of that scene, a heightening, an expression of its full romantic possibilities. There was, no doubt, a gallant Andy Hawks in the old days, and a Magnolia, and more Gaylord Ravenals than one; there was such a scene as that recorded of Julie Dozier when she was discovered to have negro blood; there was a Parthy Hawks who ran a show boat down the river, an indomitable woman who formed an anomaly among show boat proprietors; but they were never the one group who lived on the *Cotton Blossom*. Plenty of prose intermingled with the poetry of the true scene, plenty of realism with the romance. And all these things, of course, Miss Ferber knew before and while and after she wrote *Show Boat*.

But Life, here, gives way unrestrainedly to Art. And Art functions in one tone—the romantic. Some will not submit to this, and will object to a piece of melodrama here, a wild coincidence there, an unconvincing character some- where else. That will be an esthetic mistake. Let us accept the delightful lives these people lead. All in all, when you look back upon the story it is amazing how little that is exciting and complicated has happened; this is biography rather than "plot." Miss Ferber has told her story without stint, a long free- breathing story, safe from the careful selectiveness and lacunation of modern schools of writing. It never becomes sentimental; at times it is high romance, at times light romance, at times comedy; but it is never melancholy romance. There is no sighing after the snows of yesteryear. With *Show Boat* Miss Ferber establishes herself not as one of those who are inaugurating first-rate literature, but as one of those who are reviving first-rate storytelling. This is little else but an irresistible story; but that, surely, is enough.

—Louis Kronenberger, "Show Boat Is High Romance," *New York Times Book Review* (22 August 1926), excerpted in *Twentieth-Century American Literature*, ed. Harold Bloom (New York: Chelsea House Publishers, 1986), 1370–71

WILLIAM MCFEE

Miss Ferber's talent, this reviewer is irrevocably convinced, does not lie in the way of the novel at all. She writes a novel as a modern athletic girl might wear a crinoline and a bustle. She manages the trick, but she is self-conscious and filled with secret amusement over the masquerade. Why so many words? Why such a portentous enclosure for a mere story? So I imagine Miss Ferber secretly regarding the novel form. Her forte, I humbly submit, is the short story. She has the gift, and it is my belief she has the predilection, for that form of liter- ary art. But editors and publishers demand novels spun out to serial length and

Miss Ferber, who can do it, supplies the demand. That does not vitiate the argument that her short stories are remarkably good stories, while her novels are only remarkably good short stories spun out to novel length and thereby largely spoiled.

Show Boat as an example. I am prepared to confess that I am inconsistent because I read the book with excitement, not over the story, which is negligible, but over the description of life on the Mississippi in a floating theatre. The reader can take it as a sign of ignorance and incompetence, but I didn't know anything about show boats. It is to me an inexplicable thing why George W. Cable did not write a book about them, and why Mark Twain (as far as I can remember) does not allude to them. In the case of *Show Boat*, one is yanked back to the fortunes of Magnolia and her daughter Kim—named after the states of Kentucky, Illinois and Missouri because she was born on the show boat at the confluence of the Ohio and Mississippi—one returns to the story with a sigh. But of course it is the story of Magnolia and Kim which will make *Show Boat* a best seller. They are in characteristic Edna Ferber vein.

If it be demanded outright what is the real trouble with *Show Boat* as a novel it is just this, that it is written in short story tempo. That, as already stated, is Edna Ferber's natural bent. Even though she writes a novel, it goes along at a speed which leaves the author out of breath and the reviewer out of patience. A novel is not a hundred-yard dash kept up mile after mile. It is something utterly different from a short story.

But *Show Boat* is enthusiastically recommended to the four out of five Americans who have no information on the subject. Miss Ferber "got up" that subject. If anything, the book is at times heavy with information. And certainly the information in the later chapters, telling us how certain well known and practicing dramatic critics, editors and column writers foregathered at the heroine's apartment, is a bad error of judgment and taste. It is cheap, and one very nearly adds, in irritation, nasty. It is lacking in dignity, which may be important after all. Because the first part of *Show Boat* is dominated by the Mississippi, and it is a drop indeed at the end to be fobbed off with anecdotes about Alexander Woollcott.

    —William McFee, "Life on the Mississippi—New Style," *New Republic* (15 September 1926), excerpted in *Twentieth-Century American Literature*, ed. Harold Bloom (New York: Chelsea House Publishers, 1986), 1371

Margaret Lawrence

There is nothing in ⟨Edna Ferber's⟩ stories borrowed from Europe. There is no shadow of sophisticated weariness. Sometimes there are touches of naïveté, but these touches come from the author's sense of the zest for living, which is the breath of any new civilization.

She writes as if none of the authors of Europe existed. From the classical standpoint she has no style whatever. But from the vital standpoint of how style is associated with the emotion of time and place, she has perfect style.

Apart entirely from her fidelity to the rhythm of primitive pioneer story-telling, and apart entirely from her absorption in the current of the American scene, Edna Ferber is of towering importance to the School of Femininity. She belongs to the great procession—Austen, the Brontës and Eliot—who presented the feminist picture.

Serena de Jong, the heroine of her greatest book, *So Big*, belongs with Elizabeth Bennett and Jane Eyre and Maggie Tulliver. Her other women are like the other women of Miss Austen, the Brontës and George Eliot. They are the Elizabeths and the Janes and the Maggies out in a new world on the make, selling lingerie, performing on show boats, running newspapers and raising prize asparagus, struggling with emotion and finding themselves relief in action. But there is one great difference, and it is the difference between the nineteenth-century lady and the twentieth-century woman—her women are not dependent upon men for the adequate conduct of their lives. Elizabeth Bennett, had she been disappointed in Mr. Darcy after marriage, would have been in an emotional whirlwind, and Miss Austen, had she tackled such a situation, would have been hard put to it to find a neat conclusion. Little Jane Eyre, if fate had not taken the wild and fascinating Mr. Rochester by the scruff of his unrighteous neck and handed him over to her, would have been a flattened out little mortal. Poor Maggie Tulliver had to be drowned after a purgatory of isolation because she had magnetism which she could not use to her own advantage. But Serena and all the women of Edna Ferber take erotic disappointment in their twentieth-century stride and do not expect anything from men. They say to themselves—men are like that—and find plenty to do besides looking around for another hero or getting drowned. And this in spite of the fact that they are women of deep emotions and strong passionate attachments. They observe their husbands; they mother their sons and their daughters, and expect no undue amount either of love or of great stature from any of them in return. Life to them is worth what it brings in experience. They live in the feminist era in the new world.

—Margaret Lawrence, "Go-Getters," *The School of Femininity* (1936), excerpted in *Twentieth-Century American Literature*, ed. Harold Bloom (New York: Chelsea House Publishers, 1986), 1369

T. S. MATTHEWS

. . . ⟨Edna Ferber⟩ has no charm at all. Reading one of her books gives you the pleasant sense of toil vicariously accomplished. And her novels are always success stories, in spite of the threatening implications she turns up and pats neatly back into place—which makes her popular reading. She squares off at her job in workmanlike fashion and turns out a nationally advertised product that looks as sound as this year's model always does, until next year's model comes along. This time ⟨in *Come and Get It*⟩ she has elected to give the reader his money's worth by a report on the Wisconsin lumber industry. In fact, she gives double your money's worth, for the story not only ends but begins all over again, and finally peters out in a formless finish. The hero of the first part is a ruthless old self-crowned lumber king; at his death, halfway through the book, the girl whom he tried to get for himself but who had sense enough to snag his son instead becomes the centerpiece, and blossoms out into a rich vulgarian. The only point I could discover in the story was that Miss Ferber thought there was good stuff in the lass, because when the crash of the depression came, she had the gumption to cut the cackle and come home. In a pathetic attempt to justify Edna Ferber's national advertising, her publishers announce that she has now practically covered the mores of the entire United States. With what? may I ask. To paraphrase a famous disclaimer: "It's just an Edna Ferber, Mister; it don't mean nothing."

> —T. S. Matthews, "Novels by Weight," *New Republic* (6 March 1935), excerpted in *Twentieth-Century American Literature*, ed. Harold Bloom (New York: Chelsea House Publishers, 1986), 1371

JOHN BARKHAM

If you haven't read Edna Ferber's name on any new novel lately, it isn't (as you might have suspected) because she was relaxing on the royalties from *Show Boat*, *Cimarron*, *Saratoga Trunk* and other movie masterpieces made from her books. On the contrary, it was because Miss Ferber was brewing the biggest witch's broth of a book to hit the great Commonwealth of Texas since the revered Spindle blew its top. Miss Ferber makes it very clear that she doesn't like the Texas she writes about, and it's a cinch that when Texans read what she has written about them they won't like Miss Ferber either. Almost everyone else is going to revel in these pages.

For unsophisticated Easterners, *Giant* is going to be a guided tour to an incredible land unlike any they have ever seen before. (Texans, of course, have diligently fostered such a legend for years.) It outdoes anything our material culture has ever produced. Miss Ferber's Texas is the apotheosis of the grandiose, the culmination of that biggest-and-bestest cult peculiar to this side of the Atlantic. Whether it is recognizable to anyone inside of Texas is something else again. But *Giant* makes marvelous reading—wealth piled on wealth, wonder on wonder in a stunning, splendiferous pyramid of ostentation.

Her Texas was not altogether a surprise to this reviewer. Although he has not recently dallied at the Shamrock or shopped at Neiman-Marcus, he has run across oil aristocrats in the royal suites at the Savoy in London, the Grand in Stockholm and elsewhere, and had been suitably awed. And wasn't it Bob Ruark who recently told us in *Esquire* that in Texas even the midgets stood six feet high, and that you never met anybody there but rich millionaires and poor millionaires.

This is the Texas Miss Ferber has put into her bitter, brilliant, corrosive, excoriating novel. She refuses to genuflect to the lords of the oil wells or the barons of the ranches. Her Texas is a state where the skies are clamorous with four-engined DC-6's carrying alligator jewel cases and overbred furs, "where a mere Cadillac makes a fellow no better than a Mexican." An exaggeration? Perhaps, but one which Texans have put over.

It requires courage to take all this apart as scathingly as Miss Ferber has done; and in the process of so doing she paints a memorable portrait of that new American, *Texicanus vulgaris* which is all warts and wampum.

She does this by marrying her heroine, Leslie, an elegant Virginian, to Jordan Benedict 3d, head of the Reata Ranch, whose frontiers stretch into the middle of tomorrow. When "Bick" brings his lovely, naïve bride into his cattle empire, he also takes with him a host of curious readers whose prying eyes are to be dazzled by what they see. It's a world of its own, "all noise and heat, big men and bourbon, and elegantly dressed, shrill-voiced women who needed only three plumes to be presented as they stood at the court of St. James." Gradually Leslie becomes familiar with the gradations of Texas wealth: as cotton once snooted at the cattle rich, so now the cattle rich sneer at the oil rich—with Miss Ferber sneering at all of them.

For our author believes passionately that this glorification of wealth is a massive and dangerous symptom in our body politic. She makes Leslie say things like: "Here in Texas we have very high buildings on very broad prairies, but very little high thinking or broad concepts." Most of all she resents the treatment of the Mexican-American in his native Texas. To the monolithic men in cream-colored Stetsons and tooled boots whose daughters cost a heifer a day to keep in Swiss finishing schools, the Mexican is a sub-human to be used as a *vaquero* or ranch-hand but kept out of public places meant for white folks. To point her moral she makes one of the Benedict children marry a Mexican, and subjects one of them to a supreme insult at a four-motor party.

Admittedly, this novel presents the Texan larger and more chromatic than life, but life-size is large enough. And it's true that people in big empty places like to behave as the gods did on Olympus. As for bigness, says Miss Ferber militantly, it's time Texans stopped confusing it with greatness. "Are sunflowers necessarily better than violets?"

It's easy to spend hours debating the rights and wrongs of this red-hot novel. It all depends where you come from and what you think of Cadillaccum-Dallas culture. But no one can deny the explosive impact of this story. For all the slickness of its writing (and Miss Ferber is a past mistress of best seller style), *Giant* carries the kind of message that seldom finds expression in such chromium-plated prose. What's more, Miss Ferber states it with a conviction that carries the ring of sincerity. All this may make it impossible for her to revisit the great Commonwealth without the law at her hip, but at least she has written a book that sets the seal on her career.

It is possible, if other novelists rush in where Miss Ferber has not feared to tread, that the Houston-Dallas axis may replace Park Avenue-Bel Air as the symbol of opulence in our fiction. In that event, *Giant*—an October Book-of-the-Month choice—will become known as the first of our A. S. (After Spindletop) classics.

—John Barkham, "Where It's the Biggest and Bestest," *New York Times Book Review* (28 September 1952), excerpted in *Twentieth-Century American Literature*, ed. Harold Bloom (New York: Chelsea House Publishers, 1986), 1372

JULIE GOLDSMITH GILBERT

The word "whimsical" sent Ferber into a frenzy when Norman Cousins, editor of *The Saturday Review*, applied it in defense of a book review of *Giant* he had run in the magazine, to which Ferber had taken great umbrage. It was a satirical piece, written by what Ferber termed "a Texas peanut grower and press-clipping agent." Upon reading it, Ferber sent a letter protesting the fatuous and whimsical piece, and demanded that her letter be published. Cousins refused, brushing off her fury by saying that the intent of the piece was to amuse—that nobody had taken it seriously. Ferber knew the real reason of Cousins' refusal and felt it despicable enough to upbraid him once again:

"For a long time, Norman, I've wanted to write an article entitled I ONLY WORK HERE. This is not only a phrase. It is a state of mind, a degradation of the spirit, an indication of cracked morale. The waiter who gives you soiled table utensils. I only work here. Eisenhower who clasps the hand of McCarthy and stands, a captive, while Jenner throws an arm about his shoulder. I only work here. The saleswoman who shrugs off her responsibility for an error. I only work here. Norman Cousins, whose name tops the list of editors on the Saturday Review editorial page but who has a 'hands off' policy in the matter of book reviews and who doesn't think the financial backer of his magazine—a rich Texas oil man—should be mentioned in a letter of protest. I only work here.

". . . There is nothing in my novel GIANT that would call for 'whimsicality' in a review. I have said to you—and I repeat—a book review may properly be good or bad, but its tone should fit the tenor of the book. GIANT, which represents many years of intensive work, is a novel of power, purpose, and high readability, among other excellent qualifications. It does not rate whimsical treatment. Your reviewer, incidentally, is as whimsical as a bowl of oatmeal.

"It is incredible that an incident would at once be as boring and as revolting as this one has been to me. I am certain you share my feelings. In more than forty years of creative writing it is the first in my experience.

"Also, incidentally, your reviewer misspells the name of the book's leading character, points to an explorer whose name is not mentioned in the book, refutes as untrue a hideous barbecue which I myself witnessed and endured as a guest, and which was in no way considered as unusual by the local residents; and takes it upon himself to name living characters to fit the fictional characters in my book.

"Whimsical, eh?

"I now don't care whether you run a note of correction or not. No one cares—except you. And your reason for caring should be deep and clear and considered."

Needless to say Norman Cousins was not a frequent guest at Ferber's.

—Julie Goldsmith Gilbert, *Ferber: A Biography* (Garden City, NY: Doubleday & Company, Inc., 1978), 180–82

MARIA K. MOOTRY

Ferber's account of the novel's textual history is telling. *So Big* was originally serialized as "Selina" in the *Woman's Home Companion*. Ferber reports that "when the novel was serialized by Gertrude Lane . . . she so fully agreed with me about the impossibility of the title [*So Big*] as to discard it entirely. In the magazine the novel was titled Selina" ⟨*Peculiar Treasure*, 1960, 276⟩. No doubt naming the book for a heroine appealed to a woman's magazine. Yet Ferber reverts to the original when readying the manuscript for publication as a novel: "When the book was finished, I had found no title more fitting than *So Big*. I still didn't like it, but it had stuck somehow. I now think that those two short words, their familiar ring, and all the fat round curves in the S, the O, the B and the G helped to make the book a selling success" (*PT* 276). This explanation marks—and masks—a shift from a female-dominated to a male-dominated narrative—a shift that gives the novel its peculiar quality of double-centeredness.

It seems that Ferber had no confidence in her book as a domestic novel. She wrote to Russell Doubleday, her publisher: "I have promised to send you the manuscript of *So Big*, and here it is. I feel very strongly that I should not publish it as a novel. It will, as you know, appear serially in the *Woman's Home Companion*. I think its publication as a book would hurt you, as publishers, and me as an author. No one would read it. It is the story of a middle-aged woman in a Chicago truck garden. Nothing happens. The high spot is where she drives in to Chicago with a load of vegetables. . . . If you decide that it will be better not to publish I shall be entirely satisfied" (*PT* 275). But Doubleday had read it and wept; in fact, his entire staff had read it and wept. Ferber's ever-present wit is apparent in her reply: "I pictured the offices, damp with tears, the water mounting, mounting, like a scene out of *Alice in Wonderland*" (*PT* 275–76). We are left to speculate if Ferber, like her contemporary Robert Frost, was consciously or unconsciously playing a game—presenting an ostensibly celebratory, almost sentimental text to a gullible audience that would buy the product but miss her more biting, modernistic, tongue-in-cheek voice.

The title of Ferber's novel, like the narrative itself, achieves multiple resonance and a modernistic inversion. "So Big" (later "Sobig"), in addition to being Dirk's childhood nickname, refers to Selina's vision, spirit, and ambition, which are certainly bigger than those of most of her unimaginative farm neighbors, her husband, and her son. But it is a mocking title as well, critiquing jazz age excesses in business, especially brokering, that would lead to the 1929 stock market crash. The name "Dirk," which sounds like "work" and "kirk" (the Old English word for "church"), both positive ideas, also deconstructs and inverts the naming process. As a woman character in the novel tells Dirk with bitter incisiveness, his name even suggests a shallow phallic gigolo-type identity, something "dirty." Finally, because a dirk is a dagger, the name reminds us of the dangerous betraying qualities of that weapon. Is Dirk a man who stabs his mother's dreams in the back just as thousands of "successful" young men, according to Ferber, betrayed the American dream? Just who is to blame when Sobig DeJong grows up to have dreams as pitifully small as his father's marble-sized tomatoes? Certainly not Selina, who refuses to feel guilty.

—Maria K. Mootry, "Introduction" to *So Big* by Edna Ferber (Chicago: University of Illinois Press, 1995), xiv–xv

BIBLIOGRAPHY

Dawn O'Hara. 1911.
Buttered Side Down. 1912.
Roast Beef Medium. 1913.
Personality Plus. 1914.
Emma McChesney and Co. 1915.
Fanny Herself. 1917.
Cheerful, by Request. 1918.

Half Portions. 1920.
$1200 a Year. 1920.
The Girls. 1921.
Gigolo. 1922.
Old Man Minick. 1924.
So Big. 1924.
The Eldest. 1925.
Show Boat. 1926.
Mother Knows Best. 1927.
The Royal Family. 1928.
Cimarron. 1930.
American Beauty. 1931.
Dinner at Eight. 1932.
They Brought Their Women. 1933.
Come and Get It. 1935.
Stage Door. 1936.
Nobody's in Town. 1938.
A Peculiar Treasure. 1939.
Saratoga Trunk. 1941.
No Room at the Inn. 1941.
The Land Is Bright. 1941.
Great Son. 1945.
One Basket. 1947.
Bravo. 1948.
Giant. 1952.
Ice Palace. 1958.
A Kind of Magic. 1963.

DOROTHY CANFIELD FISHER

1879-1958

DOROTHY CANFIELD, named after the heroine of *Middlemarch*, was born Dorothea Frances Canfield on February 17, 1879, in Lawrence, Kansas. She and an older brother, James, were the children of James Hulme Canfield, a university professor, and Flavia Camp Canfield, an artist. A distinguished and cultivated family, they traveled widely, and Flavia kept a studio in Paris.

Graduated from Ohio State University in 1899, Dorothy went on to receive a Ph.D. in French from Columbia University in 1904, having written a dissertation on Corneille and Racine. In 1907 she married John Redwood Fisher and settled on a Vermont farm inherited from her great-grandfather. Civic-minded and dedicated to education, Fisher introduced the Montessori method of teaching to the United States and was the first president of the Adult Education Association and the first woman to serve on the Vermont State Board of Education. Morally compelled, with her husband, to volunteer during World War I, she founded a Braille press for blinded soldiers and a children's hospital in France. She later established the Children's Crusade for Children during World War II, a conflict that took Fisher's son.

Fisher's literary career began with the publication of stories and articles in popular women's magazines while she was a graduate student. Her first novel, *Gunhild* (1907), attracted little attention. *The Squirrel Cage* (1912), however, was better received and enabled her to support her family. Her husband, also a writer, became her consultant and editor as her success increased. Fisher's popular reputation grew with the publication of *The Bent Twig* (1915), *Home Fires in France* (1918), and a collection of stories based on her experiences in France during World War I, *The Day of Glory* (1919). With *The Brimming Cup* (1921), Fisher achieved wide popular and critical acclaim. It was the second most purchased novel in the country, behind Sinclair Lewis's *Main Street*. *The Home-Maker* was among the 10 best-selling novels of 1924. She received an O. Henry Memorial Award in 1944 for "The Knot-Hole," a short story published in the *Yale Review*. Fisher remained for decades one of America's best-known writers of short stories, novels, children's books and magazine articles.

As a Book-of-the-Month Club (BOMC) judge from 1926 until 1951, Fisher firmly established herself as an important figure in American letters beyond her own writing. She introduced the works of, among others, Pearl S. Buck, Isak Dinesen (Karen Blixen), and Richard Wright to American readers. Interest in her own work faded, however, with the rise of modernist critics.

In the 1980s, scholarship on the BOMC and interest in women writers increased. Several of Fisher's novels were reissued, and her correspondence with Willa Cather drew attention. A prolific letter writer, reader, author, wartime relief volunteer, and mother of two children, Fisher reveals in her letters that her literary work was produced with great effort among the many demands of household and community. She regarded it as a challenge to women to fulfill the roles of wife and mother while pursuing interests outside the home. Dorothy Canfield Fisher continued to write children's books and magazine articles until near her death in 1958.

CRITICAL EXTRACTS

ARTHUR HOBSON QUINN

It was in *The Deepening Stream* (1930) that Mrs. Fisher made her most distinct contribution to American fiction. In a way, all her earlier studies of married life seem to have been a preparation for this novel. Beginning in the West, in a university town, she describes, through the eyes of a young girl, Matey Gilbert, the desperate struggle for control between her father and mother. She had to endow the girl with an almost uncanny insight into the subtle methods by which the conflict is carried on. But the dramatic scene at Professor Gilbert's death bed needs only a loving heart to understand it. Matey Gilbert is a distinct advance beyond Marise Crittenden in *Rough Hewn* because the morbid idea of married life which Marise has gained from the relations of her parents is modified in Matey's case by her comprehension of the spiritual kinship between the husband and wife which came to the surface in a great crisis. Contrast, the life of fiction, is next established by Matey Gilbert's life in the little village on the Hudson River, where she meets her husband, Adrian Fort. Mrs. Fisher's real preference for the East is revealed by her sympathetic picture of Rustdorf, with its long-settled tradition, which comes as a revelation to a girl whose constant changes of residence have prevented the growth of roots of any kind. The Great War, to which Adrian goes as an ambulance driver, taking with him Matey and their two children, is painted without glamour. Out of Mrs. Fisher's own experience rise some very striking scenes; the description of the arrival of the first American troops, the roughneck regulars, with their proficient, professional swing; the effect upon the French of President Wilson's statement concerning the real meaning of the war; the picture of the materialists, who went over during the Peace Conference to make sure that his idealistic program would be upset; and most of all, the complete apathy that took possession of Adrian and Matey, as compared with the enthusiasm with which they went to the aid of France in 1915. In *The Deepening Stream*, Mrs. Fisher has accomplished the rare feat of making a happy marriage interesting and of depicting the growth of a woman's character consistently and naturally. ⟨. . .⟩

Throughout all Dorothy Canfield's fiction the prevailing note is that of the individual who, never underestimating the disillusioning processes of life, nevertheless finds the struggle worth while. Thoroughly as she knew the limitations of the Western town without adequate knowledge of social values, or the Eastern village where tradition ruled with a power that verged upon stagnation, or the pettiness of the French provincial, or the immovable prejudice of the Basque farmer, she has had the insight to see below the surface, and discern the rich variety of character which in any place or time reward the student of human nature. In the introduction to her collection of short stories, *The Real Motive*, she describes the dying man who, knowing how weak and futile life can be, had pretended to an optimism he did not feel, who "had showered upon a wretched world a flood of reassuring thoughts, of inspiring phrases," and who knew and dreaded the unsparing mirror which death was about to hold before him, and in which he would at last see himself as he really was— and who trembled in an awful terror. "And yet those who were with him at the last, say that at the end he cried out in a loud voice of exceeding joy."

Like Miss Cather, her wide knowledge at first hand of many sections of the United States and of some of Europe, prevented her from making those superficial generalizations which weaken the work of the satirist like Lewis, Dreiser, or Sinclair, and her knowledge of adolescence gained through her experience as a teacher, spared her from the errors of those novelists like Anderson who picture youth as a quagmire of evil. If her material seems at times to overwhelm her powers of artistic assimilation and expression, her best fiction has an acuteness of insight which will keep her place secure.

—Arthur Hobson Quinn, *American Fiction: An Historical and Critical Survey* (New York: D. Appleton-Century Company, Inc., 1936), 711–14

DOROTHY CANFIELD FISHER

What you say about *Seasoned Timber* interests me enormously. I'm touched that you were able to read it so carefully as you evidently have, for I had expected that younger women could no more read this study of a middle-aged intellectual man than middle-aged intellectual men have ever been able to read my stories of the vital young home-making women so dear to my heart. Most of the letters I have had about *Seasoned Timber* have been from men and this has seemed quite natural to me. I agree with you that there is something exasperating about Timothy's not reaching out his hand to take what he could get. And it's much more than half a loaf, you know, which one gets by accepting ordinary life. You may remember that the young Canby thought it would be very natural for his Uncle Timothy to marry the home economics teacher. And how enraged that made Timothy! I think probably Timothy's rigorous training and experience in music (his aunt's fiercely "professional" attitude, that it must be "just right," or it was nothing) may have had something to do with his attitude towards life. There may have been a confused mental "carryover" into the complex field of human relations of that tyrannical demand for perfection which alone gives distinction to artistic creativeness. Such standards ignore the obvious fact that human life is vast and diverse and rich, immeasurably beyond any art-material, and cannot be restricted and pruned off and cut down as the artist restricts and cuts down on his material to get even a little selected piece of it into the frame-work of his art. But of course one great factor in Timothy's situation was that he was just leaving physical youth behind him!

But here I go, so stirred and interested and stimulated by your letter that I'm starting off as though you were sitting here in my study, with a long evening of talk before us. It's a deep and fascinating aspect of Timothy's life— of everybody's life—which you bring up, as a result of such thoughtful reading of *Seasoned Timber* as any author couldn't but be grateful for.

It is as hard for me to resist plunging into a long talk with you about the war, as about what was the matter with Timothy Hulme's way of taking life (especial thanks for bringing that grand Browning quotation to my mind!). But I'm headed off from that too, by this new necessity to use what strength I have sparingly and cautiously because there's not enough of it to go around. It would of course take a long book to set down what comes leaping to my mind as I read your questions and observations on our world's tragic situation. But I can't let a letter to you go off without one outcry of real horror over your English rector's attitude, which seems to me as dreadful as anything ever said by Hitler. It would be poison to me, to be in the same room with a man capable of such words. And yet I don't feel that Lindbergh has any grasp at all on what the problem really is. I'm afraid he is carried away by a feeling so many of us have (don't mention this to your English rector!) of intense personal distaste for English people, and intense long-standing disapproval of British imperialism.

But I feel that, just as we must, when a great personal sorrow comes to us, make an epic effort not to let our lives be bounded and limited by that grief, but enlarge our hearts till they can harbor both faithful old sorrow and also the new joy which life is willing to bring with every dawn—so, in this terrible crisis, we must enlarge our natures till they have room in them for such personal distastes and dislikes, and *also* for acceptance of all men as (potential) partners and sharers of life. Until we accept them, there can be no partnership. We have shut the Germans out. We must not shut out even your English rector.

It seems to me that this dreadful convulsion is (or may be) part of the struggle to bring to birth a new conception of the oneness of mankind. (This was the idea Timothy was so wildly struggling to try to grasp and pass on to his young people, and by the way, this was what he *really* cared about much more than about Susan Barney!)

Now many an effort to bring new life into being, results in death. Perhaps this *may* be such an effort—just too great for the human race to achieve. We may not be able to rise above our dreadful human faults like a horse, fumbling with his nose at the latch of a gate, not able to perform the simple operation of lifting the latch and going forward. But there's a chance that, this time, we *may* learn how to lift that latch. The very violence of the convulsion may drive us to transcend what we have thought were our powers. A chance to succeed is a challenge!

—Dorothy Canfield Fisher, [16 July 1941 letter to Mary C. Jane], *Keeping Fires Night and Day: Selected Letters of Dorothy Canfield Fisher*, ed. Mark J. Madigan (Columbia, MO: University of Missouri Press, 1993), 211–12

SHARON O'BRIEN

The personal source of Claude Wheeler's humbling encounter with France ⟨in Willa Cather's *One of Ours*⟩, Cather explained in ⟨a letter to Dorothy Canfield⟩, was her trip to France with Canfield in the summer of 1902. In *One of Ours* she had tried to convey, she told Canfield, the feeling a sensitive roughneck has when he is plunged into the midst of a rich culture. It was not only his vanity that suffered, but he felt as if he had been cheated out of everything, deprived of the whole treasure of the ages just because he didn't know some language. This was a terrible experience, Cather wrote—the confrontation of an uncultivated, even primitive self with an older, tradition-filled civilization. She had tried to express this contrast in the relationship between Claude and David (Claude's sophisticated friend who is at home in French culture). That friendship, Cather confessed, was an emotional picture of herself and Canfield in France, twenty years previously. Reworking this painful experience in *One of Ours* was her revenge, she continued, since Canfield had admitted how moved she had been by Claude's and David's relationship. A month later Cather told Canfield what she had not been able to say during their 1902 trip: Canfield had never been a "roughneck" like herself because Canfield's mother and father—unlike Cather's parents—were intellectuals. Canfield had never understood why she had suffered so in the past, Cather wrote, but maybe now—with Claude as an intermediary—she could.

The wounds of a rural childhood heal slowly. By 1902 Cather was doubtless as well read as Canfield and had been imbued with a love for French literature since college days. But since her parents had not given her a comparable cultural and intellectual inheritance Cather felt excluded from the European heritage which she assumed Canfield, the child of educated, upper-class parents, enjoyed as a birthright. Canfield had received a maternal gift that Cather particularly envied. Her friend's ability to speak fluent French, to Cather the sign of inclusion in the culture she loved and admired, had first been encouraged by her mother Flavia Canfield, an artist who had taken her young daughter on several trips to Paris. Meanwhile, as Cather then thought, she had been given nothing by the women in her family, who did not paint, sculpt, or take her to foreign countries.

    —Sharon O'Brien, *Willa Cather: The Emerging Voice* (New York: Oxford University Press, 1987), 249–50

MARK J. MADIGAN

Closely related to Fisher's commitment to education was her active support of women's rights. Surprisingly, Fisher once wrote that she "was never a feminist." She explained, "It was my older generation, my father and mother, who were. I was rather (as it often goes in generations) in reaction from their extreme zeal for 'women's rights' " (DCF to Helen K. Taylor, no date). Her devotion to the cause of equal opportunity for women, though, is unmistakable. Both Fisher's fiction (most notably *The Home-Maker*, in which the protagonist, Evangeline Knapp, is a wife, mother, and the family breadwinner) and her letters speak to her strong belief that women should not be limited in their access to education and job training, nor should they be bound by societal conventions. Characteristically, in a 1946 letter to Margaret Mead, she lamented "the social pressure, invisible and tyrannical, which the United States puts upon its women and girls." The restriction of women's roles—and men's too: in *The Home-Maker*, the husband, Lester Knapp, draws great satisfaction from staying at home and caring for his children—seemed, quite simply, impractical to Fisher. She reasoned that since everyone is born with unique abilities, limitations, and temperaments, one's place should not be determined by gender. It was only when each person was in a role he or she was suited for that society could function productively, and Fisher lectured and wrote in support of that principle. As she remarked to Julia Collier Harris:

So large a majority of fathers of our girls are heart-and-soul business men, it stands to reason that the girls themselves might do better if they were not automatically shoved off into being cultured teachers . . . although goodness knows our country needs cultured teachers enough sight more than business-people. Still, folks have to do what they are best fit for, and every opportunity for women means one less chance of a square peg living miserably in a round hole all its life.

Nearly thirty years later, Fisher still worried over the obstacles women faced:

I'm very much struck by the fact that although America offers us a life astonishingly safe from most physical dangers, it plunges us into another danger which is devilishly insidious because it falls so imperceptibly about us as we live—and that is the danger of becoming held and mastered by triviality. The little things of life, of no real importance, but which have to be "seen to" by American home makers, is like a blanket smothering out the fine and great potential qualities in every one of us.

—Mark J. Madigan, "Introduction" to *Keeping Fires Night and Day: Selected Letters of Dorothy Canfield Fisher*, ed. Mark J. Madigan (Columbia, MO: University of Missouri Press, 1993), 19–20

PATRICIA RAUB

Dorothy Canfield explicitly challenges received wisdom in both *The Squirrel-Cage* (1912) and *The Home-Maker* (1924). Not only does Canfield suggest that husband and wife should share—or even exchange—the duties and responsibilities that society had traditionally assigned them, but she also advances the unorthodox idea that the less time and effort a woman spends on housework the better a wife and mother she is likely to be. In *The Home-Maker*, Evangeline Knapp is endlessly scrubbing the floors, polishing the furniture, beating the rugs, and, even though she, like her friend Mattie Farnham, automatically believes that "[h]ome-making is the noblest work anybody can do!" (199), the truth of the matter is that Eve Knapp hates housework. Because she forces herself to lavish so much of her energy on homemaking, she has no reserves of patience left to expend upon her husband and children. Lydia Emery in Canfield's *The Squirrel-Cage* is not a born housewife ⟨. . .⟩; neither is she a model—if reluctant—homemaker, as is Eve Knapp. When Lydia is left in charge of her parents' household upon her mother's illness, she proves to be an indifferent mistress. Her father is "dismayed by the thorough-going domestic anarchy that had ensued. He was partly aware that what alarmed him most was Lydia's lack of zest in the battle . . . [signaling a] failure to acquiesce in the normal, usual standard of values" (80). ⟨. . .⟩ Canfield presents Lydia's lack of interest in housekeeping as a sensible response to an unreasonable social expectation. As Lydia believes that housework demands too great a share of a woman's time, she tries to convince her *fiancé* to build their house so that it can be maintained easily—to omit carved hall panels, for example, which will be difficult to dust. Paul ignores Lydia's entreaties, as his primary goal is to construct an ornate structure assertive of his social status. Once married, Lydia confronts "all of the dismaying difficulties of housekeeping and keeping up a social position in America" (194). Lydia feels increasingly smothered by her homemaking responsibilities, and it is only Paul's death which relieves her of her burden.

While Canfield questions the emphasis that should be placed upon housework, and even hints that in some cases it may be appropriate for women to transfer their duties in the home to others and to enter the paid labor force, few other popular women novelists appear to have agreed with her. Most other writers ⟨. . .⟩ maintain that a woman's place is in the home, carrying out her traditional wifely responsibilities. In actuality, according to the U.S. Census of 1930, almost ninety percent of all married women did remain at home rather than enter the workplace. For that matter, most unmarried women stayed home as well. In the Twenties and Thirties, only about a quarter of the female population were wage earners. As the novels of the era indicate, most young, single, middle-class women were not expected to support themselves; like Lydia Emery, they were to move gracefully from their fathers' to their husbands' homes without ever being forced to venture out into the world of work. Even those middle-class families hard put to make ends meet were reluctant to send their unmarried daughters out into the work force or to encourage them to prepare themselves for gainful employment.

—Patricia Raub, *Yesterday's Stories: Popular Women's Novels of the Twenties and Thirties* (Westport, CT: Greenwood Press, 1994), 46–47

Mark J. Madigan

The distillation of ⟨Dorothy Canfield Fisher's⟩ experiences is contained in a body of work marked by far more than a technical facility with narrative. There is in Fisher's best writing a vigorous curiosity about human nature, and a judiciousness that is no less bracing for its acknowledgment of our inherent frailties.

While stylistic experimentation was never her primary concern, Fisher nonetheless contributed significantly to the genre of the short story. At her disposal were a storyteller's natural talent for plot development, an ear for the nuances of spoken language, and an eye for telling detail. Her stories are populated with an unusually broad range of characters—young, old, rich, poor, middle class, men, women, children, American, French, Spanish—all rendered convincingly. But Fisher's greatest strength lies in her ability to mine the commonplace for the revelatory. Her observation of life at hand is at once scrupulous in its detail and inviting of far-ranging interpretation.

Fisher related her observations of the human drama in direct language and with a desire to educate. With typical candor, she once declared in *The Home-Maker* that "Under its greasy camouflage of chivalry, society is really based on a contempt for women's work in the home." Such statements made Fisher's best-selling novel, which focuses on the restrictions of traditional gender roles within a marriage, one of the most controversial works of 1924, and led at least one reviewer to call it "extreme." To those familiar with Fisher's fiction, however, *The Home-Maker* should have been anything but extreme. The topics she explores therein—women's rights, marital relations, domesticity, the bonds of family that both unite and constrict, the struggle to support oneself in a capitalist society, the artistic temperament—are the same ones that had been of consistent interest to her since she began publishing short stories in mass-market magazines nearly twenty years earlier. "The Bedquilt," for example, is, on the surface, a "quiet" tale about a New England spinster, which, on a deeper level, speaks as forcefully about the condition of women and "contempt for women's work in the home" as any line from *The Home-Maker*.

In ⟨her⟩ essay, "What My Mother Taught Me," Fisher recalls the moment of inspiration for "The Bedquilt" at the Prado museum as she gazed into the eyes of one of the court dwarfs painted by Diego Velásquez:

> The subject of one of the first stories I wrote, "The Bedquilt," was as helplessly starved as the Spanish dwarf of what all human beings need for growth . . . was as humbled before her fellow-men through no fault of hers . . . as defenselessly given over to the careless mockery of those luckier than she. This by no glandular lack . . . by the social code of her time which decreed that plain women without money, who did not have husbands, who had never been admired by men, were only outcasts from the normal group . . . grotesque deformities, so that to look at them was to laugh at them!
>   . . . A message received from the marvelously painted, dark, tragic eyes of Sebastian de Morra had forced me to look deep into the faded blue eyes of Aunt Mehetabel.

The significance to Fisher of that look into Aunt Mehetabel's eyes is hard to overstate. In fashioning the character of the elderly country woman, she felt the importance of her work as a writer for perhaps the first time. The effort to understand and communicate the complexity of the human condition, begun in earnest in "The Bedquilt," would be her authorial project for the next fifty years. That understanding is at once specific to the character of Mehetabel and more expansive as it argues that the attributes of all women need to be better recognized.

The character of Mehetabel and her talent for quilting are not only convincingly rendered, but also are an effective means of voicing provocative thematic concerns. For her heroine, Fisher chose neither a radical feminist nor an avant-garde artist, but rather a character with whom even the most conservative reader could sympathize. Moreover, in quilting, she chose a craft with deep roots in American history. By embodying her message of empowerment in the unassuming Aunt Mehetabel, Fisher subverted the negative criticism that greeted more strident female characters such as Kate Chopin's Edna Pontellier. While it is true that Mehetabel is eventually honored for the magnificent quilt she creates, her initial invisibility in the Elwell home serves as a powerful metaphor for the failure of a patriarchal society to acknowledge the special skills and qualities of the women it oppresses. As Elaine Showalter has written in her essay "Piecing and Writing," "The Bedquilt" is indeed a story that reverberates with larger implications. For Showalter, it is no less than "a parable of the woman writer, and her creative fantasies."

—Mark J. Madigan, "Introduction" to *The Bedquilt and Other Stories by Dorothy Canfield Fisher*, ed. Mark J. Madigan (Columbia, MO: University of Missouri Press, 1996), 2–4

BIBLIOGRAPHY

Gunhild. 1907.
The Squirrel Cage. 1912.
The Bent Twig. 1915.
Hillsboro People. 1915.
The Real Motive. 1916.
Home Fires in France. 1918.
The Day of Glory. 1919.
The Brimming Cup. 1921.
The Home-Maker. 1924.
Her Son's Wife. 1926.
The Deepening Stream. 1930.
Basque People. 1931.
Bonfire. 1933.
Fables for Parents. 1937.
Seasoned Timber. 1939.
Four-Square. 1949.

ZONA GALE
1874-1938

ZONA GALE was born in Portage, Wisconsin, on August 26, 1874, the only child of Charles and Eliza Beers Gale. A frail, solitary, and meditative child, Gale wrote stories, poems, and literary impressions, which she kept in notebooks. In 1895, Gale graduated from the University of Wisconsin and became a reporter for the *Milwaukee Journal*, continuing her studies until she earned a master's degree in 1899. She became a highly regarded journalist and left Wisconsin in 1901 to join the staff of the New York *Evening World*, following the pattern of other midwestern writers like William Dean Howells, Willa Cather, Sherwood Anderson, and Hamlin Garland, who left small towns for New York.

In 1902, Gale became Edmund Clarence Stedman's secretary in order to pursue a career writing fiction. Her stories were soon published in *Outing*, *Smart Set*, and *Success* magazines. As part of the Stedman literary circle, Gale met the writer Ridgely Torrence. They almost married, but after two years of courtship, Gale broke off their relationship in 1904; she did, however, correspond with him throughout her life. In 1906 Gale published her first novel, *Romance Island*.

In Portage, living in her parents' home, Gale wrote collections of stories published as *Friendship Village* (1908), *Friendship Village Love Stories* (1909), *When I Was a Little Girl* (1913), *Neighborhood Stories* (1914), and *Peace in Friendship Village* (1919). In 1911, *The Delineator* magazine awarded Gale a $2000 first prize for her story "The Ancient Dawn." A novel, *Mothers to Men*, appeared that same year, followed in 1912 by a novelette, *Christmas*. The same village characters reappear in all these works, which make the characters' superstitions and bigotry appear comic and harmless.

From 1912 to 1920, Gale participated in many civic projects, including the pacifist movement; the struggle for women's suffrage; the movement for reform legislation; and the development of the Wisconsin Dramatic Society, one of the first regional theater movements. Her one-act play, *The Neighbors*, was produced in 1914 by the society.

The novel *Birth*, published in 1918, marked a change in Gale's fiction. The sweetness of the Friendship Village stories was replaced by literary realism and a strain of mysticism. *Miss Lulu Bett* (1920), judged by most critics to be her best novel, depicts a newly educated

American woman tyrannized, without options, by the small town in which she lives. The novel was adapted to the stage and won the Pulitzer Prize in 1921. Her 1923 novel, *Faint Perfume*, characteristically wavers between the mundane and the spiritual.

Gale married William L. Breese of Portage in 1928 and adopted his two daughters. She continued to write and was active in politics throughout her life: she was appointed to the University of Wisconsin's Board of Regents (1923), covered the Republican National Convention for the *Milwaukee Journal* (1930), and was appointed Wisconsin's representative to the International Congress of Women (1933). She received honorary degrees from Ripon College, the University of Wisconsin, and Rollins College. Zona Gale died in Chicago on December 27, 1938. Her last novelette, *Magna*, was published posthumously in 1939.

CRITICAL EXTRACTS

RÉGIS MICHAUD

While the Frenchman, supposedly a domestic person, makes little of family life on the stage and in his novels, the American idealizes it. The father, the mother and the child, those are the corners of his "eternal triangle." Zona Gale has gratified the tastes of that particular public. *Birth* is a work of original analysis, a good psychological document for the study of certain maladies of personality. The novel portrays a curious case of sentimental aphasia. The hero of the book is a simple sort of soul. He married a woman his superior in education. Awkward, *gauche*, even grotesque, he is at bottom the best of men. His heart is paved with good intentions, but unfortunately he knows not how to disclose them. Pitt—that is his name—acts like a man, who knowing two languages, would be incapable of translating one into the other. Failing to be able to express himself, he buries himself in a sort of psychological twilight where he vegetates and suffers in silence. Unable to express his sentiments to others, he is reduced to acting for his own benefit what was meant for them. His life is henceforward but a fiction, a novel which would never have been read had not Zona Gale played the part of the publisher. Pitt would make an excellent Pirandello character. Externally but a grotesque clown, inside goodness and delicacy incarnate, he seemed to come out of the shadows at the birth of his son. Pitt adores his child, but as a father he continues to be a victim of Freudian inhibitions. He feels every paternal sentiment, but he is unable to find the words and gestures which correspond to his emotions. Little by little the distance between father and child lengthens, and one day poor Pitt disappears, misunderstood by his own child.

The book was followed by *Miss Lulu Bett*. Zona Gale studied in it again the effects of suppression, but with new methods of dramatic simplification. Her style is lighter; her portraits are more strikingly pathetic and resemblant. Lulu Bett is a scapegoat. A Cinderella at home and a slavey, her life is that of an automaton, and yet she possesses a romantic heart. We must admire the skill with which Zona Gale was able to keep her before us halfway between tears and laughter. Every reader remembers poor Lulu's courtship by an adventurer who subsequently abandoned her, her devotion to the members of the household, her marriage to the village music-dealer, all incidents of a trivial nature, but sympathetically brought out to reveal the kind-hearted Lulu. Zona Gale's pathos is direct and familiar, almost trivial, but pervaded with delicate and deep emotions.

All inhibited people are not necessarily Ophelias or Lady Macbeths. There are many nuances to repression. Nevertheless, Lulu Bett is a romantic heroine.
    —Régis Michaud, *The American Novel To-Day: A Social and Psychological Study* (Boston: Little, Brown, and Company, 1928), 249–50

ARTHUR HOBSON QUINN

In *Birth* (1918) Miss Gale made a distinct advance in the sharpness and vitality of her fiction. Instead of the pleasant portrait of the small Wisconsin village of her earlier stories, she drew a realistic picture of the town against whose lack of understanding a fine soul in an insignificant body struggles in vain. There could hardly be imagined a more hopeless hero than Marshall Pitt when he enters Burage, a pickle salesman, undersized, inarticulate, uneducated, but with a great longing to rise spiritually and intellectually. Miss Gale with fine insight presented at once a contrast between the recognition which Rachel Arrowsmith, the woman of breeding, accords to those qualities of Pitt which lie beneath his unattractive surface, and the lack of understanding of the commonplace girl, Barbara Ellsworth, whom he marries. What wins and keeps the sympathy for Pitt is his humanity, beginning with marriage to a woman whose father's death has left her with nothing but debts, and ending with his own rescue of a dog at the cost of his life. Even when his wife deserts him and their little son for a flashy bandmaster—or when years later his son Jeffrey shows how ashamed he is of his father's insignificance, Pitt rises to the supreme degree of charity in attributing to both of them motives higher than those by which they are really actuated. Quietly he takes the blame upon himself. Pitt's growth in spiritual stature is unperceived by anyone except Rachel Arrowsmith, and even her efforts to help him are not persistent. The com-

ments of the citizens, male and female, after his death, are ironic bits of com-
placent misunderstanding:

> "Say," said Mis' Barber, "did you ever see anybody pick up the way
> Jeffrey has since his father died?"
> "Ain't he?" said Mis' True. "I've thought of that myself."
> "Why, my land," said Mis' Miles, "he's a different person. It looks
> like what he'd needed was to get rid of that little man—honestly."
> They wove this in small patterns, and when Mis' Hellie came back
> they all reverted to an old design.
> "Jeffrey ain't a bit like his father, is he?" Mis' Hellie observed with
> satisfaction.
> They gave their negatives without restraint and Mis' Monument
> Miles took up the whole story, from the first, rocking slowly and
> looking out upon the Burage Street.
> "Pitt never was much good," she began.

Burage is etched mercilessly but fairly. The picture of the town at six o'clock
is better than Sinclair Lewis's description of Main Street because it gives both
sides of the shield ⟨. . . .⟩

Whether Lewis had read *Birth* before he wrote *Main Street* I do not know,
but it is significant that he chose the surname of Rachel Arrowsmith for the
leading character in one of his later novels. ⟨. . .⟩

The fiction of Zona Gale has been progressive in matter and in form.
Beginning with the idealistic treatment of romantic material, she proceeded to
realistic pictures of familiar life. She has never lost, however, a sense of the distinction between the merely external analysis and the more searching synthesis which builds up a story that in her own words "does something to you."
There is a poet's touch constantly in her prose, and while at times it has led to
unreality, and even absurdity, it has been responsible also for flashes of insight
which atone for them. Her plays and her dramatic interests undoubtedly
sharpened her later fiction, but she is a novelist rather than a playwright. It did
not need the publication of the play *Miss Lulu Bett*, with its alternate third acts,
one of which followed the novel and the other which yielded to the necessities of production, to prove that she works best when she has her material
under her own control.

She had her own theories of fiction, found in "The Novel and the Spirit"
and "The Novel of To-morrow" in her volume of essays *Portage, Wisconsin and
Other Essays* (1928). She objected to the school of thinking which believes that
the novel of economic struggle includes all the elements of conflict, and stated
correctly: "The novel in which a crude moral struggle, either lost or won, is
the highest motif [is as] primitive in art as is the economic struggle in life." She
also remarked hopefully that: "The chief concern of the American novel of

tomorrow will be to uncover the beauty of our essential commonplace living as the novel of today has triumphantly uncovered its ugliness." In this belief she may be an optimist, but there can be no question that in her own fiction she has sought beauty in many forms, and has at times achieved it.

—Arthur Hobson Quinn, *American Fiction: An Historical and Critical Survey* (New York: D. Appleton-Century Company, Inc., 1936), 701–3, 706

IMA HONAKER HERRON

Restricted in theme to the commonplaces of narrow lives, all the Friendship stories, nevertheless, are happily optimistic in tone. The busy men and women of the town find time to enjoy the neighborliness of a limited environment. The village women, especially, are always ready to meet any emergency. Marvels of serenity and capability, they

> . . . prepare breakfasts, put up lunches, turn the attention to the gar-
> den, and all, so to speak, with the left hand; ready at any moment to
> enter upon the real business of life—to minister to the sick or bury
> the dead, or conduct a town meeting or a church supper or a birth.
> They have a kind of goddess-like competence, these women.
> ⟨*Friendship Village Love Stories*, 26⟩

Little is said of the village fathers, but one may suppose that they, too, were both competent and Samaritan-minded. Otherwise, they could not have lived in Friendship, the sweetest of villages, one, says Carl Van Doren ⟨in *Contemporary American Novelists*, 164⟩, that should stand "upon the confectionery shelf of the fiction shop, preserved in thick syrup. . . ." In all of these stories of secluded, intimate life Miss Gale varied the same device of "showing how childlike children are, how sisterly are sisters, how brotherly are brothers, how motherly are mothers, how fatherly are fathers, how grandmotherly and grandfatherly are grandmothers and grandfathers, and how loverly are all true lovers of whatever age, sex, color, or condition." While Friendship Village, with no definite location upon the printed map of the world, may once have been praised as worthy of abiding permanently in the memories of countless readers, "who in the enjoyment of its chronicles have been able temporarily to forget the latitude and longitude of their own personal cares and sorrows," it is really no haven for the modern escapist ⟨Frederick Tabor Cooper, *The Bookman* 31, no. 79, 1910⟩. The eternal saccharine might prove too strong.

Even Miss Gale herself wearied of her own idyllic creed, as her later and more mordant village criticism shows. The influence of *Spoon River Anthology* marks her complete change of style in *Birth* (1918), a novel of a small Wisconsin town. Realistic description, natural characterization, and logical plot indicate a pronounced deepening of Miss Gale's understanding of village manners. Here she has such an assemblage of types that her *dramatis personae* resemble a living picture of the eighties. The portrait of Marshall Pitt—a timid little man pitied by his son and neighbors—gives promise of what Miss Gale later was to do in *Miss Lulu Bett*. The heroine's desertion of her husband and native town in the hope of finding beauty and pleasure in the city foreshadows ⟨Sinclair Lewis's⟩ *Main Street*. For the first time in her recording of inhibited lives Miss Gale, like many of her Western contemporaries, declared in this novel her revolt from the village. ⟨. . .⟩

Miss Gale's abandonment of the Friendship formula is further evidenced in the literary maturity and undeniable artistry distinguishing her later fiction. *Preface to a Life* (1926) illustrates both the development of her fictional powers and her further change in attitude toward small town life. The revolt indicated in *Birth* and *Miss Lulu Bett* reaches a new stage in this story of Bernard Mead, a small town businessman. In sketching Bernard's experiences from his young manhood to his fifty-second birthday Miss Gale pictures life in the little town of Pauquette, near Chicago, during the era of 1900 and later. Like *Main Street*, this is a story of attempted escape from the village virus. In youth Bernard wanted to escape the monotony of life in Pauquette by working in Chicago. At his father's insistence, he remained in the town he despised; entered the family lumber business; and eventually became, to all outward appearances, a fond husband, father, and successful business man. Through the years Bernard secretly longed for Alla, with whom he corresponded at rare intervals. But always he was conscious of his ordeal: the ordeal of being surrounded constantly by too many women within his household. Finding his love for Alla in opposition to his feeling of family honor and the small town code, Bernard tried unsuccessfully to adapt himself to the role of martyr. Eventually, after a temporary mental derangement, his outlook became calmer and he ended his long conflict between moral obligation and love with the decision that his life to this point has been but a preface to richer things to come.

This novel, with later stories, such as *Yellow Gentians and Blue* (1927), contains acid sketches of small town characters far different from those of the friendly folk of Friendship Village. Unsavory gossip, hypocrisy, and other kindred marks of repressed lives fill these records sufficiently to place Miss Gale in the newer school emerging during the years following *Spoon River Anthology*. She, too, looked at the village from a new viewpoint, but never with the complete cynicism or utter futility of some of her contemporaries. As the conclusion of *Preface to a Life* suggests, she leaves a little bit of hope in her diagnosis of small town cases.

—Ima Honaker Herron, *The Small Town in American Literature* (New York: Pageant Books, Inc., 1959), 346–49

HAROLD P. SIMONSON

The two words "Portage, Wisconsin" signified life to Zona Gale. There she was born and there she was secured by ties of home and parents. These two words, written by her thousands of times, became "charged," she said, in a way unknown to the casual visitor. "It seems strange," she wrote in 1928, ten years before her death, "that the majority of the people in the United States have never heard of [Portage]." Though frequently away from it, she always returned. After coming back from a winter in New York, her second favorite city, she wrote to Hamlin Garland: "It is quite heavenly here, after my joyous season of brick and mortar." Garland, on the other hand, thought it "a drab little city," but he correctly observed that Zona Gale's imagination transformed its drabness into literature. The extent of her success may be told in Willa Cather's reaction to the town of Zona Gale's fiction: "I am haunted by Portage."

Zona Gale, like many American writers, found in small-town life the distillation of American folkways. Since Colonial times, native writers with a strong sense for locality have sought to identify the nation itself by delineating specific regions representative of American manners. Small communities, originally left in the wake of frontier expansion, held abundant material for local colorists who in the North, South, and West celebrated their own provinciality.

The Middle West had its own regionalists, who, by the 1870's, had begun to set the dominant tone which later writers followed. The best word to describe this tone is "sullen," for the representative works point again and again, both subtly and ponderously, to this quality. Joseph Kirkland, Edward Eggleston, E. W. Howe, Edgar Lee Masters, Sherwood Anderson, Sinclair Lewis—each in his own way, and Zona Gale in hers—showed the postfrontier communities as being far this side of paradise. The monotony, social and emotional curbing, tastelessness, cultural poverty, pettiness, and general stagnation took the place of what had been for the first discoverers a mythical garden. The local colorists, who came next, found more often an atmosphere of disillusionment; as a region the Middle West became for writers "a metaphor of abuse."

But life is not one tone, not even on Main Street. Zona Gale was justified in pointing out this fact, though some of her efforts at sweetness and light turned into innocuous puffballs fully deserving the criticism they received. The point, however, is that her acid little novels like *Miss Lulu Bett* and *Faint Perfume* present only part of her view. Not all her characters are singular American boobs, not all are Philistines. Even Sinclair Lewis showed his Sam Dodsworth to be a man of backbone, and many of Sherwood Anderson's "grotesques" hide an uncanny beauty. In sympathy with such writers as Ruth Suckow, Ole Rölvaag, and Willa Cather, Zona Gale wrote stories about people knit firmly together by common ties of sacrifice, humor, perseverance, and tragedy. To read her prolific work is to discover a surprisingly polychromatic writer whose little town of Portage, called by Carl Van Doren "one of the sweetest of all literary villages," is large enough to embrace a multitude of townsmen and manners.

Portage, then, takes its place with Lewis' Zenith and Gopher Prairie, Anderson's Winesburg, and Carl Van Vechten's Maple Valley. In each town the main street sliced through a cross-section of provincial America. The drama to be seen brought the small town into American literature to stay. It is true that neither Zona Gale's fame nor sensationalism equalled that of many other realists. But it is well to remember that her widely read novel *Miss Lulu Bett*, exactly contemporaneous with Lewis' *Main Street*, was hardly less influential in establishing the new direction in provincial realism; and it won for her a Pulitzer Prize when she adapted it for the stage in 1921.

—Harold P. Simonson, *Zona Gale* (New York: Twayne Publishers, Inc., 1962), 15–16

DIANNE LYNCH

⟨In⟩ 1918, Zona Gale surprised her readers and the country's literary establishment with *Birth*, a major departure from the simplicity and romance of her earlier works. In *Birth*, Gale presents to her readers a painfully realistic portrait of an uncertain little man named Marshall Pitt, a pickle salesman whose most compelling characteristic is his refusal—or inability—to recognize the cruelty and selfishness of those he loves. Even as his wife abandons him, even as his son grows ashamed of him, Pitt proves incapable of rejecting or rebuking them. In the name of love, he absorbs their anger and their disgust, certain that his own inadequacies merit their scorn. In *Birth*, Gale presents the classic human conflict between independence and commitment, between responsibility and freedom. Pitt is the ultimate martyr, a man who dies without ever having challenged those who oppressed and ridiculed him. His final words reflect his anguish and despair: "Then at dawn he opened his eyes full upon the room. It was lit by the naked flame of an unshaded lamp, and in that unwonted light, at that unwonted level, there may have seemed many people present. An odd, thin-drawn sound broke from Pitt, and he threw up his hands in their shapeless bandages. 'Say!' he whispered, and the words came like whistling. 'Am I going to die—like a fool?' " Gale's implicit answer is a resounding yes.

Two years later, in 1920, Gale returned to the themes she introduced in *Birth*. *Miss Lulu Bett* is the story of the tyranny of a family, of the superficial niceties that can mask stupid pettiness. In the character of Dwight Deacon, dentist, deacon and head of the house, Gale has created one of fiction's most obnoxious and banal of brothers-in-law; it is Deacon's chief delight to taunt Lulu Bett, to remind her as frequently as possible that she is a spinster dependent upon his goodwill for her keep. When, in an unexpected twist of fate, Lulu finds herself married to Deacon's brother Ninian, she rejoices that the marriage offers escape—from her life as a spinster, from her brother-in-law's home, from the judgmental eyes of her neighbors. But her freedom is short-lived and, when the marriage turns out to be a farce, Lulu once again must choose between her family's needs and her own. Unlike Marshall Pitt, Lulu is no martyr. As she agrees to marry Neil Cornish, she reclaims her self-respect and dignity; not surprisingly, the novel ends with hope and expectation: "The street door was closed. If Mrs. Bett was peeping through the blind, no one saw her. In the pleasant mid-day light under the maples, Mr. and Mrs. Neil Cornish were hurrying toward the railway station." Ironically, Lulu Bett has achieved a personal freedom that Zona Gale would not know until after the death of her own parents in 1923.

As readers and critics mark the 120th anniversary of Zona Gale's birth, her work continues to offer us insights into the social and familial conflicts that surrounded women's roles at the turn of the century. Like so many of the educated, middle-class women of her era, Gale's personal and political lives were a study in contradictions: She was a traditionalist and a ground breaker; a submissive, obedient daughter and an outspoken feminist; a professional newswoman and a writer of stylized romantic fiction; a political progressive and a Midwesterner wedded to the perspectives and mores of small-town America. She was, in short, the embodiment of the dilemma faced by so many women of her day, women forced to balance their education, independence and ambition against the very real demands of their families, their history and their circumscribed place in her world. For Zona Gale, like millions of her nineteenth century sisters, it was a very real dilemma, and *Birth* and *Miss Lulu Bett* resonate with its tensions. For that reason alone, these works merit our attention and our recognition.

—Dianne Lynch, "Introduction" to *Miss Lulu Bett* and *Birth*, by Zona Gale (Oregon, WI: Waubesa Press, 1994), 10–12

DEBORAH LINDSAY WILLIAMS

The ⟨Friendship Village⟩ stories do begin what will prove to be a theme in all Gale's work: the emphasis on women and women's lives. The men in these stories are background noise when they appear at all; it is the women who create the society of the village, who do its work. Reviews of the first *Friendship Village* stories were, for the most part, condemnatory of its sentimentality, a quality that Fannie Hurst called a "china shop full of quaint porcelains." Some reviewers, however, praised Gale's use of "homespun" maxims and the veracity with which she rendered the dialect of her characters. These early stories, then, connect to an earlier period in American literature, when women wrote to uplift the spirit, and the small town was the last bastion of Christian virtues.

These first collections of stories point to an interesting split between Gale's life and work, which she unified in her later work: on the one hand is Zona Gale the serious activist, who lobbies for equal rights, better education for the poor. She is a public figure, explicitly aware of, and concerned about, current social causes, the same things her male contemporaries—Garland, Sinclair, Dreiser, Lewis—are writing about. As an activist, she advocates powerfully for change, but her short stories connote an earlier, less challenging era. As a writer, Gale seems to accept the role of a woman writer from an earlier time. Her challenges to the status quo do not extend to her writing, at least at this early point in her career. This dichotomy opposes how Wharton and Cather lived and worked: they lead their lives without calling attention to their breaks from convention, and their novels—without overt political messages—challenged the accepted ideas about "proper" subject matter for the American novel: Wharton with anti-heroines like Undine Spragg, and the highly sexual Charity Royall; Cather by playing with expectations of form, in novels like *The Song of the Lark, Death Comes for the Archbishop*, and *Lucy Gayheart*.

In 1918, however, Gale's tone changed; she found a way to unify the activist and the writer. If calling for change in the gentle, sentimental tones of Friendship Village wouldn't work, she would question whether those tones were any longer possible. The bitterness of *Birth* establishes, metaphorically, Gale's new residence in a small town similar to Zenith, or Gopher Prairie. There are various explanations for Gale's abrupt change: the effect of Masters' *Spoon River Anthology*, ⟨World War I⟩ and America's participation in it, the harshness with which her pacifism was received by her beloved Portage neighbors. Critics and reviewers hailed *Birth* as a refreshing change from Friendship Village, despite her publishers' warning that the title sounded like "a treatise by Mrs. Sanger." The reviewer for the *Nation* pointed out Gale's shift in tone, saying, "Miss Zona Gale is revenging herself on Friendship Village. For years she fed its impossible legends to a public with an unlimited appetite for inexpensive sweets. But all the while she knew it to be in the same part of the physical and moral world as Spoon River and Winesburg . . . How Friendship Village must have rasped her nerves during the sweetish years!" (*Nation* 24, April 1920).

Gale's next novel, *Miss Lulu Bett*, won her even more critical accolades. Critics debated whether it or Sinclair Lewis' *Main Street*, published the same year, were the better novel. *The New Republic* reviewer of *Miss Lulu Bett*, Constance Rourke, called it "a signal accomplishment in American letters" (*The*

New Republic, August 11, 1920). The novel tells the story of Lulu Bett, 34-year-old spinster, who keeps house for her sister and her sister's husband. In many ways, *Miss Lulu Bett* is a typical 1920s indictment of what H.L. Mencken called "the booboisie," by which he meant the bourgeoisie, the middle class. Lulu is trapped by the smallminded conventionality of Warbleton, Wisconsin—represented by her sister's family, the Deacons, with whom Lulu lives; she is the "poor relation" who has nowhere else to go. Lulu is trapped by gender, economics, and social convention: she has no money, no job, no husband. Her gradual emergence from grim drudge to a woman who chooses her own version of happiness, regardless of the town's opinion, is a classic feminist awakening; Lulu is a kind of self-actualized Cinderella. With the publication of this novel, Gale finished her long writing apprenticeship, which had begun as a journalist twenty years prior; her critical success finally matched her popularity (and her sales). ⟨. . .⟩

Gale's awareness of the economic necessities facing women is as accurate as that of Wharton's, although Wharton's gaze usually does not go as far down the food chain as places like Warbleton, Wisconsin (unless we count the two "New England" novels, *Summer* and *Ethan Frome*). In part Gale's awareness comes from her familiarity and agreement with the more radical economic ideas of Charlotte Perkins Gilman, who suggested, among other things, that all women be paid for housekeeping, and that childcare be socialized. In *Miss Lulu Bett*, Gale said she created "an honest portrayal of the . . . domestically enslaved woman of her day." In creating a portrait of the "enslaved," Gale unifies her craft and her politics; Lulu is Everywoman. Gale's ease with this sort of didactic articulation separates her from Cather and Wharton (both of whom, nevertheless, admired the novel).

—Deborah Lindsay Williams, "Not in Sisterhood: Edith Wharton, Zona Gale, Willa Cather, and the American Woman Writer Re-defined," (Diss., New York University, 1995), 56–58, 62–63

BIBLIOGRAPHY

Romance Island. 1906.
The Loves of Pelleas and Etarre. 1907.
Friendship Village. 1908.
Friendship Village Love Stories. 1909.
Mothers to Men. 1911.
Christmas. 1912.

When I Was a Little Girl. 1913.
Neighborhood Stories. 1914.
The Neighbors. 1914.
Heart's Kindred. 1915.
A Daughter of the Morning. 1917.
Birth. 1918.
Peace in Friendship Village. 1919.
Miss Lulu Bett. 1920.
The Secret Way. 1921.
What Women Won in Wisconsin. 1922.
Faint Perfume. 1923.
Preface to a Life. 1926.
Portage, Wisconsin and Other Essays. 1928.
Borgia. 1929.
Papa La Fleur. 1933.
Light Woman. 1937.
Magna. 1939.

CHARLOTTE PERKINS GILMAN

1860-1935

CHARLOTTE PERKINS was born on July 3, 1860, in Hartford, Connecticut. Charlotte and her older brother were raised by their mother, Mary Fitch Perkins, after their father left the family. Gilman identified her intellectual ambitions with her mother's family, the Beechers; she was the grandniece of Harriet Beecher Stowe, author of *Uncle Tom's Cabin*. Charlotte briefly attended the Rhode Island School of Design and later worked as an art teacher and commercial artist.

In 1884, Charlotte married Charles Walter Stetson, an artist. After the birth of their daughter, she suffered from what might now be diagnosed as postpartum depression, a nervous collapse that would affect her throughout her life. In 1892, she wrote the classic short story "The Yellow Wallpaper," describing the "dark fog" that had enveloped her. The following year, she moved with her daughter to Pasadena, California, divorced Stetson, and then made an anguished decision to send her daughter to live with him and his new wife, Charlotte's friend Grace Ellery Channing. Charlotte was consequently reviled in newspaper accounts as an unnatural and unfeeling mother. Despite this, she worked as an editor, writer, lecturer, and teacher, first in Oakland and then in San Francisco.

Women and Economics, published in 1898, marked Charlotte Perkins's emergence as a prominent feminist; the book was widely read in North America and Europe and was subsequently translated into seven languages. In it, she argues that the cultural emphasis on women's sexual and maternal roles has been at the expense of their social and economic development and indeed to the detriment of the human species. The subordination of women may have been necessary in the past, she posits, but 20th-century life demands that male assertiveness and female culture work in cooperation. Only in economic independence can women be free.

Charlotte Perkins married her cousin, George Houghton Gilman, in 1900. Until his death in 1934, his support, as well as additional domestic help, allowed her to develop her socialist and feminist ideas through a range of publications and activities. In *Concerning Children* (1900), Gilman proposed new social organizations to free women from domestic subservience. *The Home* (1903) and *Human Work* (1904) propose day-care centers, remuneration for household tasks, and houses without kitchens. Gilman lectured extensively on women's

126

rights and other social issues and, in 1909, founded the journal *Forerunner*, in which, until 1916, she published editorials, poems, and fiction. In *The Man-Made World* (1911) and *His Religion and Hers* (1923), Gilman pursued the idea that the female, because she is committed to sustaining life, should take precedence over the male, who in turn is predisposed to warfare and violence. Her 1915 novel, *Herland* (first serialized in *Forerunner*), is the story of a feminist utopia and describes the ecological and ethical superiority of matriarchy over patriarchy. Gilman addressed the International Suffrage Convention in Budapest in 1913 and helped to found, with Jane Addams and others, the Women's Peace Party in 1915.

Interest in Gilman's work declined in the 1920s, and, after her husband's death, she returned to California to live near her daughter. She published her autobiography, *The Living of Charlotte Perkins Gilman*, in 1935. Suffering from cancer, she committed suicide in Pasadena, California, on August 17, 1935.

CRITICAL EXTRACTS

AMY WELLINGTON

Charlotte Perkins saw more clearly, with more imaginative insight, than any other New England girl of her day, the crippled lives of housewives and mothers, their narrow deadening circumstances; above all, their pitiful economic dependence. "In Duty Bound," one of her earliest printed poems, written when she was about twenty-one, expressed eloquently, not only the limitations of her own young life, but of all New England girlhood in that generation.

One counts it, therefore, an historic date when, on New Year's Day, 1887, Charlotte Perkins Stetson, then a young wife and mother, a busy artist and writer, went to the Public Library in Providence, Rhode Island, and, getting a new card, filled it with the names of books on women. The contemplation of women's subordinate and cruel position in life had begun to move her powerfully. Six days later, she started an article on "the distinction of the sexes."

It was not until 1890, however, with the publication of her satirical poem, "Similar Cases," that Charlotte Stetson became widely known as a writer. These original verses, with their singular high power of social satire, were first printed in *The Nationalist*, then copied and quoted wherever English-speaking people had begun to think socially and in terms of organic evolution. Other social satires in verse were quick to follow, equal in wit and forcefulness of phrase—"A Conservative," "Wedded Bliss," bright weapons for the reformer the world over!

Charlotte Stetson could communicate the thrill of horror in both prose and verse, an uncanny art, used infrequently, with a purpose, and finding its most startling expression about this time in "The Yellow Wall Paper," the story of a nerve-sick young mother's hallucination caused by loneliness and inactivity. The figure of a woman creeps from the paper of the room in which the patient is most tenderly confined, and haunts her with a secret and growing power until the day comes when she completely identifies herself with the creeping form and is mad. "The Yellow Wall Paper" has been placed by critics with the weird masterpieces of Hawthorne and Poe; but this is only a lazy classification for a story which stands alone in American fiction. For originality, both as thinker and writer, was Charlotte Stetson's outstanding quality, except, perhaps, the inspirational beauty of her thought and its joyousness, which rose from her profound perception of reality.

In 1891, one finds Charlotte Gilman (still Charlotte Stetson) making this illuminative affirmation in one of her lectures: "I am scientist enough to know that man with all his brain is an orderly product of evolution; I am naturalist enough to know that law rules everywhere, that the subtlest action of the soul is resolvable by long and careful study back to the simplest elements of life; I am poet enough to know that the natural world is divine and the divine world is natural." Her unshakable belief, then as now, (a religion formulated at the age of sixteen) was in that "force which has with slow and constant miracle turned protoplasm into personality." Her dominant desire was "the perception and transmission of applicable truth." Then, as now, she was a philosopher making pure and beautiful poetry out of her vision of the evolutionary processes of life and their continuation into a just world made perfect. Yet in California, in the early 1890's, this brave thinker and dreamer in the sun roused a persistent and even scurrilous hostility.

She had become active in the Nationalist Movement, a political sequel to Edward Bellamy's novel, "Looking Backward." Charlotte Gilman wrote and spoke for the movement, throwing, for a time, her wit and poetry, her whole dynamic power of expression, into its propaganda. Nationalism in California was quickly kindled into a blaze, but as a blaze died down. Only Charlotte Gilman caught and perpetuated its spirit in both prose and verse; and her lectures on different aspects of Nationalism were the beginning of her life-work as a sociological writer and speaker.

When one hears of Charlotte Gilman in the 1890's as a "dangerous" woman, a disrupter of family life and destroyer of the home, one turns to these early lectures which, unlike her later ones, were put on paper, and one reads: "Let me say again, a hundred times if necessary, that I believe in permanent monogamous marriage." Then: "Let me say again, a hundred times if necessary, that housework has nothing to do with love." And so "kitchen-minded" were we that in spite of the former statement, reiterated, probably, many times one hundred times, the later was interpreted as meaning the destruction of marriage. But life has a way of agreeing with Charlotte Gilman, whatever we may choose to think about it. A kitchenless home is rapidly becoming a necessity. Women's energies are thus released for every kind of service, from the preparation of food, scientifically and professionally, to the making of new philosophies; and marriage is not discontinued, the home is not disrupted. Again and again, in those early formative lectures, Charlotte Gilman reached the crux of her argument in "Women and Economics:" "The absolute first condition in the growth of the real woman is economic independence." This was a revolting thought to the majority of both men and women in the 1890's.

Wheresoever Charlotte Gilman went during those years of lonely and courageous thinking, she was a strange dynamic power. Both she and her work were marked "dangerous." She encountered the sinister hostility of a certain section of the American press, led by Ambrose Bierce. Her public speeches were distorted and often made to appear ridiculous. Her personal life was never free from blackguardly intrusion. But fear of misunderstanding, ridicule or insult never held Charlotte Gilman back from saying or doing the thing she once saw clearly ought to be said or done. "Do you expect this to succeed?" she once was asked before a particularly doubtful undertaking. No! came the answer. Yet the thing was done, in the face of almost certain failure, because some one must have the courage to make a beginning, and some day it *would* succeed.

—Amy Wellington, "Charlotte Perkins Gilman" from *Women Have Told: Studies in the Feminist Tradition* (Boston: Little, Brown, 1930), reprinted in *Critical Essays on Charlotte Perkins Gilman*, ed. Joanne B. Karpinski (New York: G. K. Hall, 1992), 67–69

SANDRA M. GILBERT AND SUSAN GUBAR

As if to comment on the ⟨. . .⟩ anxiety-inducing connections between what women writers tend to see as their parallel confinements in texts, houses, and maternal female bodies—Charlotte Perkins Gilman brought them all together in 1890 in a striking story of female confinement and escape, a paradigmatic tale which (like *Jane Eyre*) seems to tell *the* story that all literary women would tell if they could speak their "speechless woe." "The Yellow Wallpaper," which Gilman herself called "a description of a case of nervous breakdown," recounts in the first person the experiences of a woman who is evidently suffering from a severe postpartum psychosis. Her husband, a censorious and paternalistic physician, is treating her according to methods by which S. Weir Mitchell, a famous "nerve specialist," treated Gilman herself for a similar problem. He has confined her to a large garret room in an "ancestral hall" he has rented, and he has forbidden her to touch pen to paper until she is well again, for he feels, says the narrator, "that with my imaginative power and habit of story-making, a nervous weakness like mine is sure to lead to all manner of excited fancies, and that I ought to use my will and good sense to check the tendency" (15–16).

The cure, of course, is worse than the disease, for the sick woman's mental condition deteriorates rapidly. "I think sometimes that if I were only well enough to write a little it would relieve the press of ideas and rest me," she remarks, but literally confined in a room she thinks is a one-time nursery because it has "rings and things" in the walls, she is literally locked away from creativity. The "rings and things," although reminiscent of children's gymnastic equipment, are really the paraphernalia of confinement, like the gate at the head of the stairs, instruments that definitively indicate her imprisonment. Even more tormenting, however, is the room's wallpaper: a sulphurous yellow paper, torn off in spots, and patterned with "lame uncertain curves" that "plunge off at outrageous angles" and "destroy themselves in unheard of contradictions." Ancient, smoldering, "unclean" as the oppressive structures of the society in which she finds herself, this paper surrounds the narrator like an inexplicable text, censorious and overwhelming as her physician husband, haunting as the "hereditary estate" in which she is trying to survive. Inevitably she studies its suicidal implications—and inevitably, because of her "imaginative power and habit of story-making," she revises it, projecting her own passion for escape into its otherwise incomprehensible hieroglyphics. "This wall-paper," she decides, at a key point in her story,

> has a kind of sub-pattern in a different shade, a particularly irritating one, for you can only see it in certain lights, and not clearly then.
>   But in the places where it isn't faded and where the sun is just so— I can see a strange, provoking, formless sort of figure, that seems to skulk about behind that silly and conspicuous front design. (18)

As time passes, this figure concealed behind what corresponds ⟨. . .⟩ to the facade of the patriarchal text becomes clearer and clearer. By moonlight the pattern of the wallpaper "becomes bars! The outside pattern I mean, and the woman behind it is as plain as can be." And eventually, as the narrator sinks more deeply into what the world calls madness, the terrifying implications of both the paper and the figure imprisoned behind the paper begin to permeate—that is, to *haunt*—the rented ancestral mansion in which she and her husband are immured. The "yellow smell" of the paper "creeps all over the house," drenching every room in its subtle aroma of decay. And the woman creeps too—through the house, in the house, and out of the house, in the garden and "on that long road under the trees." Sometimes, indeed, the narrator confesses, "I think there are a great many women" both behind the paper and creeping in the garden,

> and sometimes only one, and she crawls around fast, and her crawling shakes [the paper] all over . . . . And she is all the time trying to climb through. But nobody could climb through that pattern—it strangles so; I think that is why it has so many heads. (30)

Eventually it becomes obvious to both reader and narrator that the figure creeping through and behind the wallpaper is both the narrator and the narrator's double. By the end of the story, moreover, the narrator has enabled this double to escape from her textual/architectural confinement: "I pulled and she shook, I shook and she pulled, and before morning we had peeled off yards of that paper." Is the message of the tale's conclusion mere madness? Certainly the righteous Doctor John—whose name links him to the anti-hero of Charlotte Brontë's *Villette*—has been temporarily defeated, or at least momentarily stunned. "Now why should that man have fainted?" the narrator ironically asks as she creeps around her attic. But John's unmasculine swoon of surprise is the least of the triumphs Gilman imagines for her madwoman. More significant are the madwoman's own imaginings and creations, mirages of health and freedom with which her author endows her like a fairy godmother showering gold on a sleeping heroine. The woman from behind the wallpaper creeps away, for instance, creeps fast and far on the long road, in broad daylight. "I have watched her sometimes away off in the open country," says the narrator, "creeping as fast as a cloud shadow in a high wind."

Indistinct and yet rapid, barely perceptible but inexorable, the progress of that cloud shadow is not unlike the progress of nineteenth-century literary women out of the texts defined by patriarchal poetics into the open spaces of their own authority. That such an escape from the numb world behind the patterned walls of the text was a flight from dis-ease into health was quite clear to Gilman herself. When "The Yellow Wallpaper" was published she sent it to Weir Mitchell, whose strictures had kept her from attempting the pen during her own breakdown, thereby aggravating her illness, and she was delighted to learn, years later, that "he had changed his treatment of nervous prostration since reading" her story. "If that is a fact," she declared, "I have not lived in vain." Because she was a rebellious feminist besides being a medical iconoclast, we can be sure that Gilman did not think of this triumph of hers in narrowly therapeutic terms. Because she knew, with Emily Dickinson, that "Infection in the sentence breeds," she knew that the cure for female despair must be spiritual as well as physical, aesthetic as well as social. What "The Yellow Wall-paper" shows she knew, too, is that even when a supposedly "mad" woman has been sentenced to imprisonment in the "infected" house of her own body, she may discover that, as Sylvia Plath was to put it seventy years later, she has "a self to recover, a queen."

—Sandra M. Gilbert and Susan Gubar, *The Madwoman in the Attic: The Woman Writer and the Nineteenth-Century Literary Imagination* (New Haven: Yale University Press, 1979), 89–92

ELIZABETH KEYSER

In *Reinventing Womanhood* Carolyn G. Heilbrun explains how literary works that purport to deal with "the nature of man" but in fact deal only with men can be reinterpreted so as to serve as models for women. Charlotte Perkins Gilman's feminist utopia, *Herland*, published in 1915, can be viewed as such a reinter-pretation of *Gulliver's Travels*, especially of the Fourth Voyage. In *Herland* Gilman uses Swift's satire on human pride in general as a model for her attack on male pride in particular, offers an explanation for the Yahoo in human nature, and, finally, suggests how that Yahoo can be eradicated.

The complete *Gulliver's Travels* and *Herland*, together with its sequel, *With Her in Ourland* (1916), share a common preoccupation or theme. When in *Ourland* Ellador, a native of Herland, visits the United States, she compares the country to Gulliver imprisoned by the Lilliputians:

> Here you are, a democracy—free—the power in the hands of the people. You let that group of conservatives saddle you with a consti-tution which has so interfered with free action that you've forgotten you had it. In this ridiculous helplessness—like poor old Gulliver—bound by the Lilliputians—you have sat open-eyed, not moving a finger, and allowed individuals—mere private persons—to help them-selves to the biggest, richest, best things in the country. . . . What can we think of a Democracy, a huge, strong, young Democracy, allowing itself to become infested with such parasites as these? (184)

Like Swift, Gilman is concerned with the way in which people fail to recog-nize their own strength, allow themselves to be enslaved, and then pride themselves on their identification with the individuals and institutions that enslave them. In *Herland*, however, Gilman follows Swift even more closely to show how women in the early twentieth century are little more than beasts of burden, a theme she anticipates in *Women and Economics* (1899). There Gilman draws an analogy between the horse in captivity and women; they both work, but their exertions "bear no direct relation to [their] living" (7). Both are depen-dent economically on the wills of their masters. She then goes on to compare women's work in the home and caring for children with the work of a horse; their labors enable men to produce more than would be otherwise possible— they are economic factors but not economically independent (13). Like Gulliver and the economically oppressed citizens of a democracy, both horses and women, through a combination of their own servility and the tyranny of others, have become so "saddled" as to have forgotten their freedom.

In *Herland* Gilman does with the sexes what Swift does with the reversal of stations and perspectives. In *Herland* the supposedly superior sex becomes the inferior or disadvantaged just as Gulliver in the first two voyages perceives himself first as the giant, then as the dwarf, and in the Fourth Voyage first as the higher, then as the lower animal. ⟨. . .⟩

Swift, like Gilman, seems to believe that rational cooperation as opposed to irrational aggression cannot take place while people are blinded by passion and that people would be less its prey were there greater similarity and equality between the sexes. But Swift, unlike Gilman, holds out little hope for humanity. Gilman, in her appropriation of the Fourth Voyage as a model, seems to be agreeing with Swift's analysis of human nature, but she also seems to be offering an explanation and solution for it. Unlike Swift, Gilman in *Women and Economics* envisions a time when "a general Disposition to all Virtues" might be as natural to us as it is to the Houyhnhnms. Once women are freed from their socio-economic bondage, "we shall no longer conceive of ethical progress as something outside of and against nature, but as the most natural thing in the world. Where now we strive and agonize after impossible virtues, we shall then grow naturally and easily into those very qualities; and we shall [again like the Houyhnhnms] not even think of them as especially commendable" (340). "The largest and most radical effect of restoring women to economic independence" will be wholeness; individualism in the sense of selfish striving will give place to individuality or the integration of the self. Then "we shall be able to feel simply, to see clearly, to agree with ourselves, to be one person and master of our own lives, instead of wrestling in such hopeless perplexity with what we have called 'man's dual nature' " (332).

In the final chapter of *Herland* Van sees the drama of human history as enacted by men and excluding women. But he also sees that for the Herlanders an equivalent drama has been enacted solely by women. The Herlander's historic panorama is more impressive than the male-dominated one—it has the same constructive elements and none of the destructive ones. But it is nonetheless partial, incomplete, as Ellador realizes. Thus she and Van choose to leave utopia, unlike Terry and Gulliver who are exiled from it. Whereas Terry was impervious to utopian values and Gulliver made despairing by them, Van and Ellador hope somehow to translate them into action. Gilman's utopia is more optimistic than its model, just as there may be more hope for man in the collective sense of men and women than there is for man in the sense of men alone.

—Elizabeth Keyser, "Looking Backward: From *Herland* to *Gulliver's Travels*," *Studies in American Fiction* 11, no. 1 (1983), 31–32, 45–46

SUSAN GUBAR

The middle chapters of *Herland* portray motherhood completely transformed, divorced from heterosexuality, the private family, and economic dependency. Maternal feeling in Herland flows "out in a strong, wide current, unbroken through the generations, deepening and widening through the years, including every child in all the land" (95). Motherhood therefore serves as a paradigm of service so that labor and nursing become the model for work. Similarly all the evils of the private home—isolation of women, amateur unhealthy cooking, the waste of labor and products, improper upbringing of children, lack of individual privacy—are avoided not by destroying the idea of home but by extending it so the race is viewed as a family and the world as its home. Redefinitions of work, of the home, of motherhood itself confuse the male visitors who had initially insisted that in any "civilized" country there "must be men" (11). Eventually they are forced to renounce not only this assumption but the definition of "civilization" that makes it possible.

"Civilized and still arboreal—peculiar people" (17). This is how Van first comments on the unique culture of Herland. His first perspective of its inhabitants is a glimpse of three girls leaping, like wood nymphs, in the branches of a huge tree. With its forests that are cultivated like farms and gardens that look like parks, Gilman's Earthly Paradise banishes wilderness, replacing it with cultivation. From Frances Hodgson Burnett's to Nancy Friday's secret gardens, the landscapes of women's fantasies have mediated between the extremes of savagery and civility that have defined women to their own bewilderment. In fact, the crucial difference between Herland and our land is the feeling Gilman strives to give us that culture there is no longer opposed to nature. This binary dualism, resulting in the domination of nature by culture, is presented in Gilman's utopia as resolved more harmoniously, through the intercession of the female. Women, considered closer to nature because of their role in perpetuating the species, break down the dichotomy between mind and matter. The architecture Gilman uses to signal art and nature thus allied includes airy gazebos, ceilingless temples, open-air theaters. Because the all-female Herlanders define the human as female, mother earth is no longer an antagonist. The implications of the mother as landscape are quite different for the two sexes, as the strong link between feminist and ecological movements suggests.

Parthenogenesis functions symbolically, then, to represent the creativity and autonomy of women, mother-daughter reciprocity, and the interplay of nature and human nature. At the same time it releases women from the female Oedipus complex, as defined by Freud: the daughter's rejection of the mother, her resulting sense of self-hatred, the extension of her desire for a phallus to desire for the man who possesses the penis. ⟨. . . By⟩ envisioning a race of woman born, Gilman valorizes the creativity of the womb which is and always has been, after all, the tangible workplace of production. As the male visitors admit the greater power of the overmothers, two of them are converted to what they call "loving up," a phrase that evokes "the stirring" within them "of some ancient dim prehistoric consciousness . . . like—coming home to mother" (152). Analyzing the imperialist project in light of this regression, Gilman implies that the white man's burden is bound up with his not being a woman. The female, far from seeming castrated or mutilated or wounded or envious of the penis, derives her energy and her assurance from the fact that, having no penis, she cannot be castrated. Gilman's radical rejection of Freud's identification of the penis with power is probably made clearest in her emphasis on the erotics of motherhood in *Herland*: "before a child comes," we are told, "there is a period of utter exaltation—the whole being is uplifted and filled with a concentrated desire" (70). Yet another consequence of Gilman's refusal of the phallic law of the fathers is her dream of a common language: linguistic activity in *Herland* is characterized by extreme lucidity, the simplicity that stimulates collectivity.

Gilman is understandably vague about how a mother tongue would constitute a different kind of linguistic activity from the father's law. Yet the very word "Herland" implies that this language, mirroring the two-in-one of mother-and-child, would allow for simultaneous expression of the self as self and the self as object. Certainly Gilman criticizes the closed revelation of the Word of God, contrasting it to the "Indwelling Spirit" of service that Herlanders worship as the accumulated mother-love of the race. ⟨. . .⟩ Gilman claims that the Christian doctrine of personal spiritual immortality is no less egocentric on the part of every man, "a singularly foolish idea . . . And if true, most disagreeable" (116). Instead of desiring to go on growing on earth forever, her heroine wants her child, and her child's child, to go on forever. Identification with the species replaces personal identity, as Gilman insists on the importance of accepting death as an aspect of life. ⟨. . .⟩ Replacing transcendent God the father with "Maternal Pantheism" (59), the Herlanders expose the narcissism of Christianity. ⟨. . .⟩

Gilman's garden of parthenogenesis replaces the Judeo-Christian garden of Genesis, by claiming that the authority of the father—biological or spiritual—is a myth fast degenerating to the status of a fiction. Writing at the turn of the century, Gilman implies that the disappearance of God reflects and perpetuates a weakening in patriarchal domination. But parthenogenesis, besides symbolizing the autonomous creativity of women, mother-daughter bonding, the secondariness of the male, and the disappearance of God, also effectively solves the problems of the pains and pressures produced from motherhood's status as a political institution in patriarchy: these include male dispensation of birth control and abortion, the economic dominance of the father and the usurpation of the birth process by a male medical establishment. In her own time, women were becoming more vocal about the risks of venereal disease, unwanted conception, dangerous parturition, and abortion. In her own life, Gilman had been profoundly afflicted by not a few of these factors. The painful experiences Gilman describes in her autobiography—of being deserted by her father at an early age, of being brought up by an economically and psychologically impoverished mother who denied her physical affection, of severe postpartum depression, shading into madness, following marriage and the birth of her daughter—are at least partially the result of the problem sexuality constituted for nineteenth-century women. In *Herland*, she gives us this experience transmuted into an enabling fantasy celebrating mother-daughter bond and hinting at her desertion of the father who, in fact, deserted her.

> —Susan Gubar, "She in *Herland*: Feminism as Fantasy," in *Coordinates: Placing Science Fiction and Fantasy*, ed. George E. Slusser, Eric S. Rabkin, and Robert Scholes (Carbondale, IL: Southern Illinois University Press, 1983), reprinted in *Charlotte Perkins Gilman: The Woman and Her Work*, ed. Sheryl L. Meyering (Ann Arbor: University of Michigan Press, 1989), 195–97

E. SUZANNE OWENS

Gilman's tale ⟨"The Yellow Wallpaper"⟩ is acknowledged by feminist critics as a study of psychology and sexual politics grounded in autobiographical realism. It is a significant work in nineteenth-century literature because of these features. But a second story exists beside the story of repression and madness we read today—a supernatural tale drawn from the best nineteenth-century Gothic conventions, particularly from Edgar Allan Poe and Charlotte Bronte. Recently, Eugenia C. Delamotte has noted the story's Gothic elements, yet Gilman's first readers reacted to "The Yellow Wallpaper" as a ghost story, a narrative combining the supernatural with aberrant psychology framed by sexual politics. ⟨. . .⟩

Before Gilman's narrator ever begins her description of the fateful yellow-papered room at the top of the house, she, an emotionally charged woman, has entered what the reader should understand as recognizable territory for ghosts, hauntings, and possessions. Furthermore, the tale has barely begun when the moon rises and a character's uneasiness is dismissed as "a draught" : the stage is set for supernatural manifestations in accordance with ghost story conventions. Understandably, the narrator is unable to dispel the "ghostliness" she feels. ⟨. . .⟩

Like many of her predecessors in ghost stories, what the narrator resists is her own identification with the haunting presence, the woman or women trapped behind the wallpaper. But if she is, in fact, suffering from the gradual and cumulative effects of a haunting, her final deterioration comes with the ghost's possession of her body, thus leading her to "creep" by daylight. The narrator reports seeing the woman from the wallpaper "on that long road under the trees" just before the narrator admits that she locks her bedroom door and creeps by daylight around the room (31). To a reader familiar with the Gothic, the events of the story suggest possession as much as they do hallucination: the narrator watches a figure appear in the pattern of the wallpaper, witnesses increased agitation in the menacing rattling of the pattern's "bars," follows this figure's movements as it appears to break loose from the bars on the wall, and finally takes on that figure's form as she begins to crawl about the bedroom floor. As ⟨Sandra⟩ Gilbert and ⟨Susan⟩ Gubar note: "Eventually, as the narrator sinks more deeply into what the world calls madness, the terrifying implications of both the paper and the figure imprisoned behind the paper begin to permeate—that is, to *haunt* the rented ancestral mansion" ⟨*The Madwoman in the Attic*, 1979, 90⟩. By the end of the story, the narrator can do nothing *but* "creep," a verb she uses six times in the last thirty lines. Her identification with the woman in the wallpaper is explicit and complete; she worries, "I suppose I shall have to get back behind the pattern when it comes night" (*Wallpaper* 35).

The narrator's cry of triumph has puzzled many critics: "I've got out at last . . . in spite of you and Jane" (36). Elaine Hedges suggests that the intrusion of the name could be a result of a printer's error, a misprint of either "Julia" or "Jennie," the housekeeper and sister-in-law residing in the house, or a reference to the narrator's real name. In the latter case, Hedges takes the line as an indication of "the narrator's sense that she has gotten free of both her husband and her 'Jane' self: free, that is, of herself as defined by marriage and society" (63). Alternatively, if we assume that the narrator's madness accounts for the events, "Jane" is the rational self giving way to the irrational. But if this is an account of supernatural possession, the voice speaking that sentence is the voice of a ghost announcing its victory over the narrator/victim, now revealed to be "Jane."

In any case, the connection to Jane Eyre is inevitable. Gilbert and Gubar read Bronte's novel as a tale of splitting psyches personified by Jane and Bertha, acknowledging the supernatural frame of the story: "In view of [the] frightening series of separations within the self—Jane Eyre splitting off from Jane Rochester, the child Jane splitting off from the adult Jane, and the image of Jane weirdly separating from the body of Jane—it is not surprising that another and most mysterious specter, a sort of 'vampyre,' should appear in the middle of the night to rend and trample the wedding veil of that unknown person, Jane Rochester" (359). Furthermore Jane Eyre's "splitting" is incited, as is Gilman's Jane's, by a scene in which she looks out across the grounds surrounding the house. Jane Eyre's fragmentation is complicated by her doubling with Bertha, whom Gilbert and Gubar call "Jane's truest and darkest double," "the angry aspect of the orphan child, the ferocious secret self Jane has been trying to repress ever since her days at Gateshead" (359–60). Like the ghostly double that finally possesses Gilman's narrator, Bertha is an angry captive, intent upon breaking free. She is finally revealed as a wild, though indistinguishable, figure running back and forth in the attic cell, where, "[she] grovelled, seemingly, on all fours" (Bronte 278), just as Gilman's narrator does at the end.

Gilman's narrator vents her destructive rage only on the wallpaper in her room, while Bertha burns Thornfield Hall to the ground. Whereas Bertha dies and Rochester lives on, however, the ending may be reversed in Gilman's story. John is said to have "fainted" at the end, as the narrator says: "so that I had to creep over him every time!" (*Wallpaper* 36). Perhaps, however, he has died from shock, a classic consequence of confronting a ghost—a fitting end for the disbeliever. The ambiguity of the ending suits the ambiguity of the story as a whole. Has the narrator merely succumbed to madness, or has something more uncanny occurred? Clearly, late nineteenth- and early twentieth-century readers, who were more familiar with the ghost story tradition, read it in those terms. But if "The Yellow Wallpaper" is truly a story of ghostly possession, are we to rejoice in the ghost's victory, or only to lament the limitations of the combined force of female worldly and otherworldly power, which can only be expressed by creeping?

—E. Suzanne Owens, "The Ghostly Double Behind the Wallpaper in Charlotte Perkins Gilman's 'The Yellow Wallpaper,'" in *Haunting the House of Fiction: Feminist Perspectives on Ghost Stories by American Women*, ed. Lynette Carpenter and Wendy K. Kolmar (Knoxville: University of Tennessee Press, 1991), 65, 70, 76–78

GARY SCHARNHORST

"The Giant Wistaria" is, in its most elementary sense, a formulaic ghost story, a terrifying diptych about an unwed mother, tormented by Puritan patriarchy, whose spirit haunts a decaying mansion. In the first section of the story, set sometime in the late eighteenth century, the unnamed woman suffers disgrace for bearing a child upon her arrival in the wilderness of the New World. Her father physically abuses her and insists that she marry a cousin, a "coarse fellow" whose proposals she had "ever shunned." He also demands that she return with him to England, abandoning her child, and that she be locked in her chamber, a captive to his authority, until she agrees to this plan. In the second and longer section of the story, set a century later, a young couple rent the old house and invite several friends for a visit. They consider the mansion "a *real* ghostly place" (482) nestled in a riot of savage nature. The grounds, "once beautiful with rare trees and shrubs," have now gone to seed and become "a gloomy wilderness of tangled shade." ⟨. . .⟩ The visitors, particularly the women, soon begin "to see bloodstains and crouching figures" (482) in the sinister landscape, including the silhouette of a woman in the trunk of the ancient wistaria. That night, the ghost of the woman appears to two of the male visitors. The next morning, one of them reports that the "poor creature looked just like" all "those crouching, hunted figures" (483) they had discerned the night before in the dark landscape. The other reveals that he followed the ghost into the cellar, where it rattled the chains of the draw-bucket in the well. Each of them mentions a small red cross the she-ghost wore on a necklace of gold. The residents of the house quickly descend to the cellar, haul the mud-laden bucket to the surface of the well, and discover in it the tiny skeleton of a month-old child. The story ends as workmen find, beneath the rotting planks of the old porch and "in the strangling grasp of the roots of the giant wistaria," the bones of a woman with "a tiny scarlet cross on a thin chain of gold" (485) around her neck.

On first reading, the story seems a chilling if rather transparent indictment of sexual oppression. By piecing together a number of disparate clues, the reader may guess the ending to the tale of tyranny and woe recounted in part one: The young woman apparently escaped from her chamber, hid under the porch, drowned her baby rather than abandon it, and then starved to death rather than submit to her father's demand that she marry for the sake of propriety and return to England. As in other works of female gothicism, the protagonist is "simultaneously persecuted victim and courageous heroine." Her literary forebear is not so much Hester Prynne of Hawthorne's *The Scarlet Letter*, however, as the maddened slave Cassy of Harriet Beecher Stowe's *Uncle Tom's Cabin*. Lest this point seem forced or contrived, note that Gilman considered Stowe, her great-aunt, "one of the world's greatest women" and her novel "a great book," the most popular and influential "work of fiction that was ever written." Like Cassy, the heroine of "The Giant Wistaria" kills her child rather than allow it to suffer ostracism or persecution. ⟨. . .⟩

⟨. . .⟩ For the record, the story is moored autobiographically: Gilman wrote it after she left her husband in Rhode Island and moved to southern California, "the Garden of the Lord," with her infant daughter; that is, both the displaced author and protagonist flee (New) England for the West. ⟨. . .⟩

When she wrote the story in the winter of 1890, Gilman was (like her character) at the center of a brewing scandal, caught in a double bind, both under fire as an irresponsibly single mother and under pressure to return east cloaked in marital respectability. "The Giant Wistaria" thus betrays the author's own predicament. As Juliann Fleenor explains, women writers have often used the gothic form "to convey fear of maternity and its consequent dependent mother/infant relationship." Whereas Cassy and the heroine of "The Giant Wistaria" kill their children, Gilman in 1894 would dispatch her daughter to live with her former husband ⟨. . . .⟩

⟨. . .⟩ ⟨Despite the parallels, however,⟩ "The Giant Wistaria" is a type of open-ended riddle rather than a closed authorial monologue, an alternative fiction which reaches across the frontier of expression. The text responds to problems of authority by declaring its own indeterminacy. The story consists almost entirely of dialogue. Events are narrated by several distinct voices, none of them privileged, a cacophony of language akin to Bakhtin's notion of *heteroglossia*. The decentralizing, centrifugal forces tearing at the discourse, Gilman's refusal to employ a single perspective or intelligence which can be trusted to observe and explain, compels the reader to sift through the fragments of debris and puzzle over the sequence of episodes. These parts, by any method of addition, yield no simple sum or symmetrical whole. Gilman's tale resolves no mysteries of historical causation, repairs no rifts in the mosaic of the past. Like the wistaria vine grown from an innocuous sprig, the past has become a Gordian knot or monstrous tangle of events which can never be straightened.

The narrative is, perhaps, all the more terrifying for the questions it leaves dangling. Who really kills the child? The heroine seems the most likely candidate, but her despotic father had earlier wished aloud that his pregnant daughter had been "cleanly drowned, than live to this end" (480). Does the heroine really hide under the porch and starve to death, or is she murdered (again, by her father?) and her body secreted beneath the loose boards? And who fathered her child? Might the heroine have been the victim of incest, given her father's insistence on abandoning the infant and returning immediately to England? None of these questions can be definitively answered on the basis of what we are told in the story, though we might reasonably expect some or all of them to be answered in a traditionally unified authorial monologue. Like other female gothicists such as Mary Shelley, Gilman amplifies the terror her story evokes by refusing to resolve it.

—Gary Scharnhorst, "Charlotte Perkins Gilman's 'The Giant Wistaria': A Hieroglyph of the Female Frontier Gothic," in *Frontier Gothic: Terror and Wonder at the Frontier in American Literature*, ed. David Mogen, Scott P. Sanders, and Joanne B. Karpinski (Madison, NJ: Fairleigh Dickinson University Press, 1993),156–61.

CAROL FARLEY KESSLER

The 1916 sequel ⟨to *Herland*⟩, *With Her in Ourland*, recounts ⟨the⟩ world survey ⟨of the previous novel's central characters⟩. Vandyck Jennings and his Herland bride, Ellador, fly eastward over our globe to view the devastation being wrought by World War I (chap. 2), to visit China and Japan (chaps. 3 and 4), but predominantly to inspect and diagnose conditions in the United States (chaps. 5–12). The contrasts between Our ways and Hers astonish Ellador into satiric commentary. Gilman utilizes a traditional antiutopian mode: satiric dialogue and travelogue from the viewpoint of a visitor from utopia. But in comparison with *Herland*, *With Her in Ourland* plods. No adventure or romance plot provides *Herland*'s momentum. Ellador decries war either as an expression of hatred and madness, or as a mode of population control; she views "human life as a thing in the making, with human beings as the maker" (44). Upon arriving in San Francisco, Ellador notes, "The very first thing that strikes me in this great rich lovely land of yours is its *unmotherliness*. We are of course used to seeing everything taken care of" (126). Ellador finds Our country untrained in democracy: she sees appalling inequities of income, egregious wastefulness in individual households, and incomprehensible greed among a corporate elite. She also finds the private sector of marriage and home life inadequate, and public transportation and communication beneath what is needed.

Throughout the novel, Gilman's racism, anti-Semitism, and ethnocentrism unfortunately surface. Especially chapter 6, called "The Diagnosis," with its xenophobic ethnocentrism, and chapter 10, (untitled) with its racial prejudice, exemplify Gilman's problems. In chapter 6, Ellador observes to Van that in the United States "you have stuffed yourself with the most ill-assorted and unassimilable mass of human material that was ever held together by artificial means" (153). From this, the chapter than rushes downhill to "Black—yes, and how about the yellow? Do they 'melt'?" (155) and "New York . . . reverts to the clan system with its Irishmen, and back of that, to the patriarchy, with its Jews" (157). Although the later chapter opens with Ellador defending an African-American against a "Southern sociologist" (263), she quickly resumes a prejudicial stance: "if they are decent, orderly and progressive, there is no problem. It is the degraded negro that is so feared" (264). For the remaining two-thirds of the chapter, she waxes anti-Semitic: "I think the Christian races have helped the Jews to overestimate their religion" (266). Ellador's solution to "the Jewish problem" is for the Jews to "leave off being Jews" (267). The pages of the chapter multiply such biased and dystopian commentary.

Feminism remains Gilman's strongest suit 〈. . . .〉

—Carol Farley Kessler, *Charlotte Perkins Gilman: Her Progress Toward Utopia* (Syracuse: Syracuse University Press, 1995), 76–77

B I B L I O G R A P H Y

The Yellow Wallpaper. 1892.
Women and Economics. 1898.
Concerning Children. 1900.
The Home. 1903.
In This Our World. 1903.
Human Work. 1904.
What Diantha Did. 1910.
The Man-Made World. 1911.
Benigna Machiavelli. 1914.
Herland. 1915.
With Her in Ourland. 1916.
His Religion and Hers. 1923.
The Living of Charlotte Perkins Gilman. 1935.

ELLEN GLASGOW

1873-1945

ELLEN ANDERSON GHOLSON GLASGOW was born on April 22, 1873, in Richmond, Virginia. The eighth of ten children of Anne Jane Gholson Glasgow and Francis Thomas Glasgow, she was born into a southern aristocratic family of wealth and social prominence. Due to her extreme shyness and painful headaches, Glasgow was irregularly schooled, but she would, throughout her life, read and travel widely in Europe and the Mediterranean. From childhood on she wrote poetry and grew intensely serious about becoming a writer, although she would later wonder why she chose prose, and not poetry.

In her novels Glasgow rebelled against the genteel tradition of sentiment and nostalgia for the antebellum South. Her realistic depiction of life in her native Virginia contrasted the old society and the new in the period following the Civil War. Her first novel, *The Descendant*, was published anonymously in 1897. Her second novel, *Phases of an Inferior Planet*, appeared shortly thereafter. During this time, reading Maupassant, Tolstoy, and Chekhov, Glasgow sought to develop what she would call a "philosophy of fiction." In *The Voice of the People* (1900), she began a series of novels that would form a social history of Virginia from 1850. The most noteworthy of the five novels written for this project are *The Battle-Ground* (1902) and *Virginia* (1913); the latter, covering the years 1884 to 1912, is a tragicomic portrait of a girl being pointlessly groomed for a genteel way of life that has all but disappeared. The other novels in the series are *The Deliverance* (1904), *The Romance of a Plain Man* (1909), and *The Miller of Old Church* (1911).

Not until 1925, with the publication of *Barren Ground*, did Glasgow gain serious attention from critics. Two comedies of manners followed: *The Romantic Comedians* (1926) and *They Stooped to Folly* (1929). *The Sheltered Life* (1932) and *Barren Ground* are generally considered her best work. *Vein of Iron* was published in 1935. For her last novel, *In This Our Life* (1941), she brought the history that had begun in 1850 with *The Battle-Ground* up to the autumn of 1939; for this novel Glasgow won the 1942 Pulitzer Prize. Glasgow collected the prefaces to her novels in a volume called *A Certain Measure* (1943), which she called a "book of self-criticism"; some of its passages are repeated in the autobiography she began in 1934.

In 1909, Glasgow had been the first woman ever to speak publicly in Virginia in favor of women's suffrage; she also helped to organize the Virginia League for Women Voters; but she was always more devoted to writing than to politics. Although twice engaged, she never married. Among her friends and acquaintances were Henry James; Marjorie Kinnan Rawlings; and Thomas Hardy, Joseph Conrad, John Galsworthy, Arnold Bennett, and their wives.

After completing *In This Our Life* in 1941, Glasgow suffered progressive heart failure and was able to write very little. She died on November 21, 1945, in Richmond.

CRITICAL EXTRACTS

H. L. MENCKEN

⟨Ellen Glasgow's philosophy⟩ is a kind of skepticism that is pungent without being harsh; at least two-thirds of it is simple tolerance. "I believe that the quality of belief is more important than the quantity, that the world could do very well with fewer and better beliefs, and that a reasonable doubt is the safety-valve of civilization."

One may applaud this platform without forgetting how seditious it must have seemed in the Virginia of thirty years ago. But Miss Glasgow, having once mounted it, did not budge an inch. Some day the history of her novels in her home-town must be written. They began as scandals of high voltage, and it was years before Richmond was ready to admit that there was anything in them save a violent enmity to the true, the good and the beautiful. As the news gradually oozed over the Potomac that they were regarded with high politeness in the North there was some reconsideration of this position, but it was not actually abandoned until comparatively recent years. To this day, indeed, Virginia is a bit uneasy about its most distinguished living daughter, and even her appearance in all the solemn panoply of Collected Works will probably leave her something of a suspicious character. For skepticism, save in a few walled towns, of which Richmond is surely not one, is still a kind of wickedness in the South. The thing most esteemed down there, whether by the hidalgos who weep for the lost Golden Age or by the peasants who sweat and pant for the New Jerusalem is the will to believe.

Frankly, I do not blame the Virginians for stopping cautiously short of taking Miss Glasgow to their arms, and covering her with proud kisses. For the plain fact is that the whole canon of her works is little more or less than a magnificent *reductio ad absurdum* of their traditional metaphysic. Thrown among them, and essentially of them despite her struggle against the bond, she has had at them at close range, and only too many of her shots have hit them in almost pathologically tender places. In her gallery all of the salient figures of the Virginia zoölogy stalk about under glaring lights and when she has done with them there is little left to know about them—and not too much that is made known is reassuring. She has, in brief, set herself the task of depicting a civilization in its last gasps, and though her people have their share of universality they are still intrinsically Virginians, and hardly imaginable outside their spooky rose-gardens and musty parlors. They remain so even when the spirit of progress seizes them, and they try to take on the ways and habits of mind of the outside world. Surely the polyandrous Edmonia Bredalbane, in *The Romantic Comedians*, seems, at first glance, to be anything but provincial. But that is only at first glance. Soon it appears that she is Virginian in every corpuscle, despite all her far rides on her witch's broomstick. One parts from her quite sure that this witch, precisely, could not have happened anywhere else on earth.

—H. L. Mencken, "A Southern Skeptic," *America* (August 1933), excerpted in *Twentieth-Century American Literature*, ed. Harold Bloom (New York: Chelsea House Publishers, 1986), 1616

ARTHUR HOBSON QUINN

Vein of Iron has not the charm of *They Stooped to Folly* or *The Sheltered Life*, but it has a great theme and great characters. It illustrates like so many of her other novels, that combination of unity and variety which has placed Ellen Glasgow in the first rank of modern novelists. Through a significant theme such as the triumph of a human soul in its struggle against fate or circumstances, treated most effectively in *The Voice of the People, The Deliverance, The Ancient Law, The Romance of a Plain Man, The Miller of Old Church, Virginia, The Builders, One Man in His Time, Barren Ground,* and *Vein of Iron,* she has secured the unity of the novel. Yet she has not forgotten that unity alone may become monotony; not only in the different novels, but within each novel she has provided sufficient variety to make each book a new creation. Her characters are sharpened, not dulled or absorbed by the theme of which they are the concrete expression. And with an inventive power fertile within the limits of her special field, she never fails to provide characters enough to produce those contrasts that are essential.

In her penetrating analysis of her own work ⟨. . .⟩, she makes a statement which is illuminating, but only half true: "I have never wanted for subjects," she says, "but on several occasions, when because of illness or from external compulsion, I have tried to invent a theme or a character, invariably the effort has resulted in failure." She probably refers to novels like *The Wheel of Life,* or the others laid in New York City, when she was dealing with themes which seem only partly established. But she certainly has invented characters, or at least has taken characters from her own experience and made them live in fiction. Her Southern gentlemen and gentlewomen, of the older or newer régime, are a varied flock; so too are her farmer folk, her store-keepers, her dressmakers, all her rustic and village characters. Her women are on the whole better drawn than her men, and no one has pictured more relentlessly the feminine tyranny which seems in her novels to make even infidelity excusable. No one has, on the other hand, surpassed her in the portraits of women whose whole life has been a generous daily sacrifice, often to the weakness of man.

Ellen Glasgow has shown a remarkable receptivity to new ideas. She began to publish when the idealistic treatment of the romantic material of Southern life had reached its climax of popular approval. She did not break sharply with the traditions of that school, but she took the best lessons it had to teach, and turned them into a new achievement. Through her the Puritan strain, always present in Virginia, which had animated Bacon's rebellion in the seventeenth century and had reached its height in the iron tenacity of Stonewall Jackson, came into its proper place in the panorama of fiction.

—Arthur Hobson Quinn, *American Fiction: An Historical and Critical Survey* (New York: D. Appleton-Century Company, Inc., 1936), 680–81

FREDERICK P. W. McDOWELL

When her inner spirit inexorably informed external reality, Miss Glasgow achieved the full perfection of *Virginia* and *The Sheltered Life*, the delicacy and ironic strength of *They Stooped to Folly* and *The Romantic Comedians*, and the bitter intensity and serene detachment of the best parts of *The Deliverance, Barren Ground, In This Our Life*, and *The Miller of Old Church*. In these novels Miss Glasgow was at least partly successful in fusing her artist's fastidious vision with appropriate outer concretions, in reconciling, to the greatest extent possible, the "truth of fiction" and the "truth of life."

An ironic detachment from experience, in conjunction with an idealistic commitment to a flexible but strongly apprehended spiritual principle operating within and outside the self, helped give her books their authentic quality. At the same time, sentimental lapses were also encouraged by this same idealism, and a lack of felt reality by this same detachment. She is at her best when, in *The Deliverance, Virginia, They Stooped to Folly*, and *The Sheltered Life*, the conditions which surround the characters merge with them in their development until inner and outer realities virtually become one and reach full fruition in this interplay. When such full identification of scene with agent is not achieved, a separation occurs between style and subject, with the result that her novels then are either overwritten or wrongly felt. Miss Glasgow's accomplishments and limitations as a writer are best suggested in her own judgment of another Southern writer, Edgar Allan Poe, whose elusive merits she contrasts with his inadequacies:

> Poe is, to a large extent, a distillation of the Southern. The formalism of his tone, the classical element in his poetry and in many of his stories, the drift toward rhetoric, the aloof and elusive intensity,—all these qualities are Southern. And in his more serious faults of overwriting, sentimental exaggeration, and lapses, now and then, into a pompous or florid style, he belongs to his epoch and even more to his South. ⟨A Certain Measure, 1943, 132⟩

Miss Glasgow is a transitional figure in the development of our literature, standing as she does between the romanticism of the local color writers and the genteel realism of Howells or Mary Wilkins Freeman on the one hand, and the revolutionary naturalism of Theodore Dreiser and the psychological immediacy of Faulkner on the other hand. Lacking the full vigor of Dreiser and Lewis, the crisp intellectuality of Mrs. Wharton, and the poetic intensity, at their best, of Sherwood Anderson and Willa Cather, she is, in her finest work, distinguished for her mordant sense of social reality and for the precision of her ironic intelligence. Of her nineteen novels, a half dozen are truly distinguished, both for their incidental insights into human nature and for their comprehensive interpretation of human life. The exactness of perception in Henry James at his best was denied to Miss Glasgow, for she never achieved James's command of the self, and consequently of medium; but at her best she explored as deeply as he the subtle relationships existing between personality and environment. The six or seven novels which represent Miss Glasgow at her best are substantial in a way that the achievement of her more erratic contemporaries is not. When all qualifications have been made, Ellen Glasgow emerges as a complex and impressive writer; and one can agree with N. Elizabeth Monroe and Maxwell Geismar that she has been underestimated.

Her talents as a craftsman of fiction are manifold: an ability to envision living characters, a sharp sense of the psychological impact of various individualities upon each other, a skill at fusing her characters with scene, a starkness and concentration of energy in her climactic episodes, an animistic sensitivity toward nature, a gift of witty and exact phrasing and of economy of characterization, and a feeling for structure and narrative pace in the novel. More important still, the creation of a believable universe from out the Virginia past in her best novels, their undeniable insight into the human heart and their pervasive spiritual light and grace, give them a permanent place in our literature. In these novels, one must acknowledge that Ellen Glasgow manifested with ironic lucidity the qualities which she most sought to express as a writer: "Humanity and distinction, reality and art" ⟨Letters, 1958, 240⟩.

> —Frederick P. W. McDowell, *Ellen Glasgow and the Ironic Art of Fiction* (1960), excerpted in *Twentieth-Century American Literature*, ed. Harold Bloom (New York: Chelsea House Publishers, 1986), 1618–19

RICHARD K. MEEKER

Two ⟨. . .⟩ stories focus on an abstract moral problem—what we now call mercy killing, or euthanasia. Two persons with no reason for living are put out of their misery with the assistance of their fellow men. Is this a crime? There are subtleties in each case which complicate the moral decision. In "A Point in Morals" an alienist is asked for a package of opium by a passenger on a train, who has botched his life and wants to commit suicide. The alienist, finally convinced by the young man's story that he has no reason for living and many reasons for dying, leaves the fatal package on the seat when he gets off the train.

Because she has effaced herself completely from the story by means of a dramatic framework, Miss Glasgow makes evaluation of the doctor's act very difficult. The story begins as a dialogue among the five characters around a dinner table on a ship: a journalist, a lawyer, an Englishman, a girl in black, and the doctor. The discussion turns to whether the saving of a human life might become positively immoral. At this point the alienist begins his story, into which he inserts the unhappy man's biography, making a story-within-a-story-within-a-story. The reaction of the audience gives us no clue as to an official interpretation. Each of the characters is ridiculed at some point. Perhaps Miss Glasgow had no stand here but merely wanted to embarrass all these sophisticated observers with a moral problem beyond the reach of science. If we assume that she disliked this alienist as much as those in the other stories, then the doctor must be labeled a monster. We should recall, however, that this is an early story, written before Miss Glasgow had rejected science in favor of philosophy.

An answer may be easier after we consider a parallel situation in the previously discussed "Jordan's End." Alan Jordan, incurably insane, dies mysteriously after an overdose of the opiate that the doctor-narrator has prescribed. The doctor knows that Jordan's wife must be to blame, but he cannot bring himself to question her. Jordan's death solves many problems and will cause none, so long as everyone remains silent. The doctor and Mrs. Jordan are described so sympathetically that one is tempted to condone this mercy killing. Taken together, the two stories reflect Ellen Glasgow's early realization that the most serious human problems lie beyond the reach of science. This theme, too, links her with Poe and with the agrarian branch of the Southern literary tradition.

—Richard K. Meeker, "Introduction" to *The Collected Stories of Ellen Glasgow* (Baton Rouge: Louisiana State University Press, 1963), 19–20

LOUIS AUCHINCLOSS

The advantages that ⟨Ellen Glasgow⟩ brought to her task and ambition were indeed considerable. Out of her wide reading she selected the mightiest and probably the best models to guide her in her recreation of the Virginia scene. She used Hardy as her master in rustic atmosphere, George Eliot as her guide in morality, Maupassant for plot, and Tolstoi for everything. She had the richest source material that any author could wish, consisting simply of a whole state and its whole history, a state, too, that occupies the center of our eastern geography and of our history and that not coincidentally has produced more Presidents than any other. And the social range among Miss Glasgow's characters is far greater than that of most twentieth-century novelists, suggesting that of such Victorians as Trollope, Dickens, Elizabeth Gaskell, and, again, George Eliot.

She not only considered every social group, but she covered wide varieties within each. In the top ranks of the old hierarchy she showed aristocrats in their glory, such as Major Lightfoot, and aristocrats in their decay, such as Beverly Brooke (in *The Ancient Law*). She showed them turning to the new world of business and dominating it, such as General Bolingbroke, and turning to the same world to be dominated and ultimately vulgarized by it, such as William Fitzroy. She showed aristocrats surviving into our own time, such as Judge Honeywell and Virginius Littlepage, having made the necessary adjustments and compromises, respectable, prosperous, but curiously unsatisfied, and she showed aristocrats like Asa Timberlake, who have been beaten into mediocrity and have failed in life without even the consolation and romance of a picturesque decay. Among the women of this world she created such magnificent anachronisms as Mrs. Blake, such noble, docile, and submissive wives as Virginia Pendleton, such apparently submissive but actually dominating mothers as Mrs. Gay, and such a reconstructed success in the North as Gabriella Carr.

In the middle ranks we find the rising businessman, Ben Starr, the risen politician, Gideon Vetch, the corrupt overseer, Bill Fletcher, the poor philosopher, John Fincastle, the "yeoman" farmers, Dorinda Oakley and Nathan Pedlar, the thriving miller, Abel Revercomb, and, among the lower orders, the "poor white" Burr family, the Starrs from whose midst Ben rises, the victims of the Richmond slums whom Stephen Culpeper is made to visit, the village prostitute and her idiot son in *Vein of Iron*, and, of course, all the Negro servants. Despite what has already been said about the limitations of Miss Glasgow's characterization of Negroes, the servants in her novels are absolutely alive and convincing. In at least one instance, that of the maid and companion to Dorinda in *Barren Ground*, the characterization is as successful as of any of the author's other women.

Miss Glasgow had the same range in scenery that she had in human beings, and she could make the transfer without difficulty from the grim mountains and valleys of *Vein of Iron* to the interminable fields of broomsedge in *Barren Ground* and thence to the comfortable mansions of Richmond and to the smaller gentility of Petersburg and Williamsburg. Highly individual in American letters is her ability to pass with equal authority from country to city, from rusticity to sophistication, from the tobacco field to the drawing room, from irony to tragedy.

Yet for all her gifts and advantages she does not stand in the very first rank of American novelists. She was unable sufficiently to pull the tapestry of fiction over her personal grievances and approbations. The latter are always peeping out at the oddest times and in the oddest places. It is strange that a novelist of such cultivation and such fecundity and one who was also such a student of her craft should not have seen her own glaring faults. How is it possible that the woman who could imagine the brilliant repartee of Edmonia Bredalbane, which annihilates every vestige of pretentiousness in Queenborough, should not have torn up the dreary sermon that is called *The Builders*? How could the author of prose which conveys all the beauty and mystery of the desolate countryside in *Barren Ground* have written the tired purple passages in earlier novels which describe the animal charm of handsome men and women in terms that might have been lifted from the very women's magazines that she so violently despised? How, moreover, could she have failed to see that her own bitterness on the subject of men was reflected in her heroines to the point of warping the whole picture of their lives? The mystery of Ellen Glasgow is not so much how she could be so good a writer as how she could on occasion be so bad a one.

—Louis Auchincloss, *Ellen Glasgow* (1964), excerpted in *Twentieth-Century American Literature*, ed. Harold Bloom (New York: Chelsea House Publishers, 1986), 1616–17

MONIQUE PARENT FRAZEE

Let us recapitulate the fate of woman in the hands of Ellen Glasgow. Virginia cherished her role of slave and perished in despair. Gabriella rebelled and flourished, but ultimately slipped back into matrimony. Dorinda fought and conquered, but in the process killed her heart and all chance of happiness.

More flexible, Ada submitted to her emotional demands and ultimately found happiness. Which of these four women reflects most the feministic spirit of the author?

Raised like Virginia and faithful to that line of conduct, free, independent, and prosperous like Dorinda, Ellen Glasgow appears as an intellectual counterpart of the latter. Proud and tortured, "the woman within" retraces the same emotional struggle; she seems to have paid the same price in her desperate search for serenity. Perhaps she found peace—happiness never. But in the light of recent progress in Women's Lib, we may venture this suggestion: today, Ellen Glasgow would *not* publish *The Woman Within*. She would not flaunt her victimization. She would not assume the part of melodramatic endurance. She probably would turn to more sensible and positive means of psychological liberation. Times have changed; new solutions, new outlets have opened that were taboo then. Divorce was still considered a catastrophe for women. We have mentioned lesbianism before: let us hasten to say that, in all of Ellen Glasgow's writings, there is not the slightest indication, even remotely subconscious, in situations, characters, imagery, commentary, or terminology, that a republic of women would be a desirable thing. There is not one of her heroines (practically all victims of men) who did not obscurely wish that males be greater so as to be more adequate mates. Contempt for men never bars women from wanting them. Then why aren't they greatest? Why are they all so uniformly mediocre, second-rate, if not scoundrels?

In that pale gallery of unimpressive men, very few are masculine enough to be rich and influential—and those who are, are tough, scornful, cruel, insensitive, like Cyrus Treadwell; most are economic failures; the lovers are weak, selfish, spineless, alcoholic. Shall we speak of a prejudice, a bias against manhood? Let us open the very first novel, *The Descendant;* the first men to appear who, we shall learn later, have good hearts and common sense, are thus depicted: a minister of the church is "small" (no comment), "ill-omened" (without any subsequent evidence of this), "chinless" (a sign of degeneracy), "ignorant" (Michael, the pig boy, will soon outwit his master's theology). The farmer who employs Michael is "a negative character" (although good and virtuous), "since to be wicked necessitates action." We may ponder on this qualifier, persistent throughout the novels as applied to men: *negative.* ⟨. . .⟩

Such is not the case, however, for a handful of older men who (with the brilliant exception of Gamaliel Honeywell, the sexagenarian "romantic comedian") escape the damning, as if age alone would confer on men dignity and psychological depth. Shall we ask Miss Glasgow whether this is due to wisdom acquired by experience or to the decline of virility? ⟨. . .⟩

⟨. . .⟩ Here we face a bias common to most women novelists, even more flagrant with feminists, this more or less conscious determination to belittle man in order to magnify woman. This is all the more regrettable as the purpose defeats itself and the demonstration comes to nought. The more mediocre the male partners, the less convincing becomes the superiority of women to dominate or defeat them.

We may wonder how these superwomen (Dorinda for example) would react to true men. But, like the radical feminists, Miss Glasgow tends to deny the existence of the species and views the superior man as a figment of female imagination and credulity. We shall not open the debate at this stage, but we may ask: what do women gain in conquering such poor terrain? We may tentatively conclude that hers is a shortcoming in creative art more than a flaw in feminism. Probably Ellen Glasgow thought obscurely with Anaïs Nin that, notwithstanding the defective quality of men, perhaps because of it, women should take the responsibility for their lives, and, by doing so, would "feel less helpless than when we put the blame on society or man. . . . To take destiny into our own hands is more inspiring than expecting others to direct our destiny for us" ⟨in L. R. Edwards, M. Heath, and L. Baskin, eds., *Woman: An Issue*, 1972, 25⟩.

—Monique Parent Frazee, "Ellen Glasgow as Feminist," in *Ellen Glasgow: Centennial Essays*, ed. M. Thomas Inge (1976), excerpted in *Twentieth-Century American Literature*, ed. Harold Bloom (New York: Chelsea House Publishers, 1986), 1620–21

LYNETTE CARPENTER

In 1916, with her father and closest sister recently dead, Ellen Glasgow returned to the family home in Richmond, Virginia, and entered into one of the most difficult periods of her life. She felt keenly the loss of her family, and the war played upon her imagination. Her physical and mental health worsened; she became even more painfully self-conscious about her deafness. She felt herself haunted by the ghosts of dead loved ones, as she described it later in *The Woman Within*: "Ghosts were my only companions. I was shut in, alone, with the past." She added, "This is not rhetoric. This is what I thought or felt or imagined, while I stood there alone, in that empty house" (237).

Yet the house was not always empty. Anne Virginia Bennett, who had nursed Glasgow's father and sister, stayed on in the house as Glasgow's private secretary. A frequent visitor was Henry Anderson, Glasgow's close friend and probable fiance. Anderson's influence on the Glasgow novels from this period, *The Builders* (1919) and *One Man in His Time* (1922), has been noted by critics and biographers, and chronicled by Anderson himself in his correspondence with the author. Rarely discussed are the contemporaneous ghost stories, written, according to Miss Bennett, at her own instigation. The differences between Glasgow's novels and her ghost stories suggest something of the

dynamics of her household at the time. More importantly, however, they portray Glasgow's exploration of the alternatives of conventional heterosexual
romance and female community. At a time when she was contemplating marriage, Glasgow wrote some of her most radical critiques of marriage in both
the novels and the ghost stories, but only the ghost stories envision the possible substitution of relationships between women for the conventional resolution of happy marriage. ⟨. . .⟩

     The ghost stories value sympathy, compassion, and sensitivity, and por-
tray these qualities as a primary source of bonds between women. These are
qualities that men neither possess, nor understand, nor value, the stories imply.
Glasgow's familiarity with a female tradition in the ghost story is suggested by
her personal library holdings at the time of her death: in addition to ⟨Emily⟩
Bronte's *Wuthering Heights* and ⟨Ann⟩ Radcliffe's *The Mysteries of Udolpho*, she
owned two of Cynthia Asquith's ghost story collections, Edith Wharton's *Tales
of Men and Ghosts* (1918) and *Ghosts* (1937), Katherine Fullerton Gerould's *Vain
Oblations* (1914), Isak Dinesen's *Seven Gothic Tales* (1934), Virginia Woolf's *A
Haunted House and Other Stories* (1944), and miscellaneous collections by Mary
Wilkins Freeman, Elizabeth Bowen, Majorie Bowen, and Vernon Lee. Perhaps
most significant among these literary influences was Edith Wharton, whose
1904 story, "The Lady's Maid's Bell," featured a compassionate lady's maid who
struggled first to understand and then to help her victimized mistress ⟨. . .⟩; if
Anne Virginia Bennett was the actual prototype for Glasgow's heroines,
Wharton's Hartley was a likely literary model.
     —Lynette Carpenter, "Visions of Female Community in Ellen Glasgow's Ghost Stories," in
     Haunting the House of Fiction: Feminist Perspectives on Ghost Stories by American Women, ed. Lynette
     Carpenter and Wendy K. Kolmar (Knoxville: University of Tennessee Press, 1991), 118, 120

JOAN SCHULZ

⟨The⟩ oppressive nature of the family for Southern women rests on its denial
to them of a separate and self-determined existence and on its demand that
they live out the dictates of the family's past. Southern women in particular are
expected to adulate and emulate the family's past as it is conveyed to them in
legends, stories, and clichés, despite their awareness of its destructive potential for their lives. As women, they are condemned to hearing, accepting, and
living by the self-destructive myths of the nature and role of women as passive, submissive, obedient, compliant, pious, and so on. They have enforced
on them a role that is limited in action and activities, restrictive in behavior
and conduct—that is, they must be beautiful, charming ornaments; must support the double standard of sexual conduct; must heed the imperatives of self-
abnegation and duty to their families; and must limit their sphere of action to

the home and family. Lastly, they are taught that, unlike a man's, a woman's source of happiness is singular and total, and is to be found only in marriage and family. In all this, they are not unlike other women in the United States, except that the demands and expectations are more exaggerated in the South because it is such an extravagantly patriarchal society. ⟨. . .⟩

Milly Burden, of Ellen Glasgow's *They Stooped to Folly* (1929), is ⟨one⟩ in the continually lengthening list of young women who ⟨like Miranda in Katherine Anne Porter's *Old Mortality*⟩ shut their ears to the voices from the family and community past, insisting on the right to selfhood involved in making their own discoveries about themselves and their world. Milly resists not only her own immediate family in the form of her mother but also the empty, restrictive, "conventional" behavior demanded of women in that society. Though Milly is not the central character in the novel, Glasgow makes her an important figure in several ways, one aspect of which is her implicit relation to two similarly "fallen women" from earlier generations. Of the three women who "stooped to folly," only Milly seems to yearn for—or even to imagine—"something" beyond living in the attic or beyond amusement, trifling, sweets, or volunteer work. For Milly (as for those other women), it is the family that serves as the repository and transmitter of those conventions against which Milly is rebelling, and it is the family, therefore, that remains the focal point of her orphaning.

Within this framework, then, both the language of Milly's rebellion and its motivation to self-determination seen in her ignoring the limiting, oppressive voices of the past and what are called in this novel, its "ideals," are strikingly similar to Miranda's in her interior reflections, as is her breaking the primary law for young women, obedience. Milly's conversation with Virginius Littlepage, a super-conservative holdover from Victorian America, who tries to play the role of surrogate father to a fatherless young woman, exemplifies the connection between the two young women. Virginius tells her:

> "The trouble is that you have learned nothing from the past, nothing
> from the experience of other women. . . . You have set out to demol-
> ish conventions before you have tested them."
>
> Her eyes had mocked him. "But you have tested them haven't you?
> And where have they led you? Could anything that we do or think
> end in a greater calamity? No, we'll have to learn the truth for our-
> selves. Nothing that the older generation can tell us will do any
> good. We refuse to accept your theories because we saw them all
> break to pieces. The truth is we are determined to think for ourselves
> and to make our own sort of ideals. Even if everything you say to me
> is true, I shouldn't consent to take my experience from you second-
> hand. I want to find out myself. I want the freedom to live my life as I
> please. I want to choose the things I believe in. . . ." (58)

Near the end of *Old Mortality*, Miranda reflects on her past and future in similar language and tone:

> Miranda walked along beside her father, feeling homeless, but not sorry for it. He had not forgiven her, she knew that. When would he? She could not guess, but she felt it would come of itself. . . . Surely old people cannot hold their grudges forever because the young want to live, too, she thought, in her arrogance, her pride. I will make my own mistakes, not yours; I cannot depend upon you beyond a certain point, why depend at all? . . . She resented, slowly and deeply and in profound silence, the presence of these aliens [i.e., her father and cousin Eva] who lectured and admonished her, who loved her with bitterness and denied her the right to look at the world with her own eyes, who demanded that she accept their version of life and yet could not tell her the truth, not in the smallest thing. "I hate them both," her most inner and secret mind said plainly, "*I will be free of them, I shall not even remember them.*" (178–79)

And then comes Porter's famous final, ironic sentence: "At least, I can know the truth about what happens to me, she assured herself silently, making a promise to herself, in her hopefulness, her ignorance" (182). While Porter questions Miranda's ability simply to walk out on the past, she does nothing to suggest that that young woman won't bravely attempt to be her own person.

Psychologists define the act of separating one's ego from one's family as an identity-forming developmental task of adolescence and recognize that girls often do not complete the separation and hence remain "daughters" forever. Miranda and Milly, both young women, demonstrate that they are determined to make this separation, but it is noteworthy that in both cases, the language, feelings, and commitment to estrangement, even deracination, go well beyond anything required of young men who make that separation almost imperceptibly and whose reintegration is far simpler in most cases.

—Joan Schulz, "Orphaning as Resistance," in *The Female Tradition in Southern Literature*, ed. Carol S. Manning (Urbana, IL: University of Illinois Press, 1993), 92–95

DOROTHY M. SCURA

The Battle-Ground was Glasgow's fourth novel, written when she was only twenty-six years old. Born in Richmond eight years after the close of the Civil War, she grew up hearing about the wartime period from members of her family and from her governess, Miss Virginia Rawlings. In *The Woman Within*, her autobiography, she recounts the story of the burning by General Hunter of "Mount Joy," her great-aunt's ancestral home in the Valley of Virginia. Given an hour to remove belongings, Glasgow's aunt chose to save family portraits

⟨38⟩. This home provided the name of the protagonist, Dan Montjoy, in *The Battle-Ground*, and Dan's grandparents saved only a portrait of the beauty of the family, Aunt Emmeline, when their home was burned by Union troops. Thus, Glasgow adapted family experiences in her fiction about the war.

And not only did she include incidents from actual participants, she also read diaries and letters, and she kept with her during the writing of the novel copies of three newspapers printed between 1860 and 1865—the *Richmond Enquirer*, the *Richmond Examiner*, and the *New York Herald*. Too, she visited the Valley of Virginia, going over all of the scenes of the novel. In her research she was, as she explains, "collecting impressions rather than facts." She designed her novel to be the "chronicle of two neighbouring families," the Amblers, including the heroine Betty Ambler, and the Lightfoots, grandparents of the hero Dandridge Montjoy ⟨*A Certain Measure*, 1943, 21, 19⟩.

Glasgow explained in *A Certain Measure* that she consciously rejected the sentimental costume romances that purported to tell the story of the 1860s and considered herself from the beginning of her career as a writer in "solitary revolt against the formal, the false, the affected, the sentimental, and the pretentious in Southern writing" (*CM*, 8). She noted, too, however, that "one cannot approach the Confederacy without touching the very heart of romantic tradition" (*CM*, 24). She attempted in *The Battle-Ground*

> to portray the last stand in Virginia of the aristocratic tradition . . . [a culture which] was shallow-rooted at best, since, for all its charm and its good will, the way of living depended, not upon its own creative strength, but upon the enforced servitude of an alien race. (*CM*, 13)

And so Glasgow saw the Confederacy as "the expiring gesture of chivalry" (*CM*, 25). In explaining her intentions in the novel, many years after publication of that work, Glasgow claimed that she grounded her novel on fact and rejected the accepted genre in the South for dealing with the War, the sentimental romance. She also confessed—in what may seem a contradiction—that in dealing with the Confederacy she was necessarily dealing with romance. ⟨. . .⟩

The novel is briefly set in Richmond in the spring and early summer of 1862. Two chapters, only twenty pages out of 512, allow Glasgow to characterize the capital of the Confederacy and to advance her plot. She brings to Richmond several characters—principally Virginia Ambler Morson, her husband Jack, and Dan Montjoy. One chapter focuses on Virginia and depicts her death along with her unborn child's death. The second chapter allows Dan Montjoy to come to terms with the memory of his long-estranged father.

In the chapter entitled "The Altar of the War God," Virginia and her child are the human sacrifices taken on the hellish "altar" of the capital of the

Confederacy. Because Virginia is the very image of her mother, and both women are the embodiment of the beautiful, gentle lady of the aristocracy, Virginia's death suggests that this figure is too fragile mentally and physically to survive the demands of the war. Glasgow's irony is evident in her treatment of the suffering and death of the innocent Virginia. The narrator explains about Virginia that "[t]here was in her heart an unquestioning, childlike trust in the God of battles—sooner or later he would declare for the Confederacy and until then—well, there was always General Lee to stand between" (*BG*, 362). Virginia's naive faith in the God of battles and in General Lee is misplaced; neither can save her from destruction on the very altar of the War God.

Also ironic is Glasgow's use of the magnolia, the beautiful, white, sweet-smelling flower that is so connected to southern romances that they are often called "moonlight and magnolia" novels. A high magnolia tree stands next to the piazza at the back of Virginia's house, and she places a rustic bench and a flower garden under this tree. This setting is designed to replicate in a small way her home Uplands in the Valley of Virginia and contrasts with the back garden which now features vegetables rather than flowers and, especially, with the view from her front window which includes the busy passing parade that is the overcrowded city of Richmond. But the scent of the magnolia becomes connected with the heat, clamor, and dust of the city, and Virginia sickens of the smell. She is pleased when a rain storm sends the petals to the ground, but new blossoms open, and she connects their perfume with the sound of cannons. On the night of her death when her mind wanders in a delirium, "the odour of the magnolia filled her nostrils," reminding her of "the scorching dust" and "the noise that would not stop" (*BG*, 367). Thus, the scent of the magnolia is intermingled with the sound and heat of war as Glasgow makes it a symbol not of romance, but of death.

> —Dorothy M. Scura, "Ellen Glasgow's *The Battle-Ground*: Civil War Richmond in Fiction and
> History," in *Rewriting the South: History and Fiction*, ed. Lothar Honnighausen and Valeria
> Gennaro Lerda (Tubingen: Francke Verlag, 1993), 186–89

CATHERINE RAINWATER

In several letters in her autobiography, *The Woman Within* (1954), Ellen Glasgow mentions reading the works of ⟨Edgar Allan⟩ Poe and ⟨H. G.⟩ Wells. In contemplating these two authors' works, she joined what has now become a wide network of writers whose art bears complex intertextual connections centering around a mutual literary debt to Poe and, frequently, also to one another. Glasgow admits to feeling a "curious . . . kinship with Poe," and although she calls Wells's novels "dull" (*WW* 203), she owned at least five of them along with an early edition of *The Outline of History* (1920). Apparently, she found the *Outline* intriguing enough to consult in more than one of its many versions. Glasgow's well-known fascination with Darwin might partly account for her interest in Wells's ideas about history, for *Outline* is firmly rooted in Darwinian evolutionary theory. This same interest in Darwinian concepts and their social and philosophical applications might also partially explain her homage to Poe in several short stories published between 1916 and 1923 and collected as *The Shadowy Third and Other Stories* (1923). Although Poe is a pre-Darwinian writer, his works anticipate important, if not biologically based, questions about human evolution and devolution, and about the existence of primitive, irrational depths beneath the surface of civilized society.

Glasgow wrote these Gothic stories suggesting Poe's and Wells's influence during the year immediately surrounding the end of the first World War—a time when Wells claims that "everyone" was in some way or another "outlining" history in response to global conditions. The tales attest to her efforts to account for the shape of things past and things to come, efforts more typically registered throughout her career in numerous realistic novels. Although Glasgow suffered extreme emotional ups and down throughout her life, several critics and Glasgow herself have observed that the years between 1910 and 1925 marked a critical period of hesitation, reassessment, and redirection of her artistic energies. She wrote short stories at this time, argues Richard K. Meeker, because she had temporarily lost a sense of a "comprehensive view of life . . . Her writings . . . contain increasing references to a world gone mad, uncivilized barbarians, and ugly deviations from human decency . . . It became increasingly hard for her to write on a large scale, to trace the causes and effects that had so fascinated her" in her earlier works. 〈"Introduction," *The Collected Stories of Ellen Glasgow*, 1963, 6〉.

Indeed, Glasgow's preface to *Barren Ground* (1925) reports a period of "tragedy" and "defeat" from which she claims to have emerged during the composition of this novel. Dismissing most of her previous work as "thin" and "two-dimensional," Glasgow declares that with *Barren Ground* she has arrived at a "turning point" in her life, and that she can now write as she had always intended to write—"of the South, not sentimentally, as a conquered province, but dispassionately, as a part of the larger world"; and "of human nature" rather than "Southern characteristics." She is sure that "different and better work is ahead." Glasgow's sense of the "large scale" and her "comprehensive view of life" had returned along with renewed confidence in "trac[ing] . . . causes and effects" in history.

Despite this renewed confidence, Glasgow never develops any systematic outline of history (indeed, she seems finally to agree with Wells that progress is the tentative result of "Will feeling about"); however, her ghost stories that address history reveal the characteristically dialectical pattern of her thought as she struggled to attain a sense of a universal pattern grounded upon some reliable authority. Between 1916 and 1923, when most of the pieces in *The Shadowy Third and Other Stories* were written and published, the ideas of Poe and Wells (in *The Outline of History*, at least) apparently served Glasgow as thesis and antithesis in the dialectical development of her own view of historical progress. All of the stories imply Glasgow's internalization of a Poe-esque vision coalescent with her own sense of a mad "world . . . [of] uncivilized barbarians, and ugly deviations from human decency," while the 1923 stories suggest the substantial role that Wells's *Outline* might have played in her development of a "comprehensive view" of it all. Indeed, Poe and Wells might be seen as "opposing angels" that "warred somewhere in the depths of [her] being" for control of Glasgow's sense of historical design. ⟨. . .⟩

In "The Shadowy Third" and "Dare's Gift," Glasgow implies that the past is a trap in which we may be caught without comprehension or means of escape. Though she innately resembles both Poe and Wells in her battle with alternating idealism and pessimism, the early stories in Glasgow's collection suggest her particular sensitivity to Poe's dystopian fears (a frame of mind in which, likewise, Wells sometimes found himself.) The stories dated 1923, however, suggest a guardedly optimistic expansion of her thought within the Wellsian frame of reference reflected in *The Outline of History*. These later stories suggest that limited transcendence of ostensibly closed personal spheres—the self, the South—is possible; Glasgow was perhaps affected by Wells's hope for a world synthesis based on tentative notions of will and progress. Indeed, in two of her 1923 stories, the "webs" and "circles" of the early works are replaced with the Wellsian trope of the "spiral" (an image that depicts the overarching pattern of historical evolution that Wells describes in the *Outline*) to represent this idea of tentative progress. ⟨. . .⟩

Glasgow's characters in her short stories do not transcend human nature, but the stories that suggest Glasgow's Wellsian frame of mind in the 1920's emphasize the possibility of a better future at the end of the expanding "spiral" of human evolution, whereas her earlier, Poe-inspired stories depict people ensnared in the "webs" of their own circumscribed personal interests and histories. Following the example of both Poe and Wells in their different ways, Glasgow apparently looked forward to the loss of the burden of self, including that portion of the burden comprised of delimiting history.

—Catherine Rainwater, "Ellen Glasgow's Outline of History in *The Shadowy Third and Other Stories*," in *The Critical Response to H.G. Wells*, ed. William J. Scheick (Westport, CT: Greenwood Press, 1995), 125–26, 131, 135–36

BIBLIOGRAPHY

The Descendant. 1897.
Phases of an Inferior Planet. 1898.
The Voice of the People. 1900.
The Freeman and Other Poems. 1902.
The Battle-Ground. 1902.
The Deliverance. 1904.
The Wheel of Life. 1906.
The Ancient Law. 1908.
The Romance of a Plain Man. 1909.
The Miller of Old Church. 1911.
Virginia. 1913.
Life and Gabriella. 1916.
The Builders. 1919.
One Man in His Time. 1922.
The Shadowy Third and Other Stories. 1923.
Barren Ground. 1925.
The Romantic Comedians. 1926.
They Stooped to Folly. 1929.
The Sheltered Life. 1932.
Vein of Iron. 1935.
In This Our Life. 1941.
A Certain Measure: An Interpretation of Prose Fiction. 1943.
The Woman Within. 1954.
Letters of Ellen Glasgow. 1958.
Ellen Glasgow's Letters to Paul Revere Reynolds. 1961.
Literary Realism or Nominalism. 1962.
The Collected Stories of Ellen Glasgow. 1963.
Ellen Glasgow's Letters to the Saxtons. 1963.
Beyond Defeat. 1966.

CAROLINE GORDON

1895-1981

CAROLINE GORDON was born on October 6, 1895, on a tobacco farm in Todd County, Kentucky. Her early education at a boys' school run by her father led to a lifelong interest in classical literature. After taking a bachelor's degree at Bethany College, West Virginia, in 1916, she taught at a high school and in 1920 became a journalist. In 1924, she met the poet Allen Tate, whom she married later that year. After moving to New York City, she became secretary to Ford Madox Ford, who encouraged and criticized her writing. In 1928, Tate won a Guggenheim Fellowship, and the couple traveled to Paris, where they met Gertrude Stein, the Fitzgeralds, and Ernest Hemingway. Returning to America in 1930, Gordon and Tate settled on Benfolly Farm in Tennessee, where Gordon completed her first novel, *Penhally*, in 1931. She would be influenced in her work by Gustave Flaubert and Henry James and by the symbolic naturalism of Dante, Carl Jung, James Joyce, and T. S. Eliot.

After winning a Guggenheim Fellowship in 1932, Gordon returned to France with her husband and worked on a second novel, *Aleck Maury, Sportsman*, which appeared in 1934. By this time the couple was back at Benfolly and active in the Agrarian movement. Two further novels date from this period, *None Shall Look Back* and *The Garden of Adonis*, as well as the short story "The Brilliant Leaves." In 1938, Gordon was writer-in-residence at Greensboro College in North Carolina, and she then moved to Princeton when her husband took a teaching position there. In 1944, she published *The Women on the Porch*, and the next year a collection of stories, *The Forest of the South*, was published, bringing together the bulk of the stories Gordon had written since 1929. Many of these later appeared, with "The Petrified Woman" (1947), "The Presence" (1948), "Emmanuele! Emmanuele!" (1954), and "One Against Thebes" (1961), in *Old Red and Other Stories* (1963).

Gordon converted to Roman Catholicism in 1947, and her religion became an important influence on her subsequent work. While her earlier writing had explored the struggle to achieve a private dignity, her novels *The Strange Children* (1951) and *The Malefactors* (1956) and her story "Emmanuele! Emmanuele!" (1954) developed the idea of giving oneself to the Church to achieve fulfillment. From this time until her death, Gordon continued to seek a way in which to combine Christian and classical elements.

Her nonfiction works include *How to Read a Novel* (1957) and *A Good Soldier: A Key to the Novels of Ford Madox Ford* (1963). Her final novel, *The Glory of Hera*, was published in 1972, and *The Collected Stories of Caroline Gordon* appeared posthumously in 1981. Gordon gave generous and untiring help to younger writers later in her career. She died on April 11, 1981, in San Cristobal de las Casas, Chiapas, Mexico.

CRITICAL EXTRACTS

FORD MADOX FORD

. . . ⟨W⟩hen I say that *Penhally* is the best American novel that I know I need not be taken as appraising. I must not be taken as saying that *Penhally* is a better novel than *The Spoils of Poynton*, or a better piece of work than *The Red Badge of Courage* or even than *The House of the Seven Gables*. It curiously unites attributes of all those works.

. . . As befits the work of a woman who has served a long apprenticeship to her art *Penhally*, though dealing with the tragedy of a race and the disappearance of a deeply in-bitten civilization, is a work of great composure and tranquility. Great art is never harrowing; its emotions are large in outline, overwhelming, gradual. It is these qualities in Mrs. Tate's work that makes me reserve for her book the epithet "novel". The novel is a thing of form and of gradual but inevitable growth into that form. It is in short a classical phenomenon, a piece of slow moulding, like the Winged Victory.

Penhally is the triumphant tragedy of a house and the vindication of a mode of life. It is an achievement at once of erudition and of sombre and smouldering passion. It is distinguished by the afterglow of the Greek-Roman-Anglo-Saxon classicism that marked the old South off from all other lands.

> He suddenly saw his father, a tall, stooped man in a suit of gray
> homespun, standing book in hand under the poplar tree. . . . "*Nunc te,*
> *Bacche, canam,*" he said, smiling, and bending took the glass from the
> boy's hand.

There is the epitome of all the civilization of the old South in those four lines on the fourth page of Mrs. Tate's book. And we may find there the reason why, until right up to the present generation, the South has hardly produced any works of art . . . and why its most prominent writers of the imagination are women. The classics have this deterrent effect on their postulants: their perfectionism, when partaken of in an atmosphere of material suavity, makes all further intellectual effort seem not only useless but contemptible. So you had the Oxford don of the English eighteenth century, with his port, his shining naperies, his silver candlesticks by whose light he read Tully, Flaccus and the *Persephone Rapta*. So you had Nicholas Llewellyn's father who in the first years of the nineteenth century emigrated from overcrowded Virginia to a then new South, in that wilderness built Penhally, and there, after that effort, sat under his poplar tree, read Virgil, drank juleps that were brought to him at intervals by a little Negro, and put upon his estate the entail that was eventually to bring Penhally to humiliation. For, in the end it became a Northern millionaires' country club.

Penhally is thus the epic of a house and its fugitive generations of inhabitants. It is an epic, not what it is fashionable to call a saga, since the doom is pronounced in the first few words. It is a novel, not a book of fiction nor a piece of "literature of escape", because it is so constructed that every word of it leads on to the appointed end. Its themes are woven and interwoven, the story progresses forward in action and back in memory so that the sort of shimmer that attaches to life attaches also to the life of the book. Just as you may be a little vague as to the men and women who attended on your youth so you may be a little vague about the innumerable names of Llewellyns of Penhally, of Rosemead or of Virginia. But the figures themselves are alive, passionate, sombre, intolerant, foolish or weak.

. . . *Penhally* differs from other historical works which are written from the outside and are at best *tours de force*—more or less cold re-constitutions. It unites itself to the living school of autobiographic writers in that it is a piece of autobiography. Mrs. Tate has from her earliest days so lived herself into the past of her race and region that her whole being is compact of the passions, the follies, the exaggerations, the classicisms, the excesses, the gallantries and the leadings of forlorn hopes that brought the Old South to its end. She does not have to document herself in order to evoke Morgan's cavalry raids or conditions of life amongst the slaves in the behollyhocked Quarters. She has so lived in the past that it is from her own experience that she distils these things.

So *Penhally* is a chronicle of reality.

—Ford Madox Ford, "A Stage in American Literature," *Bookman* (December 1931), excerpted in *Twentieth-Century American Fiction*, ed. Harold Bloom (New York: Chelsea House Publishers, 1986), 1646–47

ROBERT PENN WARREN

⟨Caroline Gordon's new novel, *Aleck Maury, Sportsman*⟩ is a simple chronicle, with no plot in the ordinary meaning of the term. But even for a reader who is no sportsman the author has managed to convey an almost unflagging excitement and a sense of participation in that delight by which Aleck Maury lives. It is difficult to account for the success of the book on this score; it can only be remarked that the author is capable of presenting a natural and social background without effort or over-emphasis, of ordering a narrative with extraordinary skill, and of maintaining suspense concerning an apparently trivial subject. The focus is rarely wrong, and the action slackens only once, in the section dealing with the Ozarks. But the real force of the novel derives from something other than the overt objective: there is the sense of a full and intense emotional life, which is never insisted upon, rarely stated, but implied, somehow, on almost every page. The birth of the first child, the drowning of the son, and the death of the wife are scenes unsurpassed in contemporary fiction for discipline of execution or fullness of effect. . . .

The story . . . is in the form of an autobiography. It is one measure of Caroline Gordon's success that her dramatic sense is able to sustain a long first-person narrative for such different characters as the pioneer woman in "The Captive," the sportsman in *Aleck Maury*, or the 'I' of "Tom Rivers." In each of these instances the style is different and appropriate, descending to the conventional only once, in "Tom Rivers," and then but momentarily. In each case the author has set herself a precise stylistic problem based on a conception of character. She has not attempted to develop a trademark or a manner; her writing is peculiarly selfless, and therein lies its cunning and its distinction. The 'I' in much work by Hemingway is always essentially the same person, whether he is writing about the war in Italy, drinking in Paris, or bullfighting in Spain; that is, he always assigns himself the same post of observation. That post of observation is selected with a high sense of strategy, and I do not mean to underrate Hemingway's very considerable literary gifts. But the style, on occasion, can become personal in a bad sense, that is, mannered and trademarked: it is the trademark only, a sort of self-parody, that he has been selling to the magazine *Esquire* and that appears in the weaker pieces of *Winner Take Nothing*. The principle by which Caroline Gordon has composed her fiction seems, theoretically at least, to be sounder, for it should define the problem of the discipline of composition on a more objective basis, a basis that should provide in future productions a great variety of effect. But for the present it can be said that the problem has been satisfactorily solved for *Aleck Maury*: the success of the book is that it is not Caroline Gordon's novel, but, after all, the autobiography of Aleck Maury.

—Robert Penn Warren, "The Fiction of Caroline Gordon," *Southwest Review* (Winter 1935), excerpted in *Twentieth-Century American Fiction*, ed. Harold Bloom (New York: Chelsea House Publishers, 1986), 1647

KATHERINE ANNE PORTER

⟨One⟩ form of opportunism is sometimes at present called "interpreting history correctly"—that is, having the foresight to get on the bandwagon and make the most of the parade. With such shabbiness Miss Gordon has nothing to do. Her ⟨None Shall Look Back⟩ is a legend in praise of heroes, of those who fought well and lost their battle, and their lives. . . .

Miss Gordon's heart is fixed on the memory of those men who died in a single, superbly fought lost cause, in nothing diminished for being lost, and this devotion has focused her feelings and imagination to a point of fire. She states clearly in every line of her story her mystical faith that what a man lives by, he must if the time comes, die for; to live beyond or to acknowledge defeat is to die twice, and shamefully. The motive of this faith is the pride of Lucifer and Miss Gordon makes no pretense, either for herself or for her characters, to the maudlin virtue of humility in questions of principle.

All-seeing as an ancient chronicler, she has created a panorama of a society engaged in battle for its life. The author moves about, a disembodied spectator timing her presence expertly, over her familiar territory, Kentucky, Georgia, Tennessee, Mississippi. Time, 1860 to 1864, dates which are, after 1776, the most portentous in the history of this country. Having chosen to observe from all points of view, rather than to stand on a knoll above the battle and watch a set procession of events through a field glass, she makes her scenes move rapidly from Federal lines to Confederate, from hospitals to prisons, to the plantations; the effect could easily have become diffuse without firm handling, and the central inalterable sympathies of the chronicler herself. She might have done the neat conventional thing, and told her story through the adventures of her unlucky young pair of lovers, Lucy Churchill and her cousin, Rives Allard. But they take their proper places in the midst of a tragedy of which their own tragedy is only a part. . . .

The Allard family is a center, or rather, a point of departure and return; in the beginning they are clearly seen, alive, each one a human being with his individual destiny, which gradually is merged with the destiny of his time and place. Their ends are symbolically exact: the old man lapses into the escape of imbecility, the old mother into perpetual blind grief, Rives into death in battle, Jim into moral dry rot, Lucy into numbness. . . .

This seems to me in a great many ways a better book than *Penhally* or *Aleck Maury, Sportsman*, Miss Gordon's other two novels. The good firm style, at once homely, rhythmical and distinguished, is in all three of them, but at its best, so far, in *None Shall Look Back*. It is true I know her story by heart, but I have never heard it told better. The effect is of brilliant, instant life; there is a clear daylight over a landscape I need not close my eyes to see, peopled with figures I know well. I have always known the end, as I know the end of so many tales of love, and heroism, and death. In this retelling, it all happened only yesterday. Those men on the field are not buried yet, those women have just put on their mourning.

—Katherine Anne Porter, "Dulce et Decorum Est," *New Republic* (31 March 1937), excerpted in *Twentieth-Century American Fiction*, ed. Harold Bloom (New York: Chelsea House Publishers, 1986), 1647–48

JAMES I. ROCKS

A reading of Miss Gordon's fiction must take into account the masterful way in which she utilizes centers of vision, particularly in works like "To Thy Chamber Window, Sweet" and *The Strange Children*. Her manipulation is as conscious and meaningful as in ⟨Henry⟩ James's best work, from which she obviously learned much, and offers excellent examples for students of the novel who want to examine the practical illustration of a working esthetic. In Miss Gordon's fiction itself there is little development to be noted in the method of handling narrative point of view. Her first story, "Summer Dust" (1929), and her first novel, *Penhally* (1931), are evidence that she mastered the technique well before marketing her fiction. The products of an apprenticeship have never appeared (if there are any). Her fiction shows that she learned her methods before beginning to publish, rather than seeking modes in the course of her writing career.

In matters of style a development, particularly in the novels, can be indicated. Style is, of course, an adjunct to point of view, because the choice of narrator determines the quality of the narration, a fact of which Miss Gordon has been completely aware, since she is careful to distinguish between levels of diction befitting the social backgrounds of her reflector characters. If a character speaks idiomatically or ungrammatically, as in "The Captive," the narration retains these qualities. Unlike her mentor James she chooses intelligences from different classes of society, choices which would reflect her opinion that the subtlety of an observer does not depend upon his belonging to the Brahmin or moneyed class, as it often does in the case of James.

The balance and cadence of Miss Gordon's style, with its emphasis on the right word and the active detail, are more reminiscent of, say, Willa Cather (not to mention Southern female writers like Katherine Anne Porter or Eudora Welty) than of ⟨William⟩ Faulkner or ⟨Thomas⟩ Wolfe. Some of Miss Gordon's characters fall into the oral tradition of anecdote tellers, but they are not orators, and even those ante-bellum gentlemen in her fiction who might be politically inclined tone down their speeches—at least as Miss Gordon styles them. More than the convolutions and ambiguities of James, ⟨Ford Madox⟩ Ford, or even ⟨Joseph⟩ Conrad, the concrete exactitude of ⟨Gustave⟩ Flaubert influenced Miss Gordon, as did the rigorous classicism of Latin and Greek authors in whom she read extensively.

Although Miss Gordon's usual style is one of clarity and precision, utilizing a simple vocabulary and short sentences, in divulging the deep recesses of her characters' minds, she occasionally writes with a style that is more fluid, rich, and varied. *The Women on the Porch* is a distinguished example of her more complex style, which is noticeable in the last three novels. In the short stories written from the mid-'forties on there is diversity, likewise, although it is rather difficult to point to any particular story which marks the beginning of a new technique or style. "Old Red," for example, which appeared quite early in her career, is as mature in form and style as anything she wrote later. The majority of her stories were written from 1929 to 1945, when the collection *The Forest of the South* was published, bringing together most of those early stories. Some of the relatively few new stories written after 1945, including "The Petrified Woman" (1947), "The Presence" (1948), "Emmanuele! Emmanuele!" (1954), and "One against Thebes" (1961), were added to numerous notable early ones for the latest collection, *Old Red and Other Stories* (1963).

In matters of style, one must look, then, at the novels (and at the stories published from her novel in progress) to find any apparent development. Miss Gordon's fiction does take on a new dimension in the mid-'thirties with *The Garden of Adonis* (1937) and "The Brilliant Leaves." Thereafter the novels are built on some mythic superstructure derived from the classics, folklore, or religion. Symbolism and archetypal patterns, the use of which she considers essential if a work of art is to endure, occur more frequently; in a story like "The Brilliant Leaves" symbolic naturalism provides a key to meaning.

Despite the mythic character of her later work she certainly does not write in the vein of Wolfe, Faulkner, or William Styron, all of whose fiction draws attention to itself through its style. Miss Gordon criticizes Faulkner for succumbing to his own rhetoric. But the same can be said of her, for her carefully wrought style is as manneristic in its own way as is Faulkner's. If we know the actual world through style, as Allen Tate says in "The Hovering Fly," if materials are defined by form, then it can be said that Miss Gordon's careful structure and style illustrate not simply her regard for precision, clarity, and order but also her fundamental view—a view appropriated in large part from Jacques Maritain—that the artist must recognize some coherent pattern out of the shifting planes of a seemingly disjointed reality.

If Miss Gordon's fiction does not illustrate a search for new narrative techniques with which to inform her materials, it does present a quest for meaning and value. She wrote her early novels and stories in order to dramatize—indirectly, to advance—the agrarian worldview, which was at that very moment receiving a certain notoriety through the social criticism of Tate and others. Her fiction was to some degree a defense of traditions on the wane, with the aim of "educating" her audience—as Ford would have the author do—to understand a culture which existed, for non-Southerners at least, only as an exotic world of fantasy. She recreated moments in history, like the Civil War, which figures directly or indirectly as the crisis in all of her fiction, and devised characters, like the Allard family—all of which would serve as components in her dramatized dialogue on the Southern ethic. But as her career progressed Miss Gordon became uneasy in her myth of conservative agrarianism and began to question it openly in later novels, such as *The Garden of Adonis* and *The Women on the Porch*, in an effort to find a more permanent, absolute system of truth. This quest—if not the idea itself of quest—is the larger theme of her fiction.

—James I. Rocks, "The Mind and Art of Caroline Gordon," *Mississippi Quarterly* (Winter 1967), excerpted in *Twentieth-Century American Fiction*, ed. Harold Bloom (New York: Chelsea House Publishers, 1986), 1651–52

ASHLEY BROWN

The five novels which culminate in *Green Centuries* have much in common. With the exception of *Aleck Maury, Sportsman*, they exhibit a consistent movement towards tragedy, although only *None Shall Look Back* fulfills the movement. And the novels are conceived in a kind of grand design against the enveloping action of history. With these five books behind her, Miss Gordon had the choice of "filling out" her subject, perhaps using some of the characters she had already invented, or else of extending it by moving to another post of observation. Her second group of novels—*The Women on the Porch* (1944), *The Strange Children* (1951), and *The Malefactors* (1956)—does both. These books are set against the history of the South, like their predecessors, but only indirectly. And their mode is finally Christian comedy. About the time that she published *The Women on the Porch* Miss Gordon was beginning to doubt whether a "regional" literature in the South would continue much longer; it was her opinion that the renaissance in letters was coming to its end. Probably with some such feeling about her subject she has steadily widened its reference. Two of the stories of this period, for example, are set in Europe and North Africa. And the last three novels, beginning with *The Women on the Porch*, are written out of a knowledge of Europe as well as the United States.

With the complexity of subject has come a new boldness of technique. These novels are more Jamesian than the earlier ones—the point of view is more strictly controlled—but they also draw extensively on the resources of poetry, such as *The Waste Land*, which lies back of *The Women on the Porch*, and

Dante's *Purgatorio*, which informs *The Malefactors* to some extent. Miss Gordon was converted to the Roman Catholic Church even before she wrote *The Strange Children*, and that fact has its obvious repercussions in her latest novels. *The Malefactors*, especially, makes the highest demands on her talent, because here she tries to dramatize the actual experience of a religious conversion in her poet-hero, Tom Claiborne.

Having remarked the technical range of Miss Gordon's novels, we should not assume that she has been the virtuoso. On the contrary, her stylistic shifts are an index to the scale of her work. Her eight novels and her stories and even her critical essays compose a genuine *oeuvre*. Using the materials accessible to her (her own life, the history of her family, the history of her region), she has built up an impressive image of Western man and the crisis which his restlessness has created. We can see one instance of this restlessness in Rion Outlaw and his dream of infinite space. But there are scarcely any institutional forms to restrain him. Chapman, the sophisticated historian in *The Women on the Porch*, is the latest version of Rion Outlaw, and *his* dream of infinite space is a nightmare. Nearly all of Miss Gordon's heroes are aware of the general plight, but Chapman and Stephen Lewis and Tom Claiborne are intensely conscious of a failing in their lives, and their meditations take the form of an interior drama.

Most of Miss Gordon's heroes (and many of her heroines) are fleeing from some kind of historical ruin—the exceptions are old Nicholas Llewellyn and Fontaine Allard and even Mister Ben Allard in *The Garden of Adonis*, but even these patriarchs cannot check the force of disruption very long. Miss Gordon seems to be saying that it was a mistake to make such an absolute commitment to the order of history. Aleck Maury perhaps understands this failure, and as a classicist and sportsman he can still act the Aeneas who will never found another Troy. But even the sportsman's instinct for ritual as a barrier against the ruins of time cannot be counted on, and Jim Carter, a flawed sportsman-hero in *The Garden of Adonis*, hardly even makes the attempt. In *The Strange Children* we see the futility (or at least the irony) of the effort to perpetuate a history already ruined. Here and even more in *The Malefactors* Miss Gordon is saying that redemption must lie in another order of existence, and of course she finally makes no secret of her Christian emphasis. But the ruin is easier to dramatize than the act of redemption.

If the imagery of flight permeates her books, what is the counter-image, the emblem of stasis, even of fulfillment? That is a natural image which most frequently takes the form of a tree. (Like Yeats she seems to arrive at this image very easily.) Perhaps the most "typical" moments in Miss Gordon's fiction occur when her heroes step out of time, as it were, and contemplate the forest. There is the moment when young John Llewellyn, shot from his horse at Shiloh, watches a young maple leaf floating through the center of the destruction. Or there is Mister Ben Allard sitting under his favorite sugar tree and dreaming of his dead sweetheart. In *The Malefactors* the symbol of the natural order becomes more than that: Claiborne "stared at the copper beech tree as if he could find the answer there," and "he had felt that those dusky boughs harbored Presences." No other American writer has so patiently described the surfaces of trees, even the striations of leaves, or made so much of them. The tree as an image of "wholeness" yields a meaning to him who contemplates it lovingly, Miss Gordon seems to say, and the moment of stasis can perhaps be an intimation of something divine. The tragedy of historical ruin could be redeemed—so the movement from *Penhally* to *The Malefactors* suggests.

> —Ashley Brown, "The Achievement of Caroline Gordon," *Southern Humanities Review* (Summer 1968), excerpted in *Twentieth-Century American Fiction*, ed. Harold Bloom (New York: Chelsea House Publishers, 1986), 1643–44

THOMAS H. LANDESS

The structure of the novel is large enough to accommodate almost any genuine talent, however undisciplined; and though the greatest novelists are skillful and learned as well as gifted, even a figure like Theodore Dreiser, whose works are sprawling and primitive like massive pueblos, has earned a permanent place in the history of American literature. But the short story demands a special piety, a studied devotion to the intricate technique of fiction; and consequently only the finest craftsmen can successfully practice this special art. For within its narrow confines one cannot play loose and free with point of view or bury a bad sentence; a writer may make up his own rules but he must follow them to the letter or incur the scorn of the perceptive reader. For this reason, no more than a handful of modern writers have produced short stories which are both technically sound and rich in fictional values.

Such a writer is Caroline Gordon, whose artistic discipline has always been adequate to control the wide range of vision she brings to her fiction. Indeed she tends to crowd into her stories more than their formal limitations would seem to permit: the total experience of a region's history, the hero's archetypal struggle, the complexity of modern aesthetics. In every instance, however, she succeeds in bringing the broad scope of her narrative into focus and in creating the ideal fictional moment, when form and subject are at war and the outcome hangs forever in the balance.

Yet there is a classic simplicity in most of her short stories, an unusual economy of incident and detail which decorously masks their essential thematic complexity. Even the prose is, for the most part, spare in its diction and syntax, particularly in the first-person narratives, dominated by a tone that is quiet and conversational, the intimate language of the piazza on a warm summer evening.

And it is in this quality that one finds a clue to the origins of Miss Gordon's narrative virtue. For she is still in touch with the oral tradition which in her formative years was a vital element of family life. Like William Faulkner and Katherine Anne Porter, with whom she has much in common, her experience of the nature of being begins in the family, with its concrete relationships, its sense of wholeness, its collective memory. In fact, many of her stories are the artistic rendition of incidents involving her father, her brother, and more distant connections, events which formed a significant part of her earliest and most important understanding of the world. For Southern writers of her generation, the family was a natural symbol of the order of existence, the basic analogue for everything of importance; and therefore it provided a key to the meaning of community, history, politics, morality, the transcendent and timeless.

Thus to render the family was to come to terms with all of these larger considerations simultaneously and to do so as concretely and as unselfconsciously as possible in the post-Cartesian world, which is, after all, the world of fiction. For if anything survived of an earlier and more coherent order, it survived in a rural agrarian society which still held fast to some concept, however dimmed, of *pietas*, the tripartite virtue which informed western civilization until the late renaissance and undergirded the works of Homer, Virgil, Dante, and Shakespeare.

It was no problem, then, for Miss Gordon and her Southern contemporaries to move, say, from family history to regional history; for they were, after all, one and the same thing, the latter almost perfectly preserved in the former. And so the reader finds in her first volume of stories *The Forest of the South* (1945) not only the Aleck Maury stories, based on the life of Miss Gordon's father, but also tales of the Civil War and Reconstruction, which undoubtedly originated in anecdotes that came to her by way of family reminiscences.

Indeed, every narrative in *The Forest of the South* and in *Old Red and Other Stories* (1963) has the unmistakable ingredients of life itself, those sharp and singular details which one immediately recognizes as containing truths beyond the province of the mere "angelic imagination." Thus Miss Gordon's fiction moves *toward* abstraction rather than proceeds from it, and is always symbolic rather than purely literal or purely allegorical. For this reason she never falsifies the world as, for example, Shirley Jackson does in order to serve the tyranny of intellect. Heart and head in Miss Gordon's work never come to blows; and neither betrays the steady, uncompromising senses, which are the primary means of fictional understanding. In other words, her artistic vision is whole and inviolable, which can be said of few modern writers.

—Thomas H. Landess, "Introduction" to *The Short Fiction of Caroline Gordon* (1972), excerpted in *Twentieth-Century American Fiction*, ed. Harold Bloom (New York: Chelsea House Publishers, 1986), 1649–50

ROBERT H. BRINKMEYER, JR.

Gordon's early work, beginning with "Summer Dust" (1929) up through her fifth novel, *Green Centuries* (1941), depicts heroic characters struggling to assert order and meaning in a shadowed world. At the heart of these heroes' solitary stands against death and disintegration lie a stoic acceptance of man's depravity and a desire to forge a code of courageous dignity. As heroic and noble as these characters are, the dark forces of life inevitably destroy them and—we understand now—their fragile edifices of order. Gordon's strong bond of sympathy with her heroes (derived primarily from her extensive early education in the classics), allowed her to maintain a healthy tension between her dark vision of existence and her need to assert some vestige of meaning amidst life's pain; this tension helped prevent her works from becoming merely shrill cries against the world's unfairness.

Sometime in the early 1940s Gordon's thought and art began to shift. With *The Women on the Porch* (1944) and several stories which followed until her conversion to Roman Catholicism in 1947, she began searching for a larger system of order which would transcend personal heroics. Where these works, like her earlier fiction, center on the difficult quests for order in a threatening word, now disorder is finally brought into check; emerging from crises of despair, Gordon's heroes arrive at the understanding that an overarching tradition exists, rooted in eternity, which can bring them the unifying order they seek. Gordon at this point seemed to be unsure of the nature of this tradition, at times suggesting it rested with Christianity (*The Women on the Porch*), at others with classicism ("The Olive Garden," reprinted, fortunately, for the first time in *The Collected Stories*). Probably because she was herself wavering between accepting one of these two traditions, she was able to keep her fiction free from easy reconciliations and heavy-handed dogma—elements which flawed Gordon's fiction during the next few years.

In 1947 Gordon joined the Roman Catholic Church, a step which gave her a tradition and authority by which to structure her life and art. With her newly embraced faith, Gordon believed, her art took on a greater depth and profundity, since it now took on what Flannery O'Connor called "the added dimension"—that is, the Church's vision of world and eternity. Whether or not Gordon's artistic vision deepened is an arguable point, but clearly her work from this period—notably her two novels *The Strange Children* (1951) and *The Malefactors* (1956) and her long story "Emmanuele! Emmanuele!" (1954)—took a new shape. While these works are more openly concerned with the transcendent, they lack the deeply felt love for heroic struggle which gave her earlier work such strength. Rather than celebrating man's valiant efforts to achieve private dignity, the post-conversion works show such struggles as rooted in vanity and destructive pride. Only by abandoning these personal struggles and by giving oneself to the Church, these works suggest, can a person achieve fulfillment and unity.

To communicate her religious vision to an audience she saw as secular and unsympathetic, Gordon adopted strategies of shock and distortion; these she hoped would compel her readers to abandon literal interpretation and look beyond to the religious message embodied in the work. Unfortunately Gordon's strategy, usually centering on a dramatic and unprepared for conversion experience near the end of the work, often appears forced and unconvincing, the result of her didacticism rather than her fidelity to human experience. The reader feels cheated rather than enlightened.

After *The Malefactors* (1956) and up until her death in 1981, Gordon struck out with her fiction in a new radical direction: she tried to merge her Christian and classical visions. Following the lead of Jacques Maritain, she developed a definition of Christian art based on archetypal patterns rather than on literal subject matter. Great literature, she now believed, "comes into being when one of those timeless patterns reveals itself in time and conflict in which human beings are involved"; and true artists are those who intuit these archetypal patterns and structure their work by them on some deep level. Works so constructed, Gordon said, were ultimately Christian because since archetypes embody the full range of human endeavor, they finally lead to the Christian mysteries. With her new theory of fiction came a renewed interest in heroes, whom she now likened to the ancient battlers; from wrestling with evil, Gordon's heroes gained knowledge which could lead them to the discovery of God. Perhaps because she was trying to accomplish too much, most of the work from this period ("One Against Thebes" is an exception), is sketchy and uneven, written as if from a tentative hand. *The Glory of Hera* (1972), her only novel from this period, suffers from these faults.

—Robert H. Brinkmeyer, Jr., "New Caroline Gordon Books," *Southern Literary Journal* (Spring 1982), excerpted in *Twentieth-Century American Fiction*, ed. Harold Bloom (New York: Chelsea House Publishers, 1986), 1644

JOHN F. DESMOND

Ashley Brown has already made a convincing case for seeing *The Malefactors* as a Christian comedy by paralleling the novel's action to that in Dante's *Purgatorio*. The novel is, indeed, a story of conversion, not only for the protagonist, Tom Claiborne, but also for most of the major characters in the book. Yet while a reading of *The Malefactors* in terms of a general comic movement toward conversion structured along Dantean lines is indeed illuminating, it does not say all about the specific configuration of image, consciousness, and action that constitutes its dramatic life. For conversion is both the theme of *The Malefactors* and its governing principle of dramatic composition. And the brilliantly seamless quality of Miss Gordon's art in this novel derives from her power to enact in the process of creation that very conversion which is its subject. Such a power of vision, I hope to show, has as its source a belief in the Christian Incarnation and Redemption. The *process* of redemption directs not only the general thematic movement of the novel, but also the process of composition itself, so that *The Malefactors* is no less than a dramatic rendition of the Christian vision of history.

This vision of history is rendered through the configuration of image, consciousness, and action in the novel, but the configuration operates within a general design comprising three orders, or levels, of reality—natural, classical, and Christian. . . . ⟨I⟩t will be helpful to recall their general lineaments. By "natural order" I mean, of course, that conception of reality which sees existence, including man in his fallen condition, as totally governed by the laws of nature—birth, fruition, death. The limitations of such a conception are obvious. The "classical order" envisions a higher world of human activity modeled on the heroic pattern and evoked through legend and memory. But even here the vision of history and the human situation, though exalted, is nevertheless circumscribed within the natural order. For as Romano Guardini has stated, "Classical man knew nothing of a being existing beyond the world: as a result he was neither able to view or shape his world from a vantage point which transcended it."

The Christian conception of history and the human situation, in sharp contrast with the natural and classical views, posits a new and higher kind of knowledge—divine revelation—which makes possible man's participation in supernatural mystery, and enables him to conceptualize his experience from a standpoint outside his world. History is revealed as having a definite beginning emanating from a personal act of God (the Creation), a factual point of transforming apotheosis (Christ's Incarnation, Death, and Resurrection), and a fixed end (the Final Judgment). With the Incarnation, human history becomes the history of Christ's penetration and transformation of the natural world, in a process of redemption moved forward by man's willing participation in it. At the core of this process is the new freedom and grace created by the Redemption, which nurtures the divine life in man. It is this vision which serves as the absolute model for both the theme *and* the artistic practice of conversion in *The Malefactors*.

Looking at the novel in terms of its general, comic movement, one can easily see how it is structured in terms of these three orders, or visions, of reality. In the course of the narrative the major characters move in and through the natural order, with its classical trappings, to a confrontation with the supernatural embodied in the Christian vision; or to state the matter differently, the world of nature in the novel is finally circumscribed and defined by the Christian perspective. One can readily see this by noting the progress of Tom Claiborne and his wife Vera from their life at Blenker's Brook early in the novel to their final anticipated reunion at Mary Farm, the land consecrated to Christian service. Their life at Blenker's Brook is a pagan and decadent submission to the natural order, a sterile round in which Vera, aided by Max Shull, indulges in an idolatrous preoccupation with nature—her prize bull, Bud—while Tom, a lapsed poet and critic, sinks into drunkenness and despair. Claiborne despises their life at Blenker's Brook, and rightly so, for he sees it accurately as a degradation of the human spirit and a travesty of the heroic ideal envisioned in classical myth. Images of a better past—both personal and mythical—constantly haunt his memory, but memory as an ordering instrument within consciousness is not enough to save him. Claiborne lacks grace; the efforts of his human will alone are useless, and his impotence as a poet is intrinsically related to his spiritual impotence as a man. Without grace, he cannot rise above the natural level of existence, whose logical end, as he well knows, is death. It is toward the reception of divine grace that Claiborne is "converted" in his return to Mary Farm at the end of the novel.

Although the general movement of *The Malefactors* is from the natural/classical to the Christian perspective, the three orders or ways of perceiving human experience are not to be seen, of course, as rigidly exclusive of one another or, from a temporal standpoint, as consecutive. To say simply that Miss Gordon evokes the natural, classical, and Christian orders as a means of defining the action of the novel does not sufficiently explain *how* these three orders, or levels, exist in dynamic relationship with each other in the work. The point, for her art—which is indistinguishable from her vision—is crucial. Merely to say that Miss Gordon uses the three orders to heighten the significance of the narrative is a crude caricature of her art. Rather, the three orders are visions of reality which exist *simultaneously* in the human consciousness as possibilities to be enacted through knowledge and choice ⟨. . . .⟩

—John F. Desmond, "*The Malefactors*: Caroline Gordon's Redemptive Vision," *Renascence* (Autumn 1982), excerpted in *Twentieth-Century American Fiction*, ed. Harold Bloom (New York: Chelsea House Publishers, 1986), 1648–49

ROSE ANN C. FRAISTAT

Gordon's affinity with ⟨Carl⟩ Jung is evident. Commenting on the archetypal nature of an incident in her short story "The Captive," she has deemed Jung "much more interesting than Freud because . . . he believes that the archetype is operating right now." By her own admission, Jungian archetypes also help to form the pattern in *The Glory of Hera*.

Through her preoccupation with vision in the later novels, Caroline Gordon investigates these archetypal structures and shows how inextricably linked are subjective and objective experience. Because perception is not merely eyesight but a larger awareness of the physical world, compounded by intuitions of an eternal order governing both nature and human society, in *The Women on the Porch*, *The Strange Children*, and *The Malefactors* Gordon often relies on exaggerated and distorted perception to suggest the importance of these intuited realities: flashbacks are sometimes hallucinatory; dreams are treated as facts, given much the same stature that Jung would bestow on them; and the imaginations of the protagonists often grant them fanciful or grotesque, but nonetheless true, images of reality. While the distortion of time and the symbolic content of these subjective experiences at first suggest dissociation, even mental collapse or immaturity, they indicate finally an enduring and universal reality that the subconscious can discover.

Frequently, the protagonists who see this complex reality are artistic, in keeping with Jung's observation that the poet "knows that a purposiveness outreaching human ends is the life-giving secret for man; he has a presentiment of incomprehensible happenings in the pleroma. In short, he sees something of that psychic world that strikes terror into the savage and the barbarian." There is nothing reductive in Jung's choice of words: "the savage" and "the barbarian" are examples of original or primal man—one who is not protected by "the shield of science and the armour of reason" and consequently is closer to subjective truths. Similarly, Gordon stresses the universality of experience between more "primitive" peoples and moderns, even implying in *Green Centuries*, for example, that there is more beauty and directness in the rituals and faith of the Indians than in those of the pioneers.

Analyzing the grotesque, William Van O'Connor has described this "American genre" as "seeking, seemingly in perverse ways, the sublime." Although his list of American writers manifesting this concern does not include Caroline Gordon, her preoccupation with the visionary affiliates her with other contemporary southern writers who employ the grotesque to correct the prevailing dissociation of feeling and thought. Gordon's characters may not be actual freaks as are, say, Cousin Lymon in ⟨Carson McCullers's⟩ *The Ballad of the Sad Café*, Hazel Motes in ⟨Flannery O'Connor's⟩ *Wise Blood*, or Popeye in ⟨William Faulkner's⟩ *Sanctuary*. Yet she does share with these writers what William Van O'Connor defines as a belief "that man carries in his unconscious mind not merely wilfulness or the need to indulge himself, but a deep bestiality and dark irrationality."

Jim Chapman's anger and jealousy turn him into a kind of monster in *The Women on the Porch*, so that he nearly strangles his wife. But the grotesque quality in Caroline Gordon's fiction is less often expressed in such outwardly violent behavior. More frequently there is a violence of revelation—a psychic

explosion as an old way of seeing the world is destroyed and a more comprehensive meaning is perceived. As in Eudora Welty's fiction, for example, where
subjective and objective worlds seem to collide whenever a character tries to
control reality, to limit it by reason or by rationalizing the inexplicable away
(e.g., "The Green Curtain," "A Memory")—dreams, memories, and intuitions in
Gordon's novels attest to a psychic reality that cannot be permanently
repressed without irreparably damaging the individual.

The strength with which the repressed subconscious erupts not only indicates how much violence the individual has done to his psyche in damming up
such powerful forces but also serves as a measure of the true awfulness and
awesomeness of those forces. Carl Jung describes the terrible encounters that
the visionary work of art seeks to record: "The primordial experiences rend
from top to bottom the curtain upon which is painted the picture of an
ordered world, and allow a glimpse into the unfathomed abyss of what has not
yet become." A confrontation with and an appreciation of mystery is the final
result. Paradoxically, that recognition of human limitation is also the realization of human possibility—"the life-giving secret for man."

—Rose Ann C. Fraistat, "The Later Novels," in *Caroline Gordon as Novelist and Woman of Letters*
(1984), excerpted in *Twentieth-Century American Fiction*, ed. Harold Bloom (New York: Chelsea
House Publishers, 1986), 1645

BIBLIOGRAPHY

Penhally. 1931.
Aleck Maury, Sportsman. 1934.
None Shall Look Back. 1937.
The Garden of Adonis. 1937.
Green Centuries. 1941.
The Women on the Porch. 1944.
The Forest of the South. 1945.
The Strange Children. 1951.
The Malefactors. 1956.
How to Read a Novel. 1957.
A Good Soldier: A Key to the Novels of Ford Madox Ford. 1963.
Old Red and Other Stories. 1963.
The Glory of Hera. 1972.
The Collected Stories of Caroline Gordon. 1981.

I N D E X